God's Word is Our Joy

Volume Five

Advent~Christmas

Lent~Easter

Cycle C

God's Word is Our Joy

Lucien Deiss, C.S.Sp.

Readings	Advent-Christmas
Prayers	Lent-Easter
Homilies	Cycle C

WORLD LIBRARY PUBLICATIONS, a division of J. S. Paluch Co., Inc.
3815 N. Willow Road, Schiller Park, Illinois, 60176

Contents

Introduction

In this book we present some homilies for the Sundays and Feasts of Advent and Christmas, Cycle C. Each Sunday or feast includes:

I. The **lectionary scriptures** for each Sunday or feast: three readings plus the responsorial psalm. It is obvious that one cannot speak about all three readings and the psalm at each Sunday or feast. What is necessary—and sufficient—is to speak enough to satisfy the community. In the early tradition (cf. 1 Tm 4, 13), the homily is called *paraklèsis*, consolation. The homily should not cause indigestion from too many biblical texts but consolation from the word of God.

In a book, however, one can offer more, so that the one who preaches can make proper choices for the benefit of the community.

Where I found it necessary or useful, I have presented some exegetical explanations that should clarify the principal biblical difficulties. The notes at the end of each chapter have been reduced to the essentials. They either justify a position or invite the reader to examine certain points more thoroughly.

II. An **introductory prayer** for the celebration. This is generally composed of a blessing (in the genre of biblical blessings) and a prayer of petition.

III. The **homily**, which represents the principal part of this work.
I have stated in another publication what a homily was in Jewish and Christian tradition.[1] In this book I wanted to follow the golden rule of the homily that Jesus formulated: "Today in your hearing, this Scripture has been fulfilled."

IV. A **concluding prayer**. This prayer responds to the word that has been actualized in the homily. It has a freer structure than the general intercessions but can be used as a source for them.

This new edition of *God's Word Is Our Joy* provides an enlarged edition of some homilies published formerly by North American Liturgy Resources. Several explanations about responsorial psalms that seemed important liturgically have been added.

I hope to present here some help not only for the deacon or priest preparing the homily but also for all communities celebrating without the presence of their priest and for all the faithful who want to improve their knowledge and love of Jesus Christ, the living Word of God.

Homily or Homily Texts

Strictly speaking, this work does not present homilies but homily texts.

There is a difference between the homily and its text, like the one that exists between the living word spoken to the assembly and the same "dead" word lying in the shroud of the pages of a book. It is also the difference that exists between a song that one sings in the assembly and the same song that one looks at in a book; an organ piece of J. S. Bach that one plays and the piece that one admires in a collection of printed music. This is to say that not one of these homilies was ever spoken as it is printed here. No homily should ever be spoken as it is printed.

If there is a fundamental difference between the homily and its printed text, between the spoken word and the written word, there is also, one must add immediately, a fundamental resemblance between the spoken homily and the printed homily.

I hope that the printed text, delivered here without life and without defense, will know how to become living and find the reader's heart.

I hesitated a long time before deciding to publish these texts. All publication leads to communication. All communication in the religious domain is formidable. The author confides in the reader. He opens his mind, filled with personal memories, his intelligence, with his own vision of the world, and also his heart. Here, communication bears upon the most precious thing that the author and the reader have in common: God.

In his *Apology of Origen,* [3] Pamphile (+c. 310) speaks in this way about his teacher:

In his research, Origen proceeded with great humility and fear of God... He recommended to the reader to verify his statements. His opinions, he knew well, were not equally probable or certain, for there are too many mysteries in the Scriptures.

I consider the ideas presented here to be simple suggestions or propositions. It is up to the readers to compare them with what they carry in their hearts to see if these ideas are true and suit them. Many paths toward the actualization of the word are possible. Before the mystery of God, all paths require our humility.

May I also add this: Each time I must speak as a priest, I begin to tremble. It is not speaking that makes me tremble; it is speaking about God, in the name of God, which is formidable. On the Last Day, may the Lord recognize as his own each of the words that are found in this book.

While writing, I thought often about Saint Augustine. In his *Confessions*, which give proof of a fascinating theological depth and which are at the same time adorned with an incomparable literary quality, he is not afraid to talk about personal ideas. He relates, for example, how his mother Monica, when she was still a young girl, "swigged" some wine in a cave and was betrayed by a servant as *meribibula*, a little drunk;[4] or how he himself, at the age of sixteen, through pure mischievousness, robbed a neighbor's pear tree to throw fruit to the pigs.[5] In that spirit, I did not want these homilies, which I delivered in simplicity, to appear solemn and excessively severe. In spite of our fears, speaking about God must remain a feast; to listen to someone speak about God must remain a joy.

An ancient proverb, born in the biblical milieu, affirms:

The best preacher
  is your heart.
The best book
  is the world.
The best teacher
  is time.
And the best friend: you do not have any friend who loves you
  as much as God loves you.

These homilies do not want in any way to take the place of the "best teacher." They simply and earnestly desire to lead you to him.

Lucien Deiss, C.S.Sp.

NOTES TO THE INTRODUCTION:

1. *God's Word and God's People* (Collegeville, MN: The Liturgical Press, 1976), pp. 123–136 and 284–309. *Celebration of the Word* (The Liturgical Press, 1993): 54–81.
2. Luke 4, 21.
3. *Apology of Origen*, Pg 17, 543.
4. *Confessions*, IX, VIII. 18. Cf. Oeuvres de Saint Augustine, vol. 14 (Paris: Desclée de Brouwer, 1962): 106. "Meribibula" means literally small drinker *(bibula)* of pure wine *(merum)*.
5. *Confessions*, II, IV, 9. Cf. op. cit., vol. 13 (1962): 344–346.

Seasons of Advent and Christmas

FIRST SUNDAY OF ADVENT

READING I   JER 33, 14-16

A reading from the book of the prophet Jeremiah

The days are coming, says the Lord, when I will fulfill the promise I made to the house of Israel and Judah. In those days, in that time, I will raise up for David a just shoot; he shall do what is right and just in the land. In those days Judah shall be safe and Jerusalem shall dwell secure; this is what they shall call her: ''The Lord our justice.''

The Word of the Lord.

RESPONSORIAL PSALM   Ps 25, 4-5. 8-9. 10. 14

R/. (1) To you, O Lord, I lift my soul.

Your ways, O Lord, make known to me;
   teach me your paths,
Guide me in your truth and teach me,
   for you are God my savior,
   and for you I wait all the day.

R/. To you, O Lord, I lift my soul.

Good and upright is the Lord;
   thus he shows sinners the way.
He guides the humble to justice,
   he teaches the humble his way.

R/. To you, O Lord, I lift my soul.

All the paths of the Lord are kindness and constancy
   toward those who keep his covenant and his decrees.
The friendship of the Lord is with those who fear him,
   and his covenant, for their instruction.

R/. To you, O Lord, I lift my soul.

Reading II   1 Thes 3, 12-4, 2

A reading from the first letter of Paul to the Thessalonians

May the Lord increase you and make you overflow with love for one another and for all, even as our love does for you. May he strengthen your hearts, making them blameless and holy before our God and Father at the coming of our Lord Jesus with all his holy ones.

Now, my brothers, we beg and exhort you in the Lord Jesus that, even as you learned from us how to conduct yourselves in a way pleasing to God—which you are indeed doing—so you must learn to make still greater progress. You know the instructions we gave you in the Lord Jesus.

The Word of the Lord.

Gospel   Lk 21, 25-28, 34-36

A reading from the holy gospel according to Luke

Jesus said to his disciples: "There will be signs in the sun, the moon and the stars. On the earth, nations will be in anguish, distraught at the roaring of the sea and the waves. People will die of fright in anticipation of what is coming upon the earth. The powers in the heavens will be shaken. After that, humanity will see the Son of Man coming on a cloud with great power and glory. When these things begin to happen, stand up straight and raise your heads, for your ransom is near at hand.

"Be on guard lest your spirits become bloated with indulgence and drunkenness and worldly cares. The great day will suddenly close in on you like a trap. The day I speak of will come upon all who dwell on the face of the earth, so be on the watch. Pray constantly for the strength to escape whatever is in prospect, and to stand secure before the Son of Man."

The gospel of the Lord.

INTRODUCTORY PRAYER

We bless you, God of hope,
because you are the light in our hearts.
We desire to see and adore your face.

We pray to you:
May your justice guide us on our path
in this time of Advent,
and may your forgiveness light our way.
May your joy inspire us to acclaim you and sing to you
with your Son Jesus Christ, who waits for us in your house,
with your Spirit, who welcomes us in your love,
forever and ever. Amen.

HOMILY

The word *Advent* means *coming.*

Advent is the time when we await and celebrate the coming of Jesus Christ. We say that the world is still in a certain darkness; not the darkness of dusk that is closing in on us, but the darkness of a dawn that is breaking, of a day that is about to be born. As in the time of Isaiah, we implore the prophet:

Watchman, how goes the night?
Watchman, how goes the night?   Is 21, 11

And the prophet Isaiah answers us with the apostle Paul:

The morning comes, and again the night.   Is 21, 12
Repent, come back to the Lord!
The night is ending;
the day is very near.Rom 13, 12

This day—this dawn—is Christ who is bursting forth in the heart of our lives.

We Christians are people of hope. When Paul speaks about the pagans, he says: "Those who have no hope."[1] We are bearers of the beauty of God which one day must burst forth upon the world. We are the people walking toward the future. We are not dreamers, that is, people who visualize marvelous tomorrows in order to escape work in the grayness of daily life. Such a dream could only be a drug. On the contrary, we work with all our strength today to build the beauty of tomorrow. We do not leave the world; we bring the world with us to meet Christ who is coming.

Advent becomes for us a time of greater reflection. We close the windows of our heart upon the world and upon its beauty; we open the interior windows of our soul upon God and upon his splendor. We become conscious that life in its plenitude is there before us. Each day is a walk not toward an end but toward a beginning, not toward a tomb but toward the feast next to the Father.

1. A Shoot of Justice

Through the mouth of his prophet Nathan, God had promised to David an eternal kingdom:

> Your house and your kingdom will endure forever before me, and
> your throne will be made firm forever. 2 Sm 7, 16

Israel had welcomed the promise like a seed of eternity, but soon claimed this promise as a right. And finally through a series of infidelities, Israel destroyed itself by its own hands. Thus the tree of Jesse, upon which the Spirit of the Lord had rested, became a rotten stem. The axe of God's judgment struck at the root. As a flower rises from a branch that one thought dead, a little shoot was going to rise in the fire of the ruin of Jerusalem in 587 and be trampled under the feet of the Chaldean occupiers.

> In those days, at that time,
> I will make rise in the house of David
> a shoot of justice. Jer 33, 15

The prophecy was realized in Jesus. He sprang up, a little shoot of justice, in the womb of Mary, the daughter of David.

This is the meaning of the prophecy that we read today in the Book of Jeremiah. This is the realization that we celebrate in this liturgy.

The Shoot of Justice in Our Life

Each time that God proclaims a prophecy, he places it in our hands so that we may realize, with his grace, its fulfillment. He always fulfills his promises. But never without us, without our cooperation. We are the people of Christ; we represent in the eyes of the world that shoot of justice which is Christ. We are the face of the Lord; we make incarnate for our brothers and sisters the face of his holiness. Having said that, our affirmation becomes very humble. It is changed into a question that weighs upon our heart. Does our life reveal the holiness of Jesus? Does our life make that shoot of justice bloom, as proclaimed by the prophet? Or does it sometimes resemble a rotten stem upon which no flower can bloom, a dried-up branch upon which no fruit can ripen?

And here our question itself becomes a prayer: Lord, in the name of your love, in the name of your faithfulness, plant your roots in our heart. Make this shoot of justice rise and bloom in our heart.

The Shoot of Justice in the Church

Out of the plenitude of Jesus, justice is poured out like a river upon the whole Church. The Church is that new Jerusalem about which the prophet affirms:

> This is the name that one will give to her;
> "The Lord is our justice."   Jer 33, 16

In returning to that prophecy, in applying it to the Church, I tremble. For I say to myself: Is my Church, in the eyes of the world, the dwelling place of the justice and of the holiness of God? Or rather does she appear, as so many sects, like a boutique of ideology? Does the whole world look toward this holy Church as the refuge of all the oppressed? Does it contemplate in her the face of God on earth?

There are people in the world who are starving for justice, thirsting for holiness. They live—rather, they survive—under intolerable political or religious or social oppressions. The Church is for them their only hope. Because of this, we pray joyfully: Blessed be you, Lord Jesus, shoot of justice, for it is you who appear to them in the face of Christians.

There are people in the world who are starving for justice, thirsting for holiness, dying for hope. They do not hope for anything from the Church; they are not waiting for any help from her. Because of this, we pray humbly: Forgive us Lord, shoot of justice, when our poor face, ravaged by our mediocrities, hides your smile from the oppressed.

There are people in the world who are starving for justice, thirsting for holiness, dying for hope. They do not even know that there is a Savior in whom to hope and that a love has burst upon the world. Because of this, we pray with all our hearts: Come, Lord Jesus, shoot of justice, fulfill your promise! Rise upon the distress of the world. Make your Church appear like a land of hope to those who beg for love!

2. The Coming of the Son of Man

This Sunday's Gospel presents an extract from the eschatological discourse, the discourse which bears upon the events of the end (*eschaton*) of time. The three synoptic Gospels—Matthew, Mark, and Luke—give this discourse particular importance since they place it just before the account of the Passion.

With Great Power and Great Glory

In this discourse Jesus utilizes the literary methods that were used in the Jewish apocalyptic tradition in his time.[3] Thus, when he affirms that one will see signs in the sun, the moon, and the stars, he is evoking the apocalyptic images of the Book of Isaiah:

> The whole army of the heavens will be dissolved.
> The heavens will be unrolled like a scroll
> and all their army will wither away.   Is 34, 4

When he announces that people will die of fear, he is joining the Apocalypse of Baruch:

> Then torpor will seize the inhabitants of the earth. They will fall
> into numerous tribulations and fall again into cruel torments.[4]

Finally, when he announces his coming on the clouds of heaven, he is citing the Book of Daniel:

> Behold, he is coming on the clouds of heaven,
> like a Son of man.Dn 7, 13

When Jesus uses the language full of images of the Jewish apocalypses of his era, he does not intend to make these images sacred, as if it were necessary to interpret them literally, no more than he intends to make the Aramaic language sacred, the language he uses when he expresses himself. He simply affirms that he will come back "with great power and with great glory."

He will appear then as the universal master of the cosmos, the one who imprisons the stars in the palms of his hands, the one who stops the flow of the centuries with a glance, the one who reigns over the invisible world of the angels and who is the eternal life of all the saints: "He will come with all his saints." It is heartening to remember that the One who was foundering in the agony of Gethsemane and in the shame of the crucifixion, the One who was going to die remains "the firstborn of all creation" and the Lord of eternities.

The Suddenness of His Coming

The last verses of our Gospel present the conclusion of the eschatological discourse according to Luke. The Evangelist gives us, in in the manner of a resume, the essence of Jesus' instructions.

Jesus insists on the suddenness of his coming. He remembers Ecclesiastes.

As the fish are caught
in the perfidious net that one throws,
and as the birds are caught in the net,
thus will the sons of earth be caught in the time of misfortune
when it will fall upon them unexpectedly.   Ecc 9, 12 (LXX)

Jesus comments:

May that day not fall upon you unexpectedly.
Like a trap, it will fall upon all the people of the earth.

This suddenness surprises the sinner in the midst of sleep. But for the
faithful one who waits for the Lord, this suddenness is rather an immense
joy. It is the suddenness of God's love. It is like meeting a friend suddenly
after a long absence. Nay, much more! It is like meeting the Friend, the
only one who loves us truly and uniquely for ourselves. Then, looking into
each other's eyes and trembling with joy, we will say: "Oh! Lord, it is
really you, the Love who created us! Blessed be you! How we have longed
to see you!"

To Appear Standing before the Son of Man

In order to experience this suddenness of love, Jesus recommends to us:

Stay awake…
in order to appear standing before the Son of man.Lk 21, 36

Christians are people wide awake and on their feet. They are watching.
They do not allow their hearts to grow heavy "in dissoluteness, drunkenness, and the cares of life." To describe these cares, Luke uses the word
merimna. The use of this term is pretty. It evokes a care that rends the heart,
that divides *(merizo)* the soul. Luke qualifies these cares of *merimnai
biotikai*, which could be translated as "worldly cares." Of course, there are
cares and concerns that are our daily bread. These cares rend our heart. But
through the openings made by them, God can enter into our heart. On the
other hand, worldly cares make openings through which the blood of our
love pours out. In the Parable of the Sower, these cares of the world
represent the thorns that stifle the Word and keep it from bearing fruit.
Luke explains:

The seeds which fell in the thorns
are those who have heard the Word,
but the cares, the riches and the pleasures of life
along the way stifle their progress.   Lk 8, 14

How many have allowed their heart to be weighed down in the cares of this world! How many have lain down, gone to sleep in mediocrity:

There once was a man who had fully succeeded in his professional life. He put together a flourishing business, directed it with cleverness, worked all the time including weekends. At eighty-one years of age he died, stricken by a heart attack, on a Sunday morning while he was checking his company invoices! Of course, God is merciful to us in all our follies. But what a folly to appear before the Lord's throne one Sunday morning, at eighty-one, with an invoice in your hand! What a folly to allow your heart to be weighed down by the cares of the world.

Pray at all Times

Jesus says to us further:

> Stay awake
> and pray at all times.   Lk 21, 36

Our prayer must be constant. It must agree in advance to submit itself to the timetable of God, which is, of course, the timetable of his love. Our prayer always embraces the time of the patience of God.

To pray at all times is not to recite prayers at all times. It is to have the eyes of your heart fixed upon Christ. Someone said to me one day: "I do not have much time to pray. Therefore, from time to time I send a call to the good God. The line is never busy. Always open."

This is true; the path to God is always open. When one calls him, there is never an angel secretary or an answering machine that says: "We have recorded your call. It will be transmitted." God always answers. Personally. Even his silence is already a presence filled with his joy and his peace. Eternally true iss his word to his faithful:

> When they call to me, I will answer them, I will be with them in
> distress.   Ps 91,15

3. All His Paths Are Love and Truth

On certain Sundays, when we meditate on the readings in order to discover which text contains the most spiritual message, which text is situated at the heart of revelation, we often hesitate. Is it the First Reading? The apostolic letter? The Gospel? Today I would lean with pleasure today toward the Responsorial Psalm.

Psalm 25 is an alphabetical psalm. Each verse begins with a letter of the Hebrew alphabet. This is a literary method used to express the totality, the plenitude of the message. [10] There is a line of this Psalm that touches the root of my heart. Remember it; you can build your whole life upon it. And if you only remember this single line from this Sunday, you will have gained infinite riches. It is written in this psalm:

> All the paths of the Lord
> are love and truth. Ps 25, 10

If only we could understand that those words are true! If only we could understand that all the paths of our life, from the first moment of our existence, when we were conceived in the kiss of our father and mother, up to this day, this precise moment when I tell you these words, are paths of love and truth! If only we could understand that the woman that the Lord placed at your side, that the man who opened his heart to you are, in their own way, paths of love and truth! That the children who are born of that love—including the most difficult—are paths of love and truth! That this path of pain on which you walk, this road of joy on which you run, this separation, this illness without end, this distress without name are paths of love and truth. In a word, all the paths of our life, at the same time sublime and foolish—sublime by the call of heaven, foolish by our shabbiness—are paths of love and of truth.

There is, above all, that path which is the most wonderful in love: the path of the coming of Christ among us.

When one thinks of the interminable path which led matter toward life, life toward man and woman, man and woman toward Christ, toward the One who is the face of the love of the Father on earth, it is especially then that one is amazed by the paths of God. Teilhard de Chardin explains:

> The prodigious expanses of time which preceded the first Christmas were not empty of Christ: they were imbued with the influx of his power. It was the ferment of his conception that stirred up the cosmic masses and directed the initial developments of the biosphere. It was the travail preceding his birth that accelerated the development of instinct and the birth of thought upon the earth. Let us have done with the stupidity which makes a stumbling-block of the endless eras of expectancy imposed on us by the Messiah; the fearful, anonymous labours of primitive man, the beauty fashioned through its age-long history by ancient Egypt, the anxious expectancies of Israel, the patient distilling of the attar of oriental mysticism, the endless refining of wisdom by

the Greeks. All these were needed before the Flower could blossom on the rod of Jesse and of all humanity. All these preparatory processes were cosmically and biologically necessary that Christ might set foot upon our human stage...When Christ first appeared before men and women in the arms of Mary he had already stirred up the world.[11]

It is in this path of Christ that we continue in our own life. We are all in genesis. We are always growing in love. Our prayer will be the one of Paul:

May the Lord give you
for each other and for all people
a love more and more intense and overflowing.   1 Thes 3, 12

It is thus that we prepare, as Paul says,

the day when our Lord Jesus
will come with all his saints.   1 Thes 3, 12

All that is necessary now to conclude this homily is to be silent in our heart. At the beginning of this Advent, how can we prepare the coming of the Lord? Perhaps we could consecrate a little more of our time, which is so precious, to prayer and even, if we listen well to the gospel, to repentance? Perhaps we could also consecrate a little more of our heart to loving our brothers and sisters more by serving them? Let us answer according to our grace. The joy that we want to put in our life is at stake.

To Christ Jesus who came among us in the humility of Bethlehem and who waits for us in heaven with all his saints, to him alone glory forever and ever.

PRAYER

We bless you, Lord Jesus,
shoot of justice announced by the prophets.
We pray to you:
Plant in our hearts your roots of justice,
make your fruits of holiness ripen there,
and come to save us.

Marana tha! Come, Lord Jesus Christ!

We bless you, Lord Jesus,
builder of the new Jerusalem
who is called: "The Lord is our justice."
We pray to you:
Lay out in your Church a land of hope
for all the oppressed of the earth,
and come to save us.

Marana tha! Come, Lord Jesus Christ!

We bless you, Lord Jesus,
path of love and truth.
We pray to you:
Lead us across the deserts of our hates,
across the twisted roads of our lies,
toward your Father, the God of love and truth,
and come to save us.

Marana tha! Come, Lord Jesus Christ!

We bless you, Lord Jesus,
suddenness of God's dawn that will rise upon the world.
We pray to you:
Awaken us from our sleep,
lest our hearts become heavy
and come to save us.

Marana tha! Come, Lord Jesus Christ!

We bless you, Lord Jesus,
Son of man, clothed in majesty,
who comes to us in the splendor of your love.
We pray to you:
Call us to join in the procession
of all the saints who welcome you,
and come to save us.

Marana tha! Come, Lord Jesus Christ!

We bless you, Lord, for that Day
when the sun, the moon, and the stars
will dance for you rounds of joy,
when the roaring of the sea will sing your praise,
because that Day will be the one
when your love will triumph.
Help us to prepare it in a holiness without reproach
by putting our life in the service of our brothers and sisters.
Come, Lord Jesus and save us
forever and ever. Amen.

NOTES TO FIRST SUNDAY OF ADVENT

1. 1 Thess 4, 13.
2. Cf. Is 11, 1-2
3. The apocalypses aim for the revelation *(apocalypsis)* of that which is hidden, ordinarily events from the end of time. This literary genre flourished in the era of Christ. Let us cite from the second century before the Christian era: *The Book of Enoch, The Apocalypse of Moses, the Testament of the Twelve Patriarchs:* from the first century before the Christian era: *The Psalms of Solomon;* from the first century therefore contemporary with Christ: *The Assumption of Moses, The Book of the Secrets of Enoch, the Fourth Book of Esdras, The Apocalypse of Baruch, The Ascension of Isaiah, The Apocalypses of Abraham, of Moses, and of Ezekiel.*
4. *The Syriac Apocalypse of Baruch,* XXV, 3. Cf. SC 144 (1969), p. 481.
5. Lk 21, 27.
6. 1 Thes 3, 13.
7. Col 1, 15, 18.
8. Lk 21, 34.
9. Mk 4, 19.
10. According to M. Mammati "alphabetization is a literary process intended to signify the plenitude of the Word, whence the perfection of the Law and the abundance of blessings" *(Les Psaumes,* I. [Paris: Desclée de Brouwer, 1966], pp. 45-46).
11. Teilhard de Chardin, *Hymn of the Universe,* trans Simon Bartholomew (New York: Harper & Row, 1965), pp. 76-77. Copyright © 1961 by Editions du Seuil, English translation, Copyright © 1965, by Harper & Row Publishers, Inc., and William Collins Sons and Co., Ltd. By permission of Harper & Row Publishers, Inc.

IMMACULATE CONCEPTION

READING I
Gn 3, 9-15. 20

A reading from the book of Genesis

After Adam had eaten of the tree the Lord God called to the man and asked him, "Where are you?" He answered, "I heard you in the garden; but I was afraid, because I was naked, so I hid myself." Then he asked, "Who told you that you were naked? You have eaten, then, from the tree of which I had forbidden you to eat!" The man replied, "The woman whom you put here with me—she gave me fruit from the tree, and so I ate it." The Lord God then asked the woman, "Why did you do such a thing?" The woman answered, "The serpent tricked me into it, so I ate it."

Then the Lord God said to the serpent:
"Because you have done this,
  you shall be banned
  from all the animals
  and from all the wild creatures;
On your belly shall you crawl,
  and dirt shall you eat
  all the days of your life.
I will put enmity between you and the woman,
  and between your offspring and hers;
He will strike at your head,
  while you strike at his heel."
The man called his wife Eve,
  because she became the mother of all the living.
The Word of the Lord.

RESPONSORIAL PSALM
Ps 98, 1. 2-3. 3-4

R/. (1) Sing to the Lord a new song,
  for he has done marvelous deeds.

Sing to the Lord a new song,
  for he has done wondrous deeds;
His right hand has won victory for him,
  his holy arm.

R/. Sing to the Lord a new song,
  for he has done marvelous deeds.

The Lord has made his salvation known:
in the sight of the nations he has revealed
his justice.
He has remembered his kindness and his faithfulness
toward the house of Israel.

R/. Sing to the Lord a new song,
for he has done marvelous deeds.

All the ends of the earth have seen
the salvation by our God.
Sing joyfully to the Lord, all you lands;
break into song; sing praise.

R/. Sing to the Lord a new song,
for he has done marvelous deeds.

READING II   EPH 1, 3-6, 11-12

A reading from the letter of Paul to the Ephesians

Praised be the God and Father of our Lord Jesus Christ, who has
bestowed on us in Christ every spiritual blessing in the heavens! God
chose us in him before the world began, to be holy and blameless in his
sight, to be full of love; likewise he predestined us through Christ Jesus
to be his adopted sons—such was his will and pleasure—that all might
praise the divine favor he has bestowed on us in his beloved.

In him we were chosen; for in the decree of God, who administers
everything according to his will and counsel, we were predestined to
praise his glory by being the first to hope in Christ.

The Word of the Lord.

GOSPEL   LK 1, 26-38

A reading from the holy gospel according to Luke

The angel Gabriel was sent from God to a town of Galilee named
Nazareth, to a virgin betrothed to a man named Joseph, of the house of
David. The virgin's name was Mary. Upon arriving, the angel said to
her: "Rejoice, O highly favored daughter! The Lord is with you.
Blessed are you among women." She was deeply troubled by his
words, and wondered what his greeting meant. The angel went on to
say to her: "Do not fear, Mary. You have found favor with God. You

shall conceive and bear a son and give him the name Jesus. Great will be his dignity and he will be called Son of the Most High. The Lord God will give him the throne of David his father. He will rule over the house of Jacob forever and his reign will be without end."

Mary said to the angel, "How can this be since I do not know man?" The angel answered her: "The Holy Spirit will come upon you and the power of the Most High will overshadow you; hence, the holy offspring to be born will be called Son of God. Know that Elizabeth your kinswoman has conceived a son in her old age; she who was thought to be sterile is now in her sixth month, for nothing is impossible with God."

Mary said: "I am the maidservant of the Lord. Let it be done to me as you say." With that the angel left her.

The gospel of the Lord.

INTRODUCTORY PRAYER

God our Father, we bless you at all times,
but especially on this day when we celebrate
the Immaculate Conception of the Virgin Mary.
You chose her before the creation of the world
to be holy and immaculate in your presence;
and you filled her with the splendor of your love.

We pray to you:
To us sinners
grant the joy of your forgiveness,
and we will celebrate with her the grace of her innocence
through Jesus Christ, her Child and our brother,
forever and ever. Amen.

HOMILY

On the path that leads us to the manger of Jesus, we naturally find his mother, the Virgin Mary.

On this day, the Church presents her to us as the woman fully redeemed and invites us to celebrate her Immaculate Conception.

The Dogma of the Immaculate Conception

The feast of the Immaculate Conception was born in the East around the ninth century. But belief in the Immaculate Conception finds its roots in ancient Christian tradition.

In the Middle Ages, the belief was engulfed in questions that had become inextricable because they were stated badly. One said that the conception of Mary's body could not be called immaculate because all human conception— according to Saint Augustine—was stained by the libido, sexual desire. On the other hand, one asked, at what moment does the soul begin to "animate" the body? Was it not later for girls than for boys? These questions make us laugh now as those who read some of our present questions will laugh later...

The prevailing position of Scholasticism was the following: Mary was not immaculate in her conception otherwise she would not have been re- deemed by Christ. But she was redeemed immediately afterwards.

It was the Scottish Franciscan John Duns Scotus (+1308), called "Doctor subtilis," who found an outlet for the theological question. He affirmed that Mary was the masterpiece of redemption because she had been sanctified not through redemption from sin, but through preservation.

On December 8, 1854, Pope Pius IX defined what had become the common faith of the Church. In doing that, he was not inventing a new truth, but rather he was cataloguing the truth that was already held in tradition. It was a work similar to that of a Council that does not define new truths, but which takes stock of those that already belong to the faith.

Here is the definition of Pius IX:

Through a special grace and privilege of almighty God, in view of the merits of Jesus Christ, Savior of the human race, the Blessed Virgin Mary, in the first instant of her conception, had been preserved and exempted from all stain of original sin.

Each term was chosen to block the way to an eventual erroneous interpretation.

Mary was redeemed in a more sublime way. More than any other creature, she therefore needed the mercy of God. Her special privilege demanded a special grace. Her more sublime redemption was the fruit of a more sublime love.

That redemption, it is said, was realized through preservation from "the stain of original sin." But the definition avoids the discussion about the nature of that stain or about the nature of original sin.

Finally, it was affirmed that Mary's conception was immaculate. This negative way of describing the mystery[1]—that conception was not "maculate," not stained—only wants to underline its positive aspect. It is the plenitude of grace. Mary was without stain because she was resplendent with the beauty of God. She was without darkness because she was illuminated by the light of God; she was without sin because she was full of grace.

Priority of the Love of God

There is a mystery about the love of God that the Immaculate Conception makes stand out in particular. It is namely the priority of that love. God is always the first to love.

John affirms in his letter:

> This is what love is:
> It is not we who loved God;
> it is he who loved us.   1 Jn 4, 10

The love of God always precedes our love. When we respond to God, we can only give back what we have already received.

This mystery shines through especially in the marvel of the Immaculate Conception. The Immaculate Conception really is a conception. In conception the child receives everything, gives nothing. It cannot give anything since its soul still sleeps in unconsciousness. It is only later that it will be able to recognize its filiation and thank its parents for the marvelous gift of existence that they have given to it.

This is incomparably truer for the plenitude of grace with which Mary was filled in her Immaculate Conception. She receives everything, gives nothing. It is only later, for example, at the Annunciation, that she will be able to respond to God through the obedience of her faith and offer to him the highest ministry that a creature can render to the Creator: to give a human body to the Word and to answer: "May it be done to me according to your Word." But as the Immaculate Conception, she remains silent. God alone is at work. He is the first to love.

God alone can love us in this way. For only He can love us before calling us to existence.

Most certainly, our parents also love us. They wanted us, conceived us, and gave birth to us. But when they conceived us, they did not even know what we would be, nor who we would be. Popular speech says quite rightly that mothers "expect a child." But they do not know its personality, nor what it will be later. They can love their child with all their heart, but their child will always remain a mystery. And this mystery will only grow after they have brought their child into the world.

But for God, it is quite different. He creates us as he loves us. When we were formed in the womb of our mother, several billion possibilities existed. A single one was realized. Who chose? Who chose us? Who wanted us and loved us as we are, including the color of our eyes, and the texture of our hair, our intelligence, our disposition, our way of approaching problems, our unique and personal way of loving? Only God can love us before calling us to existence. Because he loves us first.

What we affirm on the level of human conception is nothing, however, in comparison with the grace of spiritual existence; therefore, it is nothing in comparison with the immaculate conception of Mary's soul. In the first instant of her existence, in the very act of her coming into existence, God filled her with grace. He clothed her with the splendor of his light; he adorned her with his love.

The holy liturgy rightly proposes to us, in the Second Reading, the hymn on predestination according to the Letter to the Ephesians. Paul affirms:

> In Christ, God (the Father) chose us
> before the creation of the world
> to be holy and immaculate
> in his presence, in love.   Eph 1, 4

What is more gratuitous than this predestination "before the creation of the world"? Before the first dawn of the universe, before the round of the billions of galaxies of stars was launched, before the first sparkle of brightness for the billions of light years was lit, God thought about that little girl, about that little Galilean with a golden heart, about that Miriam who was going to build from her young woman's womb a Temple of glory for his Son! What a marvel! How can one not fall down before the love of God and bless him:

> Blessed be God
> the Father of our Lord Jesus Christ!
> He has blessed us with every spiritual blessing
> in heaven, in Christ!   Eph 1, 3

Yes, blessed be God the Father who, before the creation of the world, filled Mary with the plenitude of his love! Mary is the most sublime of his creatures, the most beautiful love of his tenderness, the most marvelous melody in his creation.

That is why she is also the creature who must thank God the most. I think that Mary must have loved this Psalm:

> Sing to the Lord a new song,
> for he has done marvels!   Ps 98, 1

She knew that among those marvels were included the marvels of her own mystery:

> The Almighty has done marvels for me.
> Holy is his name.   Lk 1, 49

Icon of the Immaculate Church

The mysteries of Mary possess an ecclesial dimension. The Virgin realizes in a unique and transcendent way the grace of the universal Church. Immaculate Mary is the icon of the immaculate Church.

The Church is without sin, but not without sinners. She is immaculate,[3] but made up of "maculated" people. She is holy "even in the heart of her sinful children in order to condemn sin in them."[4] For her holiness is not the sum of the holiness of each one of her members—that would not go very far— but rather the holiness of Christ in her.

What would we be without Christ? Paul does not mince words when he says:

> Fornicators, idolators, adulterers, sodomites, thieves, greedy,
> drunkards, slanderers, plunderers.   1 Cor 6, 9-10

That is what the Corinthians were. What did they become?

> You have been washed, you have been sanctified, you have been
> purified.   1 Cor 6, 11

> I have betrothed you to Christ as a pure virgin.   2 Cor 11, 2

With incredible audacity and I think also with a beautiful smile, Saint Ambrose affirms that the Church is a *casta meretrix*,[5] which can be translated as "chaste whore." She is a prostitute each time that she links love with money, each time that she sells herself to power, each time that she compromises herself with the glitter of the world. She becomes chaste through the kiss of Christ.

This holy and immaculate Church—where do we see her today? Nowhere except in immaculate Mary. She is the most pure and the most intense realization of the mystery of the church. When the fiancé of the Song of Songs says to his pretty brunette:

You are all beautiful, my beloved,
and without any blemish,   Song of Songs 4, 7

we know well that he is dreaming or that love is making him blind. For flawless beauty does not exist on earth, except in Mary, where it shines in her immaculate soul.

For us Christians, the holiness of Mary, like that of the Church, is an article of faith. But how can we make "those on the outside" believe in the Immaculate Conception? How can we make the holiness of the Church accessible to them?

There are not a thousand ways. There is only one argument: the holiness of Christians. It is in fleeing sin ourselves that we glorify the Immaculate Conception and make "those on the outside" believe in the holiness of the Church.

Of course, we always look for excuses. "It is the woman that you placed next to me," says Adam, "who gave me some fruit and I ate it." "It is the serpent who tricked me," says Eve, "and I ate."[7] This text from Genesis sticks to our skin. It is always the devil's fault. The devil takes the blame. But the evil is first in our heart. It is there that we must begin by glorifying the mystery of the Immaculate Mary. It is there that we must make the Church holy.

The Faith of the Humble

In the course of the ages, while the theologians were learnedly discussing the Immaculate Conception, which was then called "the pious belief," the people of simple faith were acknowledging it without difficulty. They understood instinctively that God had embellished the mother of Jesus as much as he could. Faith in the Immaculate Conception was the faith of the little ones, the privilege of the humble. Here is how this mystery was revealed to the humble Bernadette Soubirous at Lourdes, March 25, 1858:

In the early hours of March 25, 1858, the day of the Annunciation, Bernadette wakens. She feels again "impelled" to go to the grotto. Her parents would like to keep her from there. But the attraction is irresistible. They know it. They make her wait. But at five o'clock, she is on the road to the grotto.

This time she is very determined to obtain an answer for the Curé. After the rosary, Aquerò [the apparition] draws near through the inner hollow. Bernadette, overcome with joy, forces herself to ask with trembling and reverence...

Immaculate Conception

Miss, will you have the goodness to tell me who you are, please?

Aquerò smiles. She does not answer. Bernadette repeats with insistence, a second time, then a third. The apparition always smiles...but this time Bernadette will not stop [attempting to get the answer], since this is the condition placed by the Curé for building the chapel.

The fourth time, Aquerò no longer smiles. Her joined hands separate and extend toward the earth. Then she joins her hands at the top of her chest, raises her eyes to heaven and says: "Que soy era Immaculada Councepciou."

The color comes back to Bernadette's face. She hurries to the rectory, repeating these words that she does not want to risk losing (...) She avoids questions and repeats nonstop: "Immaculada Coun...cet-tiou, Immaculada Coun...cet-ciou."

She stumbles over the last two syllables. She arrives at the parish house and cries out to the Curé: "Que soy era Immaculada Councepciou."

Peyramale, the curate, reels under the shock. He gets ready to say: Little arrogant child, you are the Immaculate Conception! But the words stick in his hoarse throat (...) They finally come out: "A lady cannot bear that name! You are mistaken! You know what that means?" Bernadette shakes her head negatively. "Then how can you say it, if you did not understand?" "I repeated all along the way."

Peyramale feels all anger leave him. What strange movement swells his chest? Is he sick? These are sobs that he is holding back. "She still wants the chapel," murmurs Bernadette in the silence.[8]

May Mary accompany us on the path that leads to the Lord's manger. It is really holiness that prepares us for the coming of Christ.

Paul writes:

> May the Lord establish you firmly
> in an immaculate holiness before God our Father,
> for the day when our Lord Jesus
> will come with all his saints.   1 Thes 3, 13

Blessed be the Lord for that Day when he will welcome into his Kingdom the sinners, the stained that we are. Then, with the Immaculate, we will celebrate his love forever and ever.

CONCLUDING PRAYER

Filled with the Holy Spirit, Mary prophesied:
"Behold, all ages will call me blessed!"
We also want to fulfill the prophecy
and to bless you, God our Father,
for the marvels of love that you performed in Mary, the mother of
your Son.

Blest are you, O Lord, through eternity!

If Jesus is the rose that blooms
on the rough stem of Jesse,
you, Mary, are the rosebush that bears him.
Truly, the Lord has done marvels for you.

Blest are you, O Lord, through eternity!

If Jesus is the sun of justice
that rises on the distress of the world,
you, Mary, are its dawn.
The Lord has done marvels for you.

Blest are you, O Lord, through eternity!

If Jesus is the source of living water
that springs up into eternal life,
you, Mary, are the fountain that makes it spring.
The Lord has done marvels for you.

Blest are you, O Lord, through eternity!

If Jesus is the wheat that gives the bread
that satisfies for eternal life,
you, Mary, are the field that makes it ripen.
The Lord has done marvels for you.

Blest are you, O Lord, through eternity!

If Jesus is Immanuel, God with us,
who unites heaven and earth,
you, Mary, are his dwelling.
The Lord has done marvels for you.

Blest are you, O Lord, through eternity!

If Jesus is the Son of light
in whom the Father has put all his kindness,
you, Mary, carry him in your womb.
The Lord has done marvels for you.

Blest are you, O Lord, through eternity!

Immaculate Conception

If Jesus is the face of infinite mercy,
the tenderness of the Father who comes to us
from heaven,
you, Mary, are his Mother.
The Lord has done marvels for you.

Blest are you, O Lord, through eternity!

We praise you and we bless you,
God our Father, Lord of all marvels,
because you always love us first.
It is your love that fills the Virgin Mary with grace
in the first moment of her existence,
even before she could thank you.
It is your love that chooses her to be the mother
of your Son;
it is your love that glorifies her as the Queen of heaven.
Save us in the name of that love.
We are her children,
and Jesus is our brother forever and ever. Amen.

NOTES TO IMMACULATE CONCEPTION

1. See J. Jugie, *L'Immaculée Conception dans l'Ecriture Sainte et la Tradition orientale* (Rome, 1952), where one will find the essential point of the oriental patristic dossier.

   On the New Testament, consult *Mary in the New Testament* (Philadelphia: Fortress Press, New York: Paulist Press, Toronto: Ramsey, 1978) which gives the Protestant and Catholic positions.

2. It is to be noted that in order to signify the mystery of God, in human language the negative is often the most convenient formula. We say, therefore, that God is infinite, that is that he has no end, but it is really to affirm his sovereign grandeur. We say that he is immeasurable, that nothing can measure him, precisely because he is infinitely great.

3. Cf. Eph 5, 27.

4. Cf. Journet, *L'Eglise du Verbe incarné* (Paris: Desclée de Brouwer et Cie, 1951), p. 395.

5. *Traité sur l'Evangile de saint Luc,* III, 23. Cf. SC 45 (1956), p. 132.

6. Mk 4, 11.

7. Gn 3, 12-13.

8. Bernadette of Lourdes, in R. Laurentin, Vie de Bernadette (Paris: Ed. Desclée de Brouwer, 1978), pp. 91-93. © 1978, Desclée de Brouwer & Cie. Published in the U. S. by Winston Press, 430 Oak Grove, Minneapolis, Minn. 55403, as *Bernadette of Lourdes.* © 1979. Published in England by Darton, Longman and Todd as *Bernadette of Lourdes.* © 1979. Used with permission of Winston Press. The citations in *italics* are from authentic documents.

SECOND SUNDAY OF ADVENT

READING I

BAR 5, 1-9

A reading from the book of the prophet Baruch

Jerusalem, take off your robe of mourning and misery;
   put on the splendor of glory from God forever:
Wrapped in the cloak of justice from God,
   bear on your head the mitre
   that displays the glory of the eternal name.
For God will show all the earth your splendor:
   you will be named by God forever
   the peace of justice, the glory of God's worship.
Up, Jerusalem! Stand upon the heights;
   look to the east and see your children
Gathered from the east and the west
   at the word of the Holy One,
   rejoicing that they are remembered by God.
Led away on foot by their enemies they left you:
   but God will bring them back to you
   borne aloft in glory as on royal thrones.
For God has commanded
   that every lofty mountain be made low.
And that the age-old depths and gorges
   be filled to level ground,
   that Israel may advance secure in the glory of God.
The forests and every fragrant kind of tree
   have overshadowed Israel at God's command;
For God is leading Israel in joy
   by the light of his glory,
   with his mercy and justice for company.
The Word of the Lord.

RESPONSORIAL PSALM

Ps 126, 1-2. 2-3. 4-5. 6

R/. (3) The Lord has done great things for us;
   we are filled with joy.

When the Lord brought back the captives of Zion,
   we were like men dreaming.

Then our mouth was filled with laughter,
  and our tongue with rejoicing.

R/. The Lord has done great things for us;
  we are filled with joy.

Then they said among the nations,
  "The Lord has done great things for them."
The Lord has done great things for us;
  we are glad indeed.

R/. (3) The Lord has done great things for us;
  we are filled with joy.

Restore our fortunes, O Lord,
  like the torrents in the southern desert.
Those that sow in tears
  shall reap rejoicing.

R/. (3) The Lord has done great things for us;
  we are filled with joy.

Although they go forth weeping,
  carrying the seed to be sown,
They shall come back rejoicing,
  carrying their sheaves.

R/. (3) The Lord has done great things for us;
  we are filled with joy.

READING II   PHIL 1, 4-6. 8-11

A reading from the letter of Paul to the Philippians

In every prayer I utter, I rejoice as I plead on your behalf, at the way you have all continually helped promote the gospel from the very first day.

I am sure of this much: that he who has begun the good work in you will carry it through to completion, right up to the day of Christ Jesus. God himself can testify how much I long for each of you with the affection of Christ Jesus! My prayer is that your love may more and more abound, both in understanding and wealth of experience, so that with a clear conscience and blameless conduct you may learn to value the things that really matter, up to the very day of Christ. It is my wish that you may be found rich in the harvest of justice which Jesus Christ has ripened in you, to the glory and praise of God.

The Word of the Lord.

GOSPEL   LK 3, 1-6

A reading from the holy gospel according to Luke

In the fifteenth year of the rule of Tiberius Caesar, when Pontius Pilate was procurator of Judea, Herod tetrarch of Galilee, Philip his brother, tetrarch of the region of Ituraea and Trachonitis, and Lysanias tetrarch of Abilene, during the high-priesthood of Annas and Caiaphas, the word of God was spoken to John son of Zechariah in the desert. He went about the entire region of the Jordan proclaiming a baptism of repentance which led to the forgiveness of sins, as it is written in the book of the words of Isaiah the prophet:

"A herald's voice in the desert, crying,
'Make ready the way of the Lord,
Clear him a straight path.
Every valley shall be filled
and every mountain and hill shall be leveled.
The windings shall be made straight
and the rough ways smooth,
and all mankind shall see the salvation of God.'"

The gospel of the Lord.

INTRODUCTORY PRAYER

We bless you, God our Father,
for this time of Advent that your love offers to us.
We pray to you:
Prepare in the desert of our heart
the path of return to your Son Jesus.
The hills of our pride – bring low by your humility.
The valleys of our despair – fill with your hope.
The twisted paths of our lies –
straighten through your truth.
Let jonquils of joy bloom in our desert.
Then we will be able to celebrate the glory of your love
and worship your salvation, your Son Jesus,
our Savior and our brother. Amen.

HOMILY

1. Jerusalem, Take off Your Robe of Sadness and Misery

The First Reading is an excerpt from the book of Baruch.

It is generally admitted that this book presents an anthology of diverse pieces coming from different authors. The present excerpt is derived from Psalm 11 of the Psalter of Solomon, a writing that dates from the first century before the Christian era.[1] We find ourselves therefore in the presence of the hope of the believing community at the dawn of messianic times.

The passage is marvelous. Jerusalem must take off her robe of sadness and misery because the glory and justice of God are going to envelope her like a royal cloak. Her dispersed children gather together, summoned by the word of Holy God, and ascend on a pilgrimage toward a Jerusalem of joy.

The Fulfillment of the Prophecy

Jesus is the "Yes" in whom the Father fulfills all his promises.[2] He is the Good News that "gathers in unity the children of God dispersed" by sin.[3] He clothes the Church, his Spouse, in a cloak of light woven from glory and justice.[4] Mercy and joy escort her on the way to heaven.

Church of Jesus Christ, community of love upon which the beauty of the Lord shines brightly! Who will help us to represent this Church of love, this beauty of heaven on earth, this smile of God in the midst of the tears of the world, this light from on high upon the darkness here below, this mercy of God upon misery of the world? For it is in our hands today that the Lord has placed his beauty; it is our love that he asks today to gather together all people. It is our mercy that he invites today to escort our brothers and sisters on the road to heaven.

The Authentic Church of Jesus

One often asks the question: What are the criteria that allow us to recognize the authentic Church of Jesus Christ?

The Church of Jesus according to the prophet Baruch is the one which takes off her worn clothes of sadness and her robe of misery, who puts on the royal cloak of God's justice. A whining and tearful Church is not the Church of my Christ. Do I carry in my heart and on my face the joy of God?

30

The Church of Jesus is the one which stands erect, which looks to the east, whose face is illuminated by the rising sun. A reclining and sleeping Church is not the Church of my Christ. Is my face radiant with the light of Christ?

The Church of Jesus is the one which gathers her children together around the Word of Holy God. A Church that raises up barriers of human words between her children is not the Church of my Christ. Does my love unite my brothers and my sisters around Christ?

The Church of Jesus is the one which tears down the mountains of our pride, which tears down the hills of our bitterness, which fills the valleys of our despair. A Church that is not a path of hope is not the Church of my Christ. Am I a path of hope for my brothers and sisters?

The Church of Jesus is the one which has mercy as an escort. A Church that is not merciful is not the Church of my Christ. Am I merciful?

2. Because of What You Have Done for the Gospel

In his missionary work, Paul always wanted to keep his freedom, even independence, not wanting to be in debt to anyone. At the time of his farewell discourse to the elders of Ephesus, he affirmed with pride:

> The silver, gold or clothing of no one have I coveted. You
> yourselves know that these hands have provided for my needs
> and for those of my companions. Acts 20, 33-44

He did not accept, throughout his ministry, any gift from any community, except from the Philippians.[5] A special love bound him to that community whose foundation resembles an idyll, a story of love. I strongly suspect that Lydia, the sympathetic merchant of the purple cloth from Thyatira, was the soul of those generosities. Luke writes: She "worshipped God." That means she belonged to those who worshipped the God of the revelation of Israel, but could not observe, especially in a pagan environment, the interdicts of the Jewish tradition. When Paul arrived at Philippi, accompanied by Silas and Timothy, perhaps also by Luke, he organized a prayer meeting the day of the Sabbath on the banks of a river. Lydia was listening, but she was not understanding anything. Then, writes Luke with delight, "the Lord opened her heart in a way that she clung to Paul's words." She was baptized with all her household. Then, with typical feminine persuasion, she invited the apostles to her home by saying: "If you consider me a believer in the Lord, come stay in my house." And, Luke adds, "she urged us there."

Such are the recollections behind these words of Paul: "What you have done for the Gospel."

That generosity is going to place the Philippians on an extraordinary path.

That generosity nurtured a mutual love. To describe it, Paul uses a very vivid image. He cherishes them, he says, "in the heart of Christ Jesus."[7] Charity, therefore, places Christians in the heart of Christ.

Charity makes them progress in the knowledge of God. Indeed, all the paths of intelligence are good for reaching God. But in order to know "the love of Christ that surpasses all understanding,"[8] the humble practice of charity is the most rapid path.

Charity leads them, says Paul, "from the first day" until the "day when Christ Jesus will come."[9] It guides them on the road of eternity.

Those are the great lines that become clear from this excerpt from the Letter to the Philippians. How can we actualize them today in our lives?

Most certainly, one cannot mechanically carry over in our present communities the situation of the communities of the apostolic period. Having said that, there are, yet today, many "Lydias" who alleviate miseries, many "Pauls" who need to be helped. In her most recent letter, Sister Elizabeth, who works in the missions, writes from Angola:

> I try to save the babies. Today I distributed one and a half spoonfuls of rice to each child. I saw that all were gazing at their plates; their eyes were asking for more. I told them: "This rice comes from France; it swells up a great deal. It will give you a full plate." But none of the children were convinced.
>
> This evening, I did not make rounds (to say goodnight), because it is too painful not being able to satisfy their hunger.

For us who live in abundance, the least that we can say—or do—is this: God calls us today to share a little of our material riches, a little of our intellectual riches, a little of our riches of love. How? I do not know. It is up to us to see how we want to place ourselves in the heart of Christ, what understanding we want to acquire of his mystery, where we want to place ourselves on the road to eternity in the awaiting of the return of Christ.

3. The Fifteenth Year of the Reign of Tiberius

As a historian, Luke likes to place the history of salvation in relation to secular history. He specifies:

The fifteenth year of the reign of the emperor Tiberius.   Lk 3, 1

The emperor Augustus died August 19 of the year 14. Tiberius succeeded him. The fifteenth year of his reign corresponds, according to that era's calculations, from the first of October of the year 27 to September 30 of the year 28.

Pontius Pilate was governor of Judea.   Lk 3, 1

We know Pontius Pilate rather well through the testimonies of Flavius Josephus and Philo of Alexandria, both of them contemporaries of the time of Christ. An inscription discovered in 1961 in the excavations of Caesari bears the name of Pontius Pilate. He was prefect of Rome in Judea from the year 26 to 36.

Herod was tetrarch (prince) of Galilee.   Lk 3, 1

This son of Herod the Great, called Antipas, is equally well-known thanks to Josephus. Antipas was the murderer of John the Baptist. We find him in the accounts of the Passion.

His brother Philip was tetrarch (prince) of Iturea and
Traconitis.   Lk 3, 1

Philip was the son of Herod the Great and Mariamme II, and the first husband of Herodias (it is this Herodias who will claim the head of John the Baptist for the prize of her daughter's dance on Herod's birthday).[10]

Lysanias was tetrarch (prince) of Abilene.   Lk 3, 1

This Lysanias was not known elsewhere in the sources of secular history until the beginning of this century. Some thought to put in doubt the integrity of Luke as a historian. But in 1912, an inscription found at Abila, 30 kilometers from Damascus, was published, which mentioned his name.

Luke, then, anchors the history of salvation in the heart of human history. Not only does he write it in the very flow of history, but he also places it in a situation of confrontation. We can hardly, in fact, imagine the despotism of dying paganism and its pretensions to dominate the world. For example, in the year 9 before the Christian era, the proconsul Paulus Fabius Maximus published the following decree relative to the birthday of Augustus:

(The birthday of Augustus) gave another aspect to the entire world, whose ruin had been near if this happiness common to all people, Caesar, had not been born. Also each one can consider rightly that event as the origin of his life and of his existence, as the time in which one must not regret having been born…Providence, which regulates the course of our life, has given proof of attention and goodness and has provided for the most perfect good for life in producing the emperor, whom she has filled with virtue to make of him a benefactor of humanity…The day of the birth of god has been for the world the beginning of the good news that he bears.[11]

It would be difficult to descend lower into base flattery.

Against these kings of straw who adorn themselves with the title of god, of savior, of benefactor, Luke opposes the message of John the Baptist. There is a conversion to undergo, a salvation to expect, a forgiveness to hope for. Against the kingdom of this world and its vanity, there is the Kingdom of God and its truth. On the one hand there is the fortress of Macheront that Herod had transformed into a luxurious palace,[12] where they flaunted crowns set with precious stones and wore lavish robes woven from gold. On the other hand there is the barrenness of the banks of the Jordan where a poor fellow dressed in camel's hair was crying out in the desert:

> Repent,
> for the Kingdom of heaven is very near!   Mt 3, 2

It was in the dunes of the desert sand that a new history of the world was beginning! When the waves of time had finished shaking the kingdoms of the earth, they appeared just as they existed before God: empty shells that the tides of history abandoned on the beaches of time. The message of John the Baptist, on the contrary, carried by the eternity of the Word of God, remains contemporary to all ages.

For us, what message does this gospel bring today?

The history of salvation has cast its anchor into the shores of the history of the world. The history of my salvation has cast its anchor into the history of my life. The most important date for me is that of my birth. It is at that moment that the history of salvation began for me. And the fifteenth year of the reign of the emperor Tiberius corresponds for me very exactly to this moment when the prophet says to me:

> Prepare the way of the Lord.
> Make straight his paths!   Lk 3, 4

Tiberius, Pontius Pilate, Herod and all his clique are dead. A thousand other tyrants continue to besiege us and to threaten our freedom: tyrants of power, of money, of pleasure. Against these tyrants of death, John the Baptist continues to cry out to us:

Repent,
for the Kingdom of heaven is very near!   Mt 3, 2

Some claim: History does not lead anywhere. We affirm: History leads to God. Each of our days possesses his eternity.

The King is Coming

In conclusion, I would like to share with you this beautiful poem written by Tagore (who lived in India from 1861 to 1941).

The night darkened. Our day's works had been done. We thought that the last guest had arrived for the night, and the doors in the village were all shut. Only some said the king was to come. We laughed and said, "No, it cannot be!"

It seemed there were knocks at the door, and we said it was nothing but the wind. We put out the lamps and lay down to sleep. Only some said, "It is the messenger!" We laughed and said, "No, it must be the wind!"

There came a sound in the dead of the night. We sleepily thought it was the distant thunder. The earth shook, the walls rocked, and it troubled us in our sleep. Only some said it was the sound of wheels. We said in a drowsy murmur, "No, it must be the rumbling of clouds!"

The night was still dark when the drum sounded. The voice came, "Wake up! Delay not!" We pressed our hands to our hearts and shuddered with fear. Some said, "Lo, there is the King's flag!" We stood up on our feet and cried, "There is no time for delay!"

The king has come—but where are lights, where are wreaths? Where is the throne to seat him? Oh shame! Oh, utter shame! Where is the hall, the decorations? Some one has said, "Vain is this cry! Greet him with empty hands...!"[13]

In reading this poem by Tagore, we ask ourselves: Is our heart empty enough of ourselves to be able to welcome the King who is coming? Is it full enough of the hope of the entire world to go before the Lord? For we Christians hold the awaiting of the whole world in our hands when we hold out our hands toward God.

Soon we are going to meet God. And I rejoice for that Day. Not for what we are, not for what we have, but because we do not have anything before God. We have nothing in our empty hands. For it is into empty hands that God gives his mercy. To him glory forever and ever.

CONCLUDING PRAYER

Holy Church of the Lord,
take off your robe of sadness;
adorn yourself with the beauty of heaven,
Christ Jesus.
He is coming to save you.

> *Show us, Lord, your unfailing love;*
> *grant us your salvation.*

Holy Church of the Lord,
display your splendor everywhere under the sun;
proclaim the "Peace of justice,"
Christ Jesus.
He is coming to save you.

> *Show us, Lord, your unfailing love;*
> *grant us your salvation.*

Holy Church of the Lord,
rise up from the midst of darkness;
turn to the east where rises your sun,
Christ Jesus.
He is coming to save you.

> *Show us, Lord, your unfailing love;*
> *grant us your salvation.*

Holy Church of the Lord,
gather together your children dispersed by sin;
reunite them around the Word of Holy God,
Christ Jesus.
He is coming to save you.

Show us, Lord, your unfailing love;
grant us your salvation.

Holy Church of the Lord,
advance in joy toward your light;
receive as escorts mercy and justice,
Christ Jesus.

He is coming to save you.

Show us, Lord, your unfailing love;
grant us your salvation.

We are your Church, Lord.

Realize in us the marvels of your love.

May your beauty be our attire.

Your light, our path.

And may your mercy accompany us
up to your paradise where we will celebrate you
forever and ever. Amen.

NOTES TO SECOND SUNDAY OF ADVENT

1. Cf. J. B. Frey, art. "Apocryphes de l'Ancien Testament," Supplément au Dictionnaire Biblique, vol. 1 (1928), col. 391-392.
2. 2 Cor 1, 20.
3. Jn 11, 52.
4. Cf. Eph 5, 27.
5. Cf. 2 Cor 11, 8-9. Phil 4, 15-19.
6. It is related in Acts 16, 11-15 and took place around the year 50.
7. Phil 1, 8. Literally: "in the bowels."
8. Eph 3, 19.
9. Phil 1, 5-6.
10. Cf. Mt 14, 3-12; Mk 6, 17-29.
11. Inscription of Priére, 7 B. C. Translated by M. J. Rouffiac. Cited in B. Rigaux, *Pour une histoire de Jésus, Témoignage de l'Evangile de Luc* (Paris: Desclée de Brouwer, 1970), pp. 384-385.
12. According to the testimony of Flavius Josephus, *De Bello Judaico,* VII, 6.2. Cf. *Flavius Josephus, De Bello Judaico* vol. 2 (Munich: Kosel-Verlag, 1969), p. 106.
13. In *Gitanjali* (Song Offerings), 51 (London: Macmillan and Co., 1914), pp. 44-46. A collection of prose translations by Tagore from the original Bengali. With punctuation changes for readability. Reprinted by permission of the Trustees of the Tagore Estate and Macmillan, London and Basingstoke. Copyright 1916 by Macmillan Publishing Co., Inc., renewed 1944 by Rabindranath Tagore.

THIRD SUNDAY OF ADVENT

READING I   ZEP 3, 14-18

A reading from the book of the prophet Zephaniah

Shout for joy, O daughter Zion!
Sing joyfully, O Israel!
Be glad and exult with all your heart,
   O daughter Jerusalem!
The Lord has removed the judgment against you,
   he has turned away your enemies;
The King of Israel, the Lord, is in your midst,
   you have no further misfortune to fear.

On that day, it shall be said to Jerusalem:
Fear not, O Zion, be not discouraged!
The Lord, your God, is in your midst,
   a mighty savior;
He will rejoice over you with gladness,
   and renew you in his love.
He will sing joyfully because of you,
   as one sings at festivals.

The Word of the Lord.

RESPONSORIAL PSALM   IS 12, 2-3. 4. 5-6

R/. (6) Cry out with joy and gladness:
   for among you is the great and Holy One of Israel.

God indeed is my savior;
   I am confident and unafraid.
My strength and my courage is the Lord,
   and he has been my savior.
With joy you will draw water
   at the foundation of salvation.

R/. Cry out with joy and gladness:
   for among you is the great and Holy One of Israel.

Give thanks to the Lord, acclaim his name;
   among the nations make known his deeds,
   proclaim how exalted is his name.

R/. Cry out with joy and gladness:
   for among you is the great and Holy One of Israel.

Sing praise to the Lord for his glorious achievement;
   let this be known throughout the earth.
Shout with exultation, O city of Zion,
   for great in your midst
   is the Holy One of Israel!
R/. Cry out with joy and gladness:
   for among you is the great and Holy One of Israel.

READING II   PHIL 4, 4-7

A reading from the letter of Paul to the Philippians

Rejoice in the Lord always! I say it again. Rejoice! Everyone should
see how unselfish you are. The Lord himself is near. Dismiss all
anxiety from your minds. Present your needs to God in every form of
prayer and in petitions full of gratitude. Then God's own peace, which
is beyond all understanding, will stand guard over your hearts and
minds, in Christ Jesus.

The Word of the Lord.

GOSPEL   LK 3, 10-18

A reading from the holy gospel according to Luke

The crowds asked John, "What ought we to do?" In reply he said, "Let
the man with two coats give to him who has none. The man who has
food should do the same."

Tax collectors also came to be baptized, and they said to him, "Teacher,
what are we to do?" He answered them, "Exact nothing over and above
your fixed amount."

Soldiers likewise asked him, "What about us?" He told them, "Do not
bully anyone. Denounce no one falsely. Be content with your pay."

The people were full of anticipation, wondering in their hearts whether
John might be the Messiah. John answered them all by saying: "I am
baptizing you in water, but there is one to come who is mightier than I.
I am not fit to loosen his sandal strap. He will baptize you in the Holy
Spirit and in fire. His winnowing-fan is in his hand to clear his thresh-
ing floor and gather the wheat into his granary, but the chaff he will
burn in unquenchable fire." Using exhortations of this sort, he preached
the good news to the people.

The gospel of the Lord.

INTRODUCTORY PRAYER

We bless you, God our Father,
fountain of mercy and source of all joy.

We pray to you:
Let your joy and your mercy
triumph in our heart.
And we will await, in peace and confidence,
the coming of your Son Jesus,
our Savior and our brother
forever and ever. Amen.

HOMILY

The Third Sunday of Advent is traditionally consecrated to celebrating the joy of Advent. Traditionally, it is known as *Gaudete* Sunday, from the first word of the entrance song: "Gaudete! Rejoice!"

Our God is a God of joy. The message of Paul today is the following:

Rejoice in the Lord always.
I will say it again: Rejoice...
The Lord is near.   Phil 4, 4-5

Joy, peace, that is what you will have left when the tumult of life has been calmed, when time has been disposed of, like water running through your fingers. When you are alone, face to face with the divine, ready to meet God, when you have only yourself to offer to him, if at that moment you are in the joy of awaiting the Lord, then you are in good standing. The Lord is already in your heart; you are very near to Christmas, to that Christmas which is eternal.

We confront here an extraordinary mystery. We are all going toward our death; we have all embarked on a pilgrimage toward a country from which one does not return. Yet, we Christians affirm that we are going there in joy. For we are going not toward a death, but toward the life which is beyond death.

Joy is the first right, the most elementary right of every creature.

If God creates a robin—if he creates the robin which, every day, comes to my window to tell me its stories and to ask me for grain—that robin has an elementary right to happiness. Oh! Surely not to a happiness that touches the stars, but to the happiness of a robin.

If God creates a hedgehog—a hedgehog which adores walking on the grass of my garden at ten o'clock at night to go I do not know where—that hedgehog has a right to happiness. Not to the happiness of an angel in paradise, but to the happiness of a hedgehog.

If God creates a heart of a man, a heart of a woman, a heart of a little boy, of a little girl, if he creates a heart of a paralyzed person, a heart of a developmentally handicapped person, if he even creates a broken heart, that heart has a right to happiness. If God gives life, he must give joy.

1. The Hymn to Joy

We all know the hymn to joy by Schiller that Beethoven used to conclude his Ninth Symphony. It is the dream of universal fraternity ("All people become brothers and sisters where your gentle wings spread."). But from the time we first sang it, we have continued to redden all the countries of the earth with the blood of our wars.

All human effort toward joy and peace is blessed by God. Paul's "hymn to joy" in the letter to the Philippians outlines for us the Christian path toward joy.

> Rejoice in the Lord always!
> I will say it again: Rejoice...
> Everyone should see how unselfish you are.
> The Lord is near.
>
> Phil 4, 4-5

Joy in the Lord

Christian joy is a joy "in the Lord." There are vulnerable, fragile joys. The first adversity wounds them to death.

> They have abandoned me—says the Lord—
> me, the source of living water,
> to dig cisterns,
> cracked cisterns that do not contain water.
>
> Jer 2, 13

Everything depends upon where we place our joy. It is a question of knowing if we intend to quench our thirst with the fetid water of a cracked cistern, or if we prefer the water of a living spring. Cracked cisterns are all those assurances of happiness that we wish to have about the future! The source of living water is confidence in God alone!

> In you, Lord, is the fountain of life.
> Through your light, we see light.
>
> Ps 36, 10

Continual Joy, for the Lord is Near

Christian joy is a continual joy, for "the Lord is near." Continual joy even in suffering? Even if, like Paul at Philippi,[1] one is beaten? Even if one has a broken heart? Yes, even if one has a broken heart. For it is written:

> The Lord is near to the brokenhearted. Ps 34, 19

He is near to them, not because they have broken hearts, but because the breaking of their hearts opens them to the Lord.

Most certainly, there are days when joy becomes a struggle, sometimes even a mystery. Then we must seek the joy of God in the midst of our sadness, seek his peace in the midst of our anxieties. Whenever we seek God, we are already dwelling in the midst of his joy.

Joy of Prayer

Christian joy is moreover a joy of prayer. One must pray without ceasing, says Paul, in thanksgiving and supplication.

Continual prayer is our continual look upon God. The psalmist says:

> My eyes are fixed on the Lord,
> for he frees my feet from the trap. Ps 25, 15

We are walking in a jungle where a thousand traps are set under steps, where a thousand cracked cisterns are open under our feet. More than ever, does not the most elementary prudence consist in watching where we place our feet? The psalmist answers us: No! The prudence of earth really consists in looking at the earth, with its traps and its cisterns. And you fall in them. The prudence of heaven consists in looking at heaven. And the Lord leads your steps.

Happy are they who walk toward the Lord, their eyes fixed on heaven, praise in their mouth! Their entire life will be a path of joy.

2. Daughter of Zion, Rejoice

There are prophets that we know and that we like more than others. Zephaniah is one of those. His ministry is placed between the years 640-630. It has been, therefore, twenty-seven centuries that the Good News has been proclaimed.

> Daughter of Zion, rejoice,
> for the Lord is in you
> as a mighty Savior! Zep 3, 14-15

Zephaniah addresses himself to the "Daughter of Zion." The community of the Covenant is personified as a young girl, as a fiancée. God loves his people as a man loves his fiancée, as a man cherishes his wife. This Daughter of Zion will become, in the New Testament, the Church of Jesus Christ, "pure virgin, fiancée of Christ."[2]

The Ecclesial Symphony of the Two Choirs of the Old and New Testament

It is this text of Zephaniah that serves as the foundation of Gabriel's message at the Annunciation. Here are the similarities as they appear between the Greek text of the Gospel of Luke and the Greek translation of the prophecy of Zephaniah:

Zephaniah 3, 14-18	Luke 1, 28-33
Rejoice,	Rejoice,
daughter of Zion.	"Full of grace."
The Lord is in you.	The Lord is with you.
Do not fear, Zion.	Do not fear, Mary.
The Lord	You will conceive
is in your womb,	in your womb.
the king of Israel.	He will reign
as a mighty Savior.	You will give him
	the name of Jesus (Savior).

The ecclesial symphony of the two choirs of the Old and of the New Testament attains here one of its summits. The message of Gabriel is cast, almost word for word, in the prophecy of Zephaniah. This message shows us, in the Virgin of the Annunciation, the Daughter of Zion, the most pure and most intense realization of the mystery of the Church.

Do Not Fear, I Am with You

One might say, "It is nice to see the relationship between Mary and the Daughter of Zion on the biblical level. But on the practical level, what does that mean to us?"

This is a valid question. I answer: On the practical level, that is, in our daily life, Zephaniah reveals to us an extraordinary message that unsettles our life. In fact, if the Daughter of Zion represents the Church, which is the community of the Covenant, and if the Virgin of the Annunciation fulfills the prophecy of Zephaniah, it also said to each one of us, since we belong to that Church. And furthermore, if God speaks to us not only through the Bible, but also through the events of our life,[3] each event, like each word of the Bible, becomes for us a kind of Annunciation.

Someone has just learned that he has an incurable illness, that the advent of his life is touching its end; this is for him an "annunciation." God tells him through the ministry of Zephaniah: "Do not fear! The Lord is with you." A family has just experienced a great joy, like the return of a child from the captivity of drugs or hate; this is for them an "annunciation." God says to them: "Rejoice! The Lord is with you." Someone has just lost a loved one, a husband, a wife, a child. God says again: "Do not fear! I am with you."

Of course we do not have to face such extreme situations every day. But each day that God gives to us—with its clouds and its banality, with its sunshine and its enthusiasm—is already in itself a word of God. Each day is already in some way an annunciation. Each day, God invites us to receive Christ, to make him born in our heart, to incarnate him in our life. And each day brings to us the joyful message of Zephaniah: Rejoice. The Lord is with you.

The mystery of the Annunciation is thus at the center of our life. The prophecy of Zephaniah, addressed originally to the "Light Remnant,"[4] which has survived the torments of the Assyrian wars, actualized later in the Virgin of the Annunciation, gives to us the key to understanding today our own life.

The God of Dance

The finale of Zephaniah is marvelous. It is written:

> The Lord will renew you through his love.
> He will dance for you with shouts of joy
> as in the days of feasting.   Zep 3, 17-18

Madeleine Delbrel has a very nice passage on the dance of God.[5]

> If there are many holy people who do not like to dance,
> There are many saints who need to dance,
> So happy were they to be alive:
> Saint Theresa with her castanets,
> Saint John of the Cross with an Infant Jesus in his arms,
> and Saint Francis before the Pope.
> If we were pleased with you, Lord,

We would not be able to resist
This need to dance, which unfurls upon the earth.
And we would come to guess
Which dance it would please you to have us dance
By taking up the steps of your Providence.
For I think that perhaps you have enough
Of people who always speak of serving you with airs of captains,
Of knowing you with airs of professors,
Of reaching you with rules of sport,
Of loving you with a worn-out love.

One day when you wanted a little something else,
You invented Saint Francis,
And you make of him your juggler.
Allow us to invent of ourselves
Joyful people who dance their life with you.

To be a good dancer, with you as elsewhere,
it is not necessary
To know where dancing leads.

It is necessary to follow, to be lively, to be light,
And especially not to be stiff.

It is not necessary to ask you for explanations
Of the dance steps that would please you.

It is necessary to be like an extension
Of you, agile and alive,
And to receive through you the transmission
of the orchestra's rhythm.
It is not necessary to want to move forward at all cost,
But to welcome the turn, the sidestep.
It is necessary to know how to stop and glide instead of walk.
And those would only be foolish steps
If the music did not make of them a harmony.

But we forget the music of your spirit,
And we make of our life a gymnastic exercise.
We forget that, in your arms, life dances.
That your Holy Will is one of inconceivable fantasy,
And that it is of monotony and of boredom only for old souls
Who are wallflowers at the joyous dance of your love.

Lord, come invite us.
We are ready to dance for you this errand to be done,
These accounts, dinner to be prepared, this evening
when we will be sleepy.
We are ready to dance for you the dance of work,
The one of heat, later the one of cold.
If certain tunes are often in a minor key we will not tell you
That they are sad;
If others make us a little breathless, we will not tell you
That they are exhausting.
And if some people jostle us, we will take it with a smile,
Knowing well that this always happens while dancing.

Lord,
…teach us to put on our humanity each day
Like a ballgown that will make us love
All its details as indispensable jewels from you.

Make us live our life,
Not like a game of chess where everything is calculated,
Not like a match where everything is difficult,
Not like a theorem that racks our brain.
But like a feast without end where meeting with you revives.
Like a ball, like a dance,
In the arms of your grace,
In the universal music of love.

Lord, come invite us.

3. The Coming of Christ

We all know what it is to wait. Waiting is always somewhat a waste of time. We know about waiting at the bus stop, waiting at the dentist's office. We sometimes even say: We are only biding our time.

None of these "waitings" reveals to us what it means to wait for Christ.

What Must We Do?

Sometimes, we dream of marvels to accomplish for the Kingdom. Sometimes, also, Christians pursue their pastors—as if they were soothsayers—with their questions: "What must we do?"

Luke answers us in today's Gospel through the voice of John the Baptist. To the crowds that come to ask him: "What must we do?" John answers: Share!

> The one who has two coats,
> let him share with the one who has none.
> And the one who has something to eat,
> let him do the same! Lk 3, 11

To the publicans who ask: "What must we do?" John answers:

> Do not demand anything more
> than what is fixed for you. Lk 3, 13

To the soldiers who come to ask him: "And what must we do?" he answers:

> Be content with your pay. Lk 3, 14

In this way then, the marvel that God proposes to us is to fulfill our daily duty in simplicity. It is thus that we place our heart in the awaiting of the Lord.

Baptism in the Holy Spirit and Fire

Luke places the baptism of John opposite that of Jesus. The former is made in water, the latter, in the Holy Spirit and fire.

The verb *"to baptize"* keeps here its early meaning: "to plunge into." It is probable that the early text declared:

> He [being the Messiah] will baptize you
> in spirit [which could mean wind] and in fire. Lk 3, 16

Actually, several old witness omit the adjective "holy." The word spirit (*ruah* in Hebrew, *pneuma* in Greek) assumes the different meanings of *wind, breath,* and *spirit.* In the Orient (even today in Africa), to winnow the wheat, one throws the grains into the air with the winnowing fork. The wind sorts out the chaff, which is carried off, from the grain which falls on the threshing-floor.

For us then, the wind of the winnowing field is the image of the Spirit or the breath of God. This wind comes upon us, separating the useless chaff in our life from the grain which serves the Kingdom. That is to say, today's Gospel signifies that the coming of Jesus is judgment.

Christ comes at each moment of our life - each moment in judgment and introduces us into the presence of the Lord. May it be filled with the service of his glory!

CONCLUDING PRAYER

Paul says to us today:
"Rejoice without ceasing!"
But how can we rejoice, Lord,
when small children are dying of hunger?
You answer us:
"Give them a little of your bread,
and with them you will be forever in joy!"

> *Be our joy, Lord our God,*
> *and keep us in your peace.*

"Rejoice without ceasing!"
How can we rejoice, Lord,
when our brothers and sisters are unjustly imprisoned?
You answer us:
"Free them from their chains,
and with them you will be forever in joy!"

> *Be our joy, Lord our God,*
> *and keep us in your peace.*

"Rejoice without ceasing!"
How can we rejoice, Lord,
when our brothers and sisters are dying in despair?
You answer us:
"Share your hope with the hopeless,
and with them you will be forever in joy!"

> *Be our joy, Lord our God,*
> *and keep us in your peace.*

"Rejoice without ceasing!"
How can we rejoice, Lord,
when our brothers and sisters are dying in solitude?
You answer us:
"Take my presence to all your brothers and sisters,
and with them you will be forever in joy!"

> *Be our joy, Lord our God,*
> *and keep us in your peace.*

We bless you, Lord Jesus.
You said to us:
"There is more in giving
than in receiving."
Teach us this joy day after day,
and keep us next to you in peace
forever and ever. Amen.

NOTES TO THIRD SUNDAY OF ADVENT
1. Cf. Acts 16, 22-23.
2. Cf. 2 Cor 11, 2. See my article "Mary, Daughter of Zion" in *Assemblée du Seigneur,* 80 (Bruges, Biblica, 1966) pp. 29-51, and my book *Mary, Daughter of Zion* (Collegeville, MN: The Liturgical Press, 1972).
3. God reveals himself in events and in words. Cf. Constitution *Dei Verbum,* 2. See my book *God's Word and God's People* (Collegeville, MN: The Liturgical Press, 1974), pp. 273-279.
4. Cf. Zep 3, 11-13.
5. Madeleine Delbrel, *Nous autres, gens des rues* (Paris: Ed. du Seuil, 1966) pp. 89-92. © 1966, Editions du Seuil. Reprinted with permission of the publisher.

FOURTH SUNDAY OF ADVENT

READING I

Mi 5, 1-4

A reading from the book of the prophet Micah

Thus says the Lord:
You, Bethlehem-Ephrathah
too small to be among the clans of Judah,
From you shall come forth for me
one who is to be ruler in Israel;
Whose origin is from of old,
from ancient times.
(Therefore the Lord will give them up, until the time
when she who is to give birth has borne,
And the rest of his brethren shall return
to the children of Israel.)
He shall stand firm and shepherd his flock
by the strength of the Lord,
in the majestic name of the Lord, his God;
And they shall remain, for now his greatness
shall reach to the ends of the earth;
he shall be peace.

The Word of the Lord.

RESPONSORIAL PSALM

Ps 80, 2-3. 15-16. 18-19

R/. (4) Lord, make us turn to you,
let us see your face and we shall be saved.

O shepherd of Israel, hearken,
from your throne upon the cherubim, shine forth.
Rouse your power,
and come to save us.

R/. Lord, make us turn to you,
let us see your face and we shall be saved.

Once again, O Lord of hosts,
look down from heaven, and see;
Take care of this vine,
and protect what your right hand has planted
[the son of man whom you yourself made strong.]

R/. Lord, make us turn to you,
   let us see your face and we shall be saved.

May your help be with the man of your right hand,
   with the son of man whom you yourself made strong.
Then we will no more withdraw from you;
   give us new life, and we will call upon your name.
R/. Lord, make us turn to you,
   let us see your face and we shall be saved.

READING II   HEB 10, 5-10

A reading from the letter of Paul to the Hebrews

On coming into the world Jesus said:
   "Sacrifice and offering you did not desire,
   but a body you have prepared for me;
   Holocausts and sin offerings you took no delight in.
   Then I said, 'As is written of me in the book,
   I have come to do your will, O God.'"
   First he says,
   "Sacrifices and offerings, holocausts and sin offerings
   you neither desired nor delighted in."
   (These are offered according to the prescriptions of the law.)
   Then he says,
   "I have come to do your will."
   In other words, he takes away the first covenant to establish the
   second.

By this "will," we have been sanctified through the offering of the body
of Jesus Christ once for all.

The Word of the Lord.

GOSPEL   LK 1, 39-45

A reading from the holy gospel according to Luke

Mary set out, proceeding in haste into the hill country to a town of
Judah, where she entered Zechariah's house and greeted Elizabeth.
When Elizabeth heard Mary's greeting, the baby stirred in her womb.
Elizabeth was filled with the Holy Spirit, and cried out in a loud voice:

"Blessed are you among women and blessed is the fruit of your womb. But who am I that the mother of my Lord should come to me? The moment your greeting sounded in my ears, the baby stirred in my womb for joy. Blessed is she who trusted that the Lord's words to her would be fulfilled."

The gospel of the Lord.

INTRODUCTORY PRAYER

Blessed among women be the Virgin Mary
who carries in her heart, Jesus, Immanuel!
Blessed be Jesus, the Child of her love,
who makes John the Baptist tremble with joy
in the heart of his mother.
And blessed be God our Father who comes to visit us
in giving his Son Jesus
to be our Savior and our brother.
To him the love and praise of our lives
forever and ever! Amen

HOMILY

1. The Messiah Will Come from Bethlehem

The prophecy of the Book of Micah about Bethlehem. Ephrathah was dear to the community. It is the one that Matthew cites when the Magi come to inquire about the place of birth of the little king.[1]

The ministry of the prophet Micah is placed toward the middle of the eighth century (around 740). But the prophecy that is proposed to us is more recent. It seems to date from the postexilic period and could come from the priestly tradition of the fifth century.[2] It will have been introduced to this epoch in the collection of Micah's prophecies.

The Prophecy and its Fulfillment

The points of this text which spontaneously catch our attention, are the following:

"After a time of destitution," that is, after the agony that was the ruin of Jerusalem and the exile, a royal shepherd will rise up from Bethlehem, the city of David.

He will gather together all his brothers and sisters, and his power will extend unto the ends of the earth.

He himself will be peace.

This deliverance will be realized "on the day when she who must give birth will give birth."

The Christian faith has recognized in the Davidic shepherd the royal child born in the midst of the sheep of Bethlehem, and in the mother who must give birth "not only the privileged young girl, the mother of the Messiah, but also the community of eschatological times."[3]

To Fulfill the Prophecy Today

In speaking about prophecies, Blaise Pascal affirmed that "in those promises each one finds what he has in the depths of his heart."[4]

Some carry in their heart apologetic cares, and this prophecy can confirm their faith: Jesus is really born in Bethlehem, as the prophecy had foretold. Others also carry in their heart the care of the prophecy that always remains to be fulfilled.

How, in fact, can we proclaim today the prophecy of the Book of Micah? How can we affirm that Jesus, the Messiah, has fulfilled it if the Church, which incarnates this Messiah on earth, does not gather together in her love all the people of good will? As we proclaim the prophecy of the book of Micah, that Christ is the true Shepherd, that he brings the peace of heaven unto the ends of the earth, we pledge the Church to be a source of peace everywhere that she exists. As we make people believe the prophecy that the Church is a land of hope, we pledge ourselves to be bearers of the hope of all the unfortunate on earth.

For the Church is each one of us. It is in our hands that God places today the fulfillment of the prophecy of the Book of Micah.

2. Here I Am, My God, to Do Your Will

In the heart of Christ dwell all the marvels of God's wisdom and love. If only we could get into that heart, read in it his thoughts, conform our heart to it...

Here the Letter to the Hebrews gives us access to the heart of Christ. It teaches us what was the prayer of incarnation of Christ Jesus:

> In coming into the world, Christ said:
> "You did not want sacrifices or offerings...
> You did not accept holocausts
> or sin offerings.
> Then I said:
> 'Here I am, my God,
> I have come to do your will.'"   Heb 10, 5-7

Christ's prayer of incarnation is cast in Psalm 40 and, through that Psalm, into the whole of God's Word. It affirms the rejection of purely ritual sacrifices and the superiority of the spiritual sacrifice which resides in obedience to the will of God.

This superiority of spiritual sacrifice is inscribed in the heart of biblical prophecy. Ten centuries before Christ, the prophet Samuel was affirming:

> Does the Lord delight in holocausts
> as much as he delights in obedience to the word?
> No, obedience is preferable to sacrifices,
> and docility is preferable to the fat of rams.   1 Sm 15, 22

Exterior sacrifice is not rejected, but it is valid only as long as it expresses interior devotion. If the rite degenerates into formalism, it cannot express the heart.

Now it is precisely in this spiritual offering that the sacrifice of Jesus was perfect. The prayer "Here I am, my God, I have come to do your will" illuminates all his life and transforms it into a sacrifice of praise. It joins the "Yes, Father, for such is your good pleasure" of the hymn of jubilation; it prepares the prayer of the agony: "Into your hands I commit my spirit!"[6]

It was especially on the cross that the spiritual offering was particularly intense and transformed agony and death into a word of love. Outwardly, the crucifixion was a nameless slaughter, and the executioners did not have the least idea of offering a sacrifice. Inwardly, it was a sacrifice of love to the Father: "He offered himself blameless to God in a perfect spirit."[7]

The sacrifice of Christ illuminates our whole life. For our life, no more than the life of Christ, appears like a sacrifice. Some of our sufferings, some of our illnesses are also nameless slaughters, and there are spiritual agonies worse than butcheries. Then the sacrifice of Christ reveals to us that our life, even in the thickness of its banality, is precious before God. For in Christ and in union with him, we too can offer our life "as a living sacrifice, holy and pleasing to God."[8]

Happy the one who makes the will of God the light of his life. Happy the one who can pray in this way: "You did not want sacrifices, or offerings, or religious practices, or Masses, or my prayers. Then I said: 'Here I am, Lord, with this pain that is crushing my heart, with this joy that makes me laugh with enthusiasm, with this situation whose only out is a prison door, with this illness whose only escape is the grave. Here I am, Father to do your will.'"

Happy the one whose only faith, whose only love, whose only religious practice is this "Yes, Father!" For then the boat of his life will reach the ocean of freedom. Nowhere are we more at peace than in that will. For it is a will of love.

Anne—52 years old, married, six children—has fought against cancer for five years. She said: "I want to look death in the eyes." One day when I brought her Communion, she said the prayer of Jesus: "Yes, Father, for such is your good pleasure!" Then, all of a sudden, like after a night of great storms, a dawn of immense peace rose in her. She looked God in the eyes. They were eyes of love.

3. The Visitation of Mary

In the account of the Visitation, Luke uses a literary method well-known in the Judeo-Christian environment, a method called midrash. It describes the evangelic event by using the accounts of the Old Testament. Luke tells here about Mary's visit by using the texts of the account of the transfer of the ark of the Covenant.[9]

We remember the event. David had taken the ark back from the Philistines, had entrusted it to the house of Abinadab, then to the house of Obed-Edom, and then had it taken up to the "City of David."

The points of contact with the Lukan text are the following:

Luke 12	Samuel 6
In those days,	On that day...
Mary arose	David arose
and left	and left
for a town of Judah	for Baalah of Judah
John danced with joy in	David and his people
the womb of his mother	Danced with joy before
the ark	the ark

Elizabeth was filled with the Holy Spirit	The Lord blessed the whole house of Obed-Edom
Whence to me this that comes to me the mother of the Lord	How would come to me the ark of the Lord
Mary stayed with her (Elizabeth) about three months	The ark stayed in the house three months

Beyond this game of references, which can seem pleasant on the biblical level, there is the message. It shines with an infinite beauty.

Mary, Ark of the Covenant

Mary is the ark of the Covenant of the New Testament. And the glory that dwells in her is the child Jesus whom she carries in her heart.

Following her, every Christian imitates the mystery of the Daughter of Zion. We carry the Lord. We must carry him to his brothers and sisters. Like Mary, we must be a source of blessing for them.

May we be sources of blessing for our brothers and sisters! May each one of our meetings with them augment their happiness and make their hearts dance with joy, as John the Baptist danced in the womb of Elizabeth! May we always be people whom one is happy to have met, because one has met the Lord in us.

Every pregnant woman imitates in a special way the mystery of Mary. "Whoever receives one of these little ones in my name," says Christ Jesus, "receives me."[10] A pregnant woman is like an ark of the Covenant. She must celebrate this mysterious presence in her. And it is her husband who, in their mutual love, enables her to carry Christ in her. Is this mystery not the most beautiful thing that God can say to us in our life?

Mother of the Lord

Mary is the mother of the Lord. Elizabeth is the mother of the servant. Now here it is the mother of the Lord who is going to visit the mother of the servant and serve her.

Jesus is "Teacher and Lord."[11] He also came to serve us, his servants.

We Christians must always be the first to go before our brothers and sisters. First to serve them. First to give. First to forgive.

Blessed among All Women

Filled with the Holy Spirit, Elizabeth cried out in a loud voice:

You are blessed among women,
and the fruit of your womb is blessed!   Lk 1, 42

Mary is blessed among all women; she is the woman most loved by God on earth, the most beautiful with the very beauty of God.

The expression "blessed among women" must be understood according to biblical tradition. It shines like a diamond in the history of the chosen people.

It is found first in the Book of Judges, in connection with Jael.[12] It was the bitter time of the Canaanite oppression. Roused by the prophetess Deborah, Israel takes up arms and fights the enemy armies led by Sisera. Sisera flees seeking to save his life. Jael receives him in her tent, puts him to sleep with her kind attentions, and while he is sleeping, exhausted with fatigue, she seizes the pike of the tent, approaches him quietly, and runs it through his temple. Deborah, in a canticle of wild lyricism and savage beauty, then sings the triumph of Jael:

Blessed among women be Jael,
among women who live in tents,
blessed be she...
May all your enemies perish, O Yahweh,
and those who love you, may they be like the sun
when it rises in its might.   Jgs 5, 24, 31

The war song that celebrates a ferocious battle is actually a song of love. "Those who love you" like Jael, it is meant, fight for you, Lord. For the wars of Israel are your wars, and its victories, your triumphs. Jael is blessed among women because she took part in your battle.

The expression "blessed among women" is read a second time in the Book of Judith. Judith's victory over Holofernes is similar to that of Jael over sisera. The parallel with the Lukan text is even more striking:

Luke 1, 42	Judith 13, 18
You are blessed	You are blessed
among women	above all the women
on earth	
and blessed is	and blessed is
the fruit of your womb.	the Lord God.

With the power of the Word of God and also, it must be said, with a supreme craft which had to make him smile with ease, Luke affirms then that Mary is not only the new Judith, but that "the fruit of her womb" is at the same time "the Lord God!" He could not state more clearly the divinity of Jesus.

The biblical image of Mary "blessed among women" does not refer to a pretty Madonna in a blue robe studded with stars of gold, but rather to Jael, the fighting woman triumphing over Sisera, to Judith the intrepid woman, victorious over Holofernes. The woman blessed among women is the one who fights with the most violence the forces hostile to God and those of evil and sin. From the Book of Genesis to the Book of Revelation,[13] Mary is in all the wars that we undertake against sin. She is blessed among women because she is the strongest against evil. She is beautiful among women because she is the most victorious. Her beauty is her triumphant battle. And her victory is that of God in her.

Blessed Be the Fruit of Your Womb

Elizabeth addresses Mary:

> Blessed is the fruit of your womb! Lk 1, 42

This blessing echoes the prophecy of Deuteronomy:

> The Lord your God will keep the Covenant and the love that he promised to your fathers.
> He will love you, bless you, multiply you.
> He will bless the fruit of your womb. Dt 7, 12-13

In Mary, God did not simply fulfill the prophecy of Deuteronomy; he surpassed it more than the wildest hope could have imagined. His Son is not simply the child of the blessing; he is the Blessed One from whom every blessing comes. Thus, in the maternal womb of a young woman, God came into the world. It is this womb that gives birth to the new creation.

Blessed be God who creates for us these marvels of love in Mary! To him glory forever and ever.

CONCLUDING PRAYER

O Wisdom
coming from the mouth of the Most High,
you govern the universe with strength and kindness:
come to teach us the path of truth.

Lord Jesus Christ, come save your people.

O Master,
Shepherd of your people Israel,
you reveal yourself to Moses in the burning bush
and give him your law on Mount Sinai:
come to redeem us through the power of your arm.

Lord Jesus Christ, come save your people.

O Branch of Jesse,
Standard of peoples and kings,
whom the world implores:
come to deliver us, Lord, do not delay any longer.

Lord Jesus Christ, come save your people.

O Key of David
and Scepter of the house of Israel,
what you close no one can open;
what you open no one can close:
come to free those who are imprisoned in darkness.

Lord Jesus Christ, come save your people.

O Rising Sun,
Splendor of eternal light
and sun of justice:
come to illuminate
those who are seated in the shadow of death.

Lord Jesus Christ, come save your people.

O King of the universe,
desired by all nations
and cornerstone that unifies the peoples:
come to save those whom you molded from clay.

Lord Jesus Christ, come save your people.

Fourth Sunday of Advent

O Immanuel,
our King and our lawgiver,
hope of nations and our Savior:
come to save us, Lord our God.

Lord Jesus Christ, come save your people.

NOTES TO FOURTH SUNDAY OF ADVENT

1. Mt 2, 6. Cf. Jn 7, 42.
2. Cf. B. Renaud, Structure et attaches littéraires de Michée IV-V, Cahiers de la Revue Biblique, 2. (Paris: Ed. Gabalda, 1964), p. 118.
3. B. Renaud, op. cit., p. 118.
4. Cf. J. Steinmann, Pensées de M. Pascal (Club des Libraires de France, 1961), p. 332.
5. Heb 10, 5-7 cites Ps 40, 6-8 following the Greek translation.
6. Mt 11, 26 and Lk 23, 46. Cf. Jn 5, 30; 8, 29.
7. Heb 9, 14.
8. Rom 12, 11.
9. Cf. 2 Sm 6. Cf. R. Laurentin, Les Evangiles de l'Enfance du Christ (Paris: Desclée de Brouwer, 1982), pp. 73-75. The comparison is made between the Greek of Luke and that of the Septuagint. In connection with the dance of David (2 Sm 6, 16), the Greek translation called Symmaque, utilizes the word skirtan, a word that Luke utilizes in connection with the "dance" of John in the womb of Elizabeth (Lk 1, 44).
10. Mt 18, 5.
11. Jn 13, 13.
12. Cf. Jgs 4 and 5.
13. Cf. Gn 3, 15 and Rv 12.
14. This prayer is inspired from the antiphons of the Magnificat (called the "Great O antiphons") of the week which precedes Christmas. The biblical references are the following: Ex 3 and 24. Sir 24, 3. Ws 7, 26; 8, 1. Is 5, 25; 9, 1; 22, 22. Ezek 34, 24. Hag 2, 8. Mt 1, 23. Eph 2, 14. Rev 3, 7.

CHRISTMAS

Mass at Midnight

READING I   Is 9, 1-6

A reading from the book of the prophet Isaiah

The people who walked in darkness
  have seen a great light;
Upon those who dwelt in the land of gloom
  a light has shone.
You have brought them abundant joy
  and great rejoicing,
As they rejoice before you as at the harvest,
  as people make merry when dividing spoils.
For the yoke that burdened them,
  the pole on their shoulder,
And the rod of their taskmaster
  you have smashed, as on the day of Midian.
For every boot that tramped in battle,
  every cloak rolled in blood,
  will be burned as fuel for flames.
For a child is born to us, a son is given us;
  upon his shoulder dominion rests.
They name him Wonder-Counselor, God-Hero,
  Father-Forever, Prince of Peace.
His dominion is vast
  and forever peaceful,
From David's throne, and over his kingdom,
  which he confirms and sustains
By judgment and justice,
  both now and forever.
The zeal of the Lord of hosts will do this!

The Word of the Lord.

RESPONSORIAL PSALM

Ps 96, 1-2. 2-3. 11-12. 13

R/. (Luke 2:11) Today is born our Savior, Christ the Lord.

Sing to the Lord a new song;
  sing to the Lord, all you lands.
Sing to the Lord; bless his name.

R/. Today is born our Savior, Christ the Lord.

Announce his salvation, day after day.
  Tell his glory among the nations;
Among all peoples, his wondrous deeds.

R/. Today is born our Savior, Christ the Lord.

Let the heavens be glad and the earth rejoice;
  let the sea and what fills it resound;
  let the plains be joyful and all that is in them!
Then shall all the trees of the forest exult.

R/. Today is born our Savior, Christ the Lord.

They shall exult before the Lord, for he comes;
  for he comes to rule the earth.
He shall rule the world with justice
  and the peoples with his constancy.

R/. Today is born our Savior, Christ the Lord.

READING II

Ti 2, 11-14

A reading from the Letter of Paul to Titus

The grace of God has appeared, offering salvation to all people. It trains us to reject godless ways and worldly desires, and live temperately, justly, and devoutly in this age as we await our blessed hope, the appearing of the glory of the great God and of our Savior Christ Jesus. It was he who sacrificed himself for us, to redeem us from all unrighteousness and to cleanse for himself a people of his own, eager to do what is right.

The Word of the Lord.

GOSPEL   LK 2, 1-14

A reading from the holy gospel according to Luke

In those days Caesar Augustus published a decree ordering a census of
the whole world. This first census took place while Quirinius was
governor of Syria. Everyone went to register, each to his own town.
And so Joseph went from the town of Nazareth in Galilee to Judea, to
David's town of Bethlehem—because he was of the house and lineage
of David—to register with Mary, his espoused wife, who was with
child.

While they were there the days of her confinement were completed.
She gave birth to her first-born son and wrapped him in swaddling
clothes and laid him in a manger, because there was no room for them
in the place where travelers lodged.

There were shepherds in the locality, living in the fields and keeping
night watch by turns over their flock. The angel of the Lord appeared to
them, as the glory of the Lord shone around them, and they were very
much afraid. The angel said to them: "You have nothing to fear! I come
to proclaim good news to you—tidings of great joy to be shared by the
whole people. This day in David's city a savior has been born to you,
the Messiah and Lord. Let this be a sign to you: in a manger you will
find an infant wrapped in swaddling clothes." Suddenly, there was with
the angel a multitude of the heavenly host, praising God and saying,
"Glory to God in high heaven,
peace on earth to those on whom his favor rests."

The gospel of the Lord.

INTRODUCTORY PRAYER

Glory to God in the highest
and peace on earth to all of us
on this Christmas day!
God, our Father in heaven, loves us.
He shows his goodness and his tenderness
in giving us today his Son Jesus
to be our Savior and our brother,
and he lights in the heart of those who seek him
the love and the joy of the Holy Spirit.
Yes, glory to our Father forever and ever. Amen.

HOMILY

When Paul speaks about the mystery of Christmas, he uses these marvelous words (the liturgy presents them in the Second Reading of the Mass at Dawn):

> God our Savior has manifested
> his goodness and his tenderness for people.[1]   Ti 3, 4

Christmas is the coming of the beauty and the love of God upon our world. The tenderness of God, today, has taken a human face. The face of a small child of Bethlehem. Tradition loved to repeat this affirmation like a refrain: "God became man in order that man might become God."

Today, one must add the following: moreover, God became a small child. And what a child! A baby in a manger! The festive acclamation that was sung in the Temple during triumphant celebrations:

> Yes, the Lord is good,   Ps 100, 5

today is murmured before a crèche. Paul's theology is verified in a stable. That is where Luke leads us today. What a spectacle!

A young mother, her eyes shining with fatigue, who is arranging her hair, a father who finds himself alone with his pretty wife and baby, who never stops straightening the stable to make himself useful in some way, shepherds who bring cheese and perhaps also some curdled milk, sheep who look at their shepherds while bleating, a donkey who is eyeing his manger changed into a cradle, an adorable swaddled baby whom one calls Savior, Christ and Lord: This is the manifestation of the goodness and the tenderness of God. This is the most fantastic birth in the history of humanity, the one which changed the face of the world! This is how far God humbled and compromised himself with us! This is Immanuel!

Luke's account is wonderful. So wonderful that we might ask: Is it really true?

Such a question honors the Word of God. For it is based upon confidence in the Gospel's veracity.

What is absolutely certain on the level of history is Joseph, Mary and the baby named Jesus. Or further: A young Galilean woman, accompanied by her husband, gives birth to a little boy while on a journey.

You will say to me: "That is not very much." I will answer: "It is nevertheless the essential!"

As for all the other elements, it is suitable to analyze them point by point.

1. Analysis of Luke's Account

As he does for the beginning of the public life of Jesus,[2] Luke, as a historian, inserts the history of salvation into secular history:

> In those days
> appeared a decree from the emperor Augustus
> ordering the census of all the earth.   Lk 2, 1

Secular history has not given us, till now, a record of such a census which would have been universal. But we know about partial censuses. They took place in different provinces. We suppose that Luke, with a certain freedom, had globalized these partial censuses into a universal census.

As for Quirinius, who is presented as the governor of Syria, we know him through other witnesses and through inscriptions. But our present knowledge does not allow us to place this census that Luke, with an excess of precise details, affirms to have been the first.

Let us note, from the beginning, the contrast between the foolish pretension of Augustus who, through this census, wanted to affirm himself emperor "of all the earth"—this earth which belongs to God alone,[3]—and the humility of the little king to whom the angel will give the royal titles of "Savior" and of "Lord."

The City of David

> Joseph…went up to Judah,
> to the city of David called Bethlehem.   Lk 2, 4

In the goal to fix the taxes on familial properties, the census had to take place in the city of origin. It is astonishing that Bethlehem is called here "the city of David." In reality, according to biblical language, this title belongs uniquely to Jerusalem.

It seems that Luke gives a prophetic value to the title "City of David." He seems to allude to a part of the prophecy of the Book of Micah about Bethlehem-Ephrathah, a prophecy that Matthew cites explicitly in the story of the Magi.[4] Luke calls to mind also the prophecy of the angel of the Annunciation: "The Lord God will give him the throne of his father David."[5] By being born in Bethlehem, the Messiah is not only born in the city of his fathers; he also asserts himself "Son of David."

The Firstborn Son

> She brought her firstborn son into the world.   Lk 2, 7

The expression "her firstborn son" is somewhat solemn, almost surprising. When speaking to the shepherds, the angel will be more simple and will say: "You will find a baby *(brephos)*[6] swaddled and asleep in a manger." The quality of "firstborn" indicates his consecration to God. Luke explicitly mentions this consecration when he speaks about the presentation of Jesus at the Temple and cites the law concerning firstborns.[7] (In itself, the term "firstborn" does not necessarily include other children. This is confirmed by a Jewish inscription for a young woman who died giving birth to her firstborn child.[8])

No Room for Them

> There was no place for them in the common room.   Lk 2, 7

The word *katalyma* can designate either a common room, like the one where Jesus celebrated Passover, or, here, a place open to travelers. It can be translated as *caravansérail, khân.* The translation "inn" is less suitable, for Luke uses the word *pandocheion* to designate an inn.[9]

It could be said "They did not have their place in the common room."[10] A common room is not a suitable place for a woman about to give birth. In any case, the distress of Joseph at not finding any place for Mary in his native village had to be extreme. It announces the poverty of the One who, later, will not have a rock upon which to rest his head.[11] Jesus was born somewhere on the way, in the wind, under the stars.

The Cave, the Donkey and the Ox

Jesus was born in a place where a manger for animals was found. One can think about those caves that are found in the vicinity of Bethlehem which serve, still today, as refuges for the flocks.

The cave was certified from the middle of the second century by Justin and in the Protevangelion of James.[12] Origen, a century later, testifies to the solidity of this tradition when he writes:

> We can show, conforming to the evangelic story of his birth in Bethlehem, the cave where Jesus was born, and in the cave, the crèche where he was wrapped in swaddling-clothes. And what one shows is famous in the country, even among strangers to the faith, since in reality in that cave was born this Jesus that Christians worship and admire.[13]

As for the ox and the donkey, we recognize them coming in the writings of the prophet Isaiah:

The ox recognizes its owner
and the donkey, his master's manger.
Israel does not know anything,
my people has not understood anything.   Is 1, 3

This text, one willingly concedes, poetic. However, it does not furnish any solid biblical argument to give the ox the right to stand next to the manger and to breathe on the child.

In return, the donkey—or the ass according to the Protevangelion of James—had every chance to have been at the feast. Since the most ancient times, it was the ordinary mount for the countries of the Middle East. It had the honor of carrying Mary and her royal child from Nazareth to Bethlehem. How could Mary have been able to travel the distance otherwise? Probably this donkey was used on all their trips.

As for the lambs, their presence is more than probable. What shepherd, invited by God himself to such a marvelous birth, would not have thought to offer a lamb?

One can also imagine that those good shepherds had a piety as enlightened as it was practical, and that they had therefore thought to come to the aid of the holy family by bringing it other small presents such as curdled milk and cheese from their flocks. I know well that this hypothesis has nothing to do with strict exegesis. Neither does it present a sublime theology. But it seems to me that it suggests the sublimity of the mystery of Christmas: on the one hand, there is the God of glory and majesty whom we worship while trembling; on the other hand, there are the shepherds, the sheep, and the cheese. Between the two, there is the simplicity of the crèche. God manifested himself in the heart of that poverty.

The Angel of the Lord, the Glory of the Lord

The angel of the Lord approached
and the glory of the Lord
enveloped them in its light.   Lk 2, 9

There is a certain redundance to the expressions *angel of the Lord* and *glory of the Lord*. These expressions are borrowed from Old Testament vocabulary.

The expression *angel of the Lord* can designate either God himself or a messenger of God. In some ancient accounts, these two meanings overlap. Therefore, in the account of the "annunciation" of Samson, Manoah and his wife see the angel of the Lord ascend in the flame of the sacrifice; then Manoah cries out: "We have seen God."[14]

The expression *glory of the Lord* also designates God as he manifests himself as resplendent majesty, radiant holiness and glorious power. God manifests himself in this way in the fire at Sinai, in the cloud of the desert of the Exodus, and in the Temple of Solomon.

On the historical level, Luke affirms then that God revealed himself to the shepherds. But the "how" of that revelation—it could be by a heavenly messenger or by a message of an interior thought—is not explained to us. No representation of the angel or the glory of the Lord is possible for us. Those who depict the angels with wings of light are no more right or wrong than those who depict them without wings, since nothing in the text allows us to depict them.

I, who believe in angels, that is in spiritual creatures born from the beauty of God and adorned with his light, do not see why God would not have sent his friends the angels in a perceptible manner to sing to the little *bréphos,* the baby, and to enchant the shepherds.

Night of Light

> Shepherds were spending the night in the fields
> guarding their flocks…
> The glory of the Lord enveloped them in its light.   Lk 2, 8-9

There is a vivid contrast between the night that covers the shepherds, the fields, and the sheep and the glory of the Lord that envelopes the shepherds in its light. The night of the shepherds is transfigured into the light of God; the darkness of the world is inhabited by the brightness of heaven. The night of Christmas becomes a "night of light."

It is this light that contributed to fixing the feast of Christmas around the winter solstice, when the nights are at their longest duration and the days again begin to lengthen.[15]

It is for that reason also that Mass takes place in the heart of the night to signify that Jesus, the light of the world, is born in the midst of our darkness and illuminates it with his brightness.

The Message of the Angel

In reading the message of the angel to the shepherds, we would like to congratulate the messenger: "Oh! Angel of the Lord, blessed be you! You truly have a good theology. You know Luke's vocabulary well! You announce the Good News exactly as Luke would have announced it in his delightful vocabulary!"

> I announce to you a Good News. Lk 2, 10

The word *euagelizein,* to announce a good news, is typical of Lukan vocabulary. It appears ten times in the Gospel and fifteen times in the Acts of the Apostles, compared with only one time in Matthew and never in Mark or in John.

> A great joy for all the people. Lk 2, 10

With the coming of Jesus, the joy of God erupts into the world. The first word of the Angel to the shepherds is a word of joy.

Here again, we find ourselves in the presence of a specifically Lukan theme. While Matthew is often solemn, while Mark mentions joy only one time (!) in his Gospel (in 4, 16), Luke makes messianic joy the companion of the messianic ministry of Jesus.[16]

> Today is born to us a Savior,
> who is Messiah, Lord,
> in the city of David. Lk 2, 11

The titles of Savior, Messiah and Lord are at the heart of Christian faith. But they create difficulties on the level of Luke's text.

No other parts of the Synoptics give the title "Savior" to Jesus. But Luke utilizes it with pleasure in Acts [17] and Paul uses it in his Letters.[18] It is also found in Johannine literature and in the Second Letter of Peter.[19] It is a question of a title of honor in the Greek churches. This title is in opposition to the pretensions of the pagan emperors who presented themselves as "Saviors" of their people.

The titles of *Christ* and *Lord* also belong to the apostolic preaching. In his homily on Pentecost, Peter affirms:

> God made him Christ and Lord,
> this Jesus whom you have crucified. Acts 2, 36

These titles in some way anticipate the Resurrection. They place Mary's baby in the light of Easter. There is nothing to prevent the angel from revealing to the shepherds the divinity of the *bréphos* lying in the manger, or from giving to the shepherds a revelation of his future Resurrection. But the ways of God ordinarily respect the delays of human progress and processes. Mary herself submitted to that law of faith; she indicated that she did not always understand the mysterious path of her child.[20]

It seems therefore more reasonable to think that Luke profited from the angel's message to affirm here the faith of the Christian community in the lordship and messiahship of Jesus, its Savior.

Let us note, finally, the actuality of the angel's message: "Today is born to you a Savior." The adverb "today" appears eleven times in Luke compared with one time in Mark, eight times in Matthew and never in John.

Glory to God

As it ought to be, the angels sing a hymn in honor of the little king. Two translations are possible.

The first is the one we know through the text of the Mass:

> Glory to God in the highest heaven,
> and peace on earth to people whom he loves.   Lk 2, 14

The expression "to people whom he loves" translates the Greek *en anthrôpois eudokias,* literally *to people of his kindness,* that is, "to people to whom he grants his kindness," his love. The old translation "to people of good will" copies the Latin but does not do justice to the original Greek. Of course, good will is always highly commendable, especially for welcoming the peace of God that comes to us from heaven, but the present text does not speak about it.

The second translation is presented in three parts:

> Glory to God in the highest heaven,
> and on earth, peace,
> to people, kindness (of God).

This translation is rather close to the acclamation that Luke reproduces on the day of the Palms:

> In heaven, peace,
> and glory in the highest!   Lk 19, 38

One can suppose that the two versions were circulating in the early community.

2. The Mystery of Christmas

The first welcome that Jesus received was the welcome from Mary. The heart of Our Lady was the first cradle of the Lord; her humility and her obedience were the two arms that rocked him.

The mystery of humility! For nine months, the womb of a young woman, of a poor girl of Galilee, was the center of the universe for God and for his angels! It is there, in the obscurity of the insignificant village of Nazareth, that the new heavens and the new earth were prepared for eternity!

Mary knew the humble progress of a little one in the womb of its mother, that path that God created in his marvelous wisdom. She felt the first signs of his presence, the first flutters. And the child, like all babies in the womb of their mother, recognized very early the voice of Mary. One day, smiling, she said to Joseph: "The baby, I felt him move in me!" And Joseph, who was the tenderest of all the husbands on earth, answered her with one of those phrases in which people clothe their tenderness: "Miriam, you are wonderful!"

On that Christmas day, Jesus surely does not appear as a wonder. He is a baby who cries and who suckles, whose mystery no one suspects. Mary is the most informed; she knows better than anyone the mystery that rests upon that child.

Maternity of Faith

Mary will remain eternally the most perfect model of the welcome of Jesus, the Word of God. She received that Word in obedience of her faith, clothed him in the garment of flesh and presented him to the world. She was so much the servant of that Word that she deserved to become his mother.

Tradition insists on the spiritual dimension of that maternity. Mary conceived Christ *prius mente quam ventre,* it was said, that is "more through her soul than through her body."[21] Augustine explains: "Faith is in her soul; Christ is in her womb."[22]

Following her, we are invited today to welcome that Word of God in the obedience of our faith. We clothe him in the garment of our human words or even in the example of our life, and we present him to our brothers and sisters. We ourselves become a revelation of Christ to the world.

On the one hand, the vocation of Mary is absolutely unique and no one can reproduce the mystery of the one who is blessed among women. On the other hand, every Christian vocation is a marian vocation, a call to share her mystery, as Jesus himself invites us to do:

> My mother and my brothers and sisters are those who listen to the Word of God and put it into practice.   Lk 8, 21

Now Mary is proclaimed blessed precisely for her faith, her faith that put into practice the word of God:

> Happy the one who believed that word the Lord had said to her would be accomplished.   Lk 1, 45

This is the first of the evangelic beatitudes, the one that was proclaimed at the dawn of salvation. Mary is the first of this new people who are the people of faith. A woman restored in her original dignity, she is, in the new paradise, the one who makes amends for Eve's mistake. She is presented to us in this way by one of the oldest traditions, according to the testimony of Irenaeus of Lyons:

Eve, seduced by the discourse of an angel, turns away from God and betrays his word. Mary hears the Good News of truth from an angel and bears God in her womb for having obeyed his word. Eve had disobeyed God; Mary consented to obey God.

Thus the virgin Eve had for an advocate the virgin Mary. The human race, enchained by a virgin, was freed by a virgin. Virginal obedience balances virginal disobedience.

This admirable text dates from the end of the second century.[23] The mystery of Christmas, for Mary as for the rest of us, remains the mystery of our faith that welcomes Christ Jesus.

A Maternity of Love

This maternity of faith was also a maternity of love. Everything that there can be of passion, but also of tenderness, in an ordinary human procreation, everything that there can also be of God's love in nuptial love, is found in Mary, but purified by the Holy Spirit, sublimated by the purity of the Spirit. Virginal conception does not signify conception without love. Quite the contrary: of all conceptions, this one was the most filled with love because it was above all, illuminated by divine love.

Christian tradition loves to explain why Mary conceived by the Holy Spirit:

> Mary conceived of the Holy Spirit.

It is not that she received from the Holy Spirit the seed for conception. But through the love and the operation of the Holy Spirit she furnished, from her virginal flesh, the substance necessary for the divine childbirth.

The love of the Holy Spirit burned indeed in her heart in a unique way. Also the power of the Holy Spirit worked marvels in her flesh. And because the love of the Holy Spirit in her heart was unique, the working of the same Spirit in her flesh was without equal.[24]

Oh! if each human conception could be—this is the least that one could desire—a gesture of fully human love! If it could also be, as it was for Mary, the result of a dialogue with the Holy Spirit! If each child, like Jesus, could be a child of love!

We will pray today for all the children who are neither desired nor loved, also, for those who conceived them without loving them, and for those who reject them. We will also bless the Lord for all the children who are born from a beautiful love, and for all those who light their tenderness in the flame of the Holy Spirit. May the Lord transform their life into an eternal Christmas!

The Welcome of Joseph

I like Joseph.

For the governor Quirinius, Joseph represents only the registration number of the census under which he had to register. For Christians, Joseph is the one who loved Mary, the Nazarene, and who, in loving her, learned to love Jesus. And it is the reciprocal love of Joseph and Mary that welcomed the Lord into our midst. Their love was the door of entry of Jesus into our world.

An old Christmas carol from Champagne (France) dating from the sixteenth century says very prettily:

> Joseph married very well
> to the Daughter of Jesse!
> It was quite a new thing
> to be a mother and a maiden.
> Joseph married very well
> to the Daughter of Jesse!

Yes, Joseph truly married well. He was lucky. All marriages are not successful. All wives are not angels; all husbands are not saints. Some loves fade, distill their weariness into boredom, sometimes into bitterness. Other loves become cruelly violent. And upon all of them rests this mist of vanity that covers all human realities, even the most beautiful, with a cloak of sadness.

> Vanity of vanities, says Qoheleth,
> everything is vanity!   Eccl 1, 2

Everything is vanity except to love God and to serve him. And it was exactly there that the story of Joseph was marvelous. It was a love that never knew the wrinkle of boredom or the shadow of sin. It was a love upon which the sun of the first paradise always shone. Never more will one be able to love as Mary and Joseph loved each other since their human love identified itself fully with their love for God. If Eve was given to Adam to be a helper who is like him, what more marvelous helper could Joseph have received than Mary, the new Eve, the woman fully redeemed through grace, the woman most loved by God on earth...

Mystery of Humility

Have you noticed the humble position of Joseph in the infancy accounts of Luke? He is named once in the account of the Annunciation—really Luke could not have done less if he wanted to give a father on earth to that child which came from heaven!—He is named twice in the account of the birth.[25]

What a contrast with Zachariah who, at the birth of John, sings his Benedictus that has no end! And at the circumcision on the eighth day, with ostentation he gives the name to the child. Joseph is not even mentioned at the circumcision of Jesus! Luke writes quite frankly: "He (the child) was named with the name of Jesus." It was, however, to Joseph that came the right to name him according to what the angel had said to him: "You will name him with the name of Jesus."[26]

In human conception, the man exercises his sexual power which becomes creative fertility. He triumphs over death by that life that he kindles in his own life and by that child who carries into creation the image of what he is himself. To that child born of his joy and loving, he gives a name, position and personality. But here before this Child of infinite riches, Joseph remains in great poverty. He possesses the richest treasure of heaven and of earth; he is very close to God but remains very humble! Only one single time in the Gospel of Luke will one say of Jesus: "Is he not the son of Joseph?"[27]

Better than anyone, Joseph knows that the identity card of that Child that he welcomes into his family surpasses his. When he was registered in Bethlehem, he was asked:

- Married?

- Yes, Miriam of Nazareth.

- How many children?

- One, a boy, Jehoshua.

What a family! We say: Jesus, Mary and Joseph. In Bethlehem, they said: Joseph, Mary and the little one.

As for material poverty, it confines one to misery. John the Baptist, Forerunner of the Messiah, was born in the dwelling of a priest. Jesus the Messiah was born in a stable. "There was no room for them": What inn or what hotel has ever refused a rich couple?

What a contrast also between the fiesta that the neighbors and relatives of Elizabeth organize to celebrate the birth of John and the solitude that surrounds the birth of Jesus: Mary and Joseph are alone to welcome the Messiah; only the shepherds and the sheep make them welcome.

The Success of a Life

We are worth what our heart is worth. A life weighs before God what its relationship with the Lord is worth.

The heart of Joseph weighed heavy in the balance of God. His relationship of love was beaming with poverty, with humility and with obedience. Joseph made a success of his life; Jesus lived under his roof.

His nuptial love, on the other hand, was illuminated by the woman most loved by God on earth. The success of a family is the quality of its love capable of welcoming God. What family was more successful than the one chosen by God to welcome Jesus?

Who today cares about the emperor Augustus, who "took a census of all the earth," who was celebrated by Virgil and Horace, acclaimed as "savior" and as "god" and whose birthday was celebrated as a "good news"? Whereas the blessed names of Jesus, Mary and Joseph are murmured by all the faithful of the world.

There have always been, throughout the ages, families that lived the ideal of Nazareth. Christmas is their feast. Ignored by people, they are cherished by God. They live without fame or riches, but their holiness dominates the course of the world. They have made a success of the most extraordinary story of a family: to make their love an intimacy with God, to open it day after day upon the infinity of God.

The Welcome of the Shepherds

Jesus received a third welcome from the shepherds.

The sheep, the ox, the donkey, the shepherds who smell of milk and cheese: the scene is bucolic, and is a part of the Christian folklore. In fact, the presence of the shepherds at the manger reveals the heart of the evangelic message.

In official circles of theology in Israel, shepherds did not have good "press." We know, in fact, of several lists of trades that were considered as contemptible[28] and that would not attract, one would say, "a sign of blessing," not even the least blessing. These were the trades of thieves, because they exposed to theft those who practiced them: such as the trades of donkey driver, of camel driver, and of sailor. Other trades made the observance of the law of the Sabbath or of ritual purity difficult: such as the trades of tanner (because of contact with the hides of dead animals), of usurer, and of publican. The shepherds belonged to this group. Taking care of animals day after day, they could not observe the law of the Sabbath rest; not frequenting the synagogues, they were presumed to be ignoring the Law. Suspicion weighed upon them, for they could cheat on the products of the flock or even—who knows?—lead the animals into strange practices. In a word, they had a true trade of "sinners." Sinners they were not before God, but they were considered such by those who classified themselves precisely among the "just."

When Luke writes that the glory of God enveloped the shepherds in its light, the community of the so-called just had to tremble with indignation. That the Lord's glory humbled itself with sinners, was that not contrary to all the rules of religious propriety that one had attached to God?

It was taught in the rabbinical schools:

> When two faithful sit down together and the words of the Law
> are between them, then the glory of God dwells with them.[29]

And here the glory was resting on common shepherds, professional sinners ignorant of the Law. It was as intolerable as imagining the Messiah eating with publicans and sinners.[30]

It is precisely because the Good News will be offered later to the publicans and sinners that it was announced here, like a first fruit, to the shepherds of Bethlehem.

These shepherds, who are so likeable in their folklore, pose a serious problem for us today. An old Christmas carol sings joyfully:

> If Jesus came back to the world...
> he would be able to come back to our house.

I am no longer so sure of that...Question: Does the Church recognize herself as enough of a sinner to be able to be invited to the manger? Does our community recognize itself as sinful enough to be able to hope for a similar invitation?

Angelus Silesius said:

> Oh! if your heart could become a manger,
> God would become again a child on this earth.[31]

Is our heart humble enough to become today, on this day of Christmas, a manger for the Child Jesus?

The Sign of God

There are many signs of God's presence in the world. But some signs are more meaningful than others. Some can be considered as better than others, especially if they have been chosen by God.

Here, the sign chosen by God is his poverty, his destitution:

> Here is the sign which has been given to you:
> You will find a newborn babe
> swaddled and lying in a manger.   Lk 2, 12

It is written in the Psalm:

> The Lord stands at the right hand of the poor.   Ps 109, 31

Each time that we meet a poor person, we can see the Lord at his right hand. But here, the poor one is the Lord himself, who became a little child.

To Marvel at God

God reveals himself to the shepherds. The shepherds then respond to God:

> They glorified and praised God
> for all that they had seen and heard.   Lk 2, 20

Their response is a praise, an announcement of Christ:

> They made known the word
> that had been spoken to them concerning the child.
> And all those who heard marveled
> at what the shepherds said to them.   Lk 2, 17-18

Whoever has met God in his life can no longer suppress his amazement.

If only we could marvel unceasingly at the splendor of our God and lead the world in praise to his love!

In beginning this homily, I emphasized that when Paul speaks about the mystery of Christmas, he affirms that "God manifested his goodness and his tenderness for people." The word "goodness," *chrèstotès,* used by Paul, had great success in the Christian community. When one sang the acclamation of the Psalm:

> The Lord is good, *chrèstos.*   Ps 100, 5

one could play on the pronunciation and understand "The Lord is *christos,*" Christ. In other words, the goodness of God is his Christ. And the one who belongs to Christ, was called not only *christianus,* Christian, but also, according to the testimony of Tertullian,[32] chrestianus, good. The Christian is the one who is "good."

Who today will give a face to the goodness of God? Who will loan to Jesus his heart and his hands so that the tenderness of God may continue to reveal itself on our earth? Who, through an entire life of love, will see to it that Christmas is not simply a joy of one day, but the continual feast of the Church until the day when we will celebrate together in heaven with Mary, Joseph, the angels, the shepherds and all those who have been good on earth, that One alone who is infinitely good and who today became our brother? To him glory forever and ever.

CONCLUDING PRAYER

> Heaven and earth, O Lord, glorify you unceasingly.
> On this day of your holy birth, we also want to praise you
> and celebrate the splendor of your love.
>
> *Glory to God in the highest!*
>
> May they glorify you for us, O Lord—
> the Virgin Mary who gave birth to you,
> and Joseph the carpenter
> who welcomed you into his arms.

Glory to God in the highest!

May they glorify you for us, O Lord—
the desire of the patriarchs, the exultation of the prophets,
the prayer of the saints and the humble in heart
who prepared the way of your coming among us.

Glory to God in the highest!

May they glorify you for us, O Lord—
the manger where, as a little child, you lay
and the donkey and ox who warmed you.

Glory to God in the highest!

May they glorify you for us, O Lord—
The angels who sang of your birth in the night,
and the brightness of heaven that burst forth
in our darkness.

Glory to God in the highest!

May they glorify you for us, O Lord—
the shepherds who came in haste to pay you homage,
and the sheep who looked with wide eyes
at their little shepherd come from heaven.

Glory to God in the highest!

May they glorify you for us, O Lord—
humble Bethlehem, the city of David,
and the little children who died for you.

Glory to God in the highest!

May they glorify you for us, O Lord—
the star that rose for you in the sky of the East,
and the long journey of the Magi who came to worship you.

Glory to God in the highest!

May they glorify you for us, O Lord—
the gold, incense, and myrrh of their offering,
and especially their joy of meeting your face.

Glory to God in the highest!

May they glorify you for us, O Lord—
old Simeon who took you in his arms,
and the prophetess Anna whose smile you were
in the evening of her old age.

Christmas — Mass at Midnight

Glory to God in the highest!
On this day (at this time) of your holy birth,
we also want to glorify you, O Lord.
Illuminate our night with the dawn of your love.
And when the hour of our death comes,
grant that we may be born in heaven, for the joy
of an eternal Christmas. Amen.

NOTES TO CHRISTMAS

1. Paul uses the word *chrèstotès,* goodness, which also means: amiability, honesty with a connotation of nobleness. The affirmation: "God is good, *chrèstos*" is "the major acclamation of the cult in Israel." C. Spick, *Notes de lexicographie nèo-testamentaire,* vol. 2 (Gottingen: Vandenhoeck & Ruprecht, 1978), p. 972. As for the other word used by Paul, it is the word *philantrôpa* that we know well and whose early meaning is here: tenderness (of God) for people.
2. Cf. Lk 3, 1-2.
3. Cf. Ps 24, 1. The enumeration of the people undertaken by David, 2 Sm 24, 1-10, is considered as a "great mistake" (v. 10).
4. Mt. 2, 6 citing Mi 5, 1-3.
5. Lk 1, 32.
6. Lk 2, 12. Luke freely uses this word (1, 41, 44; 2, 12, 16; 18, 15) that neither Mark nor Matthew nor John uses.
7. Lk 2, 12 citing Ex 13, 2.
8. Cf. J. Frey, "La signification du terme de *prôtokos* d'après une inscription juive," in *Biblica,* XI (1930), pp. 373-390.
9. Cf. Lk 22, 11 and 10, 34.
10. This is the meaning given by E. Delebecque, *Evangile de Luc* (Paris: Ed. "Les Belles Lettres," 1976), p. 13.
11. Cf. Lk 9, 58.
12. Cf. Dialogue with Tryphon, 78 (around 155-164). *Protevangelion of James,* 18-20.
13. Origen, *Contre Celse,* I, 51. SC 132 (1967), p. 215 - *Contre Celse* dates from 248 (Cf. P. Nautin, *Origen* [Paris: Beauchesne, 1977], p. 376).
14. Jgs 13, 20-22.
15. The date of December 25th appears for the first time in Rome between 325-354. Christmas took the place of the pagan feast *Natalis Solis invicti,* birthday of the emperor, venerated as the triumphant Sun, and also of the birthday of the god Mithra.
16. See L. Deiss, *Synopse* (Paris: Desclée de Brouwer, 1991), p. 345-346.
17. Acts 5, 31; 12, 23.
18. Phil 3, 20; Eph 5, 23; 2 Tm 1, 10; Ti 1, 4; 2, 13; 3, 6.
19. Jn 4, 42; 1 Jn 4, 14. 2 Pt 1, 1, 11; 2, 20; 3, 2, 18.
20. Cf. Lk 2, 50.

21. Augustine, *Sermo* 215, *In redditione Symboli,* 4. Pl 38, 1074.
22. *Sermo 196, In natali Domini,* 1. Pl 38, 1019
23. *Against the Heresies,* V, 19, 1.
24. Hugh of Saint Victor (1096-1141), *De Beatae Mariae virginitate,* 2. Pl 176, 872 AC.
25. Cf. Lk 1, 27; 2, 4 and 16.
26. Lk 2, 21. Mt 1, 21.
27. Lk 4, 22.
28. Cf. J. Jeremias, *Jérusalem au temps de Jésus* (Paris: Ed. du Cerf, 1967), pp. 399-410.
29. Cf. Strack-Billerbeck, *Kommentar zum Neuen Testament aus Talmud und Midrasch,* vol. 1 (Munich: C. H. Beck, 1961), p. 794.
30. Cf. Mt 9, 11.
31. Angelus Silesius (1624-1677), cited by J. Chuzeville in *Les mystiques allemands du XIIIe au XIXe siecle* (Paris: Ed. Grasset, 1935), p. 268. © 1935, Editions Bernard Grasset. Reprinted with permission of the publisher.
32. Cf. C. Spick, *op. cit.,* p. 976

HOLY FAMILY

READING I

SIR 3, 2-6. 12-14

A reading from the book of Sirach

The Lord sets a father in honor over his children;
  a mother's authority he confirms over her sons.
He who honors his father atones for sins;
  he stores up riches who reveres his mother.
He who honors his father is gladdened by children,
  and when he prays he is heard.
He who reveres his father will live a long life;
  he obeys the Lord who brings comfort to his mother.
My son, take care of your father when he is old;
  grieve him not as long as he lives.
Even if his mind fail, be considerate with him;
  revile him not in the fullness of your strength.
For kindness to a father will not be forgotten,
  it will serve as a sin offering— it will take lasting root.

The Word of the Lord.

RESPONSORIAL PSALM

Ps 128, 1-2. 3. 4-5

R/. (1) Happy are those who fear the Lord
  and walk in his ways.

Happy are you who fear the Lord,
  who walk in his ways!
For you shall eat the fruit of your handiwork;
  happy shall you be, and favored.

R/. Happy are those who fear the Lord
  and walk in his ways.

Your wife shall be like a fruitful vine
  in the recesses of your home;
Your children like olive plants
  around your table.

R/. Happy are those who fear the Lord
  and walk in his ways.

Behold, thus is the man blessed
  who fears the Lord.
The Lord bless you from Zion:
  may you see the prosperity of Jerusalem
  all the days of your life.
R/. Happy are those who fear the Lord a
  nd walk in his ways.

READING II   COL 3, 12-21

A reading from the Letter of Paul to the Colossians

Because you are God's chosen ones, holy and beloved, clothe yourselves with heartfelt mercy, with kindness, humility, meekness, and
patience. Bear with one another; forgive whatever grievances you have
against one another. Forgive as the Lord has forgiven you. Over all
these virtues put on love, which binds the rest together and makes them
perfect. Christ's peace must reign in your hearts, since as members of
the one body you have been called to that peace. Dedicate yourselves to
thankfulness. Let the word of Christ, rich as it is, dwell in you. In
wisdom made perfect, instruct and admonish one another. Sing
gratefully to God from your hearts in psalms, hymns, and inspired
songs. Whatever you do, whether in speech or in action, do it in the
name of the Lord Jesus. Give thanks to God the Father through him.

You who are wives, be submissive to your husbands. This is your duty
in the Lord. Husbands, love your wives. Avoid any bitterness toward
them. You children, obey your parents in everything as the acceptable
way in the Lord. And fathers, do not nag your children lest they lose
heart.

The Word of the Lord.

GOSPEL   LK 2, 41-52

A reading from the holy gospel according to Luke

The parents of Jesus used to go every year to Jerusalem for the feast of
the Passover, and when he was twelve they went up for the celebration
as was their custom. As they were returning at the end of the feast, the
child Jesus remained behind unknown to his parents. Thinking he was
in the party, they continued their journey for a day, looking for him
among their relatives and acquaintances.

Holy Family

Not finding him, they returned to Jerusalem in search of him. On the third day they came upon him in the temple sitting in the midst of the teachers, listening to them and asking them questions. All who heard him were amazed at his intelligence and his answers.

When his parents saw him they were astonished, and his mother said to him: "Son, why have you done this to us? You see that your father and I have been searching for you in sorrow." He said to them: "Why did you search for me? Did you not know I had to be in my Father's house?" But they did not grasp what he said to them.

He went down with them then, and came to Nazareth, and was obedient to them. His mother meanwhile kept all these things in memory. Jesus, for his part, progressed steadily in wisdom and age and grace before God and people.

The gospel of the Lord.

INTRODUCTORY PRAYER

On this day we celebrate
the Holy Family of Jesus, Mary and Joseph.
We want to bless you, God our Father,
source of all families in heaven and on earth.
You created in the heart of Joseph
his love for Mary, his wife.
And you ignited tenderness in the heart of Mary
for Joseph, her husband.

We pray to you:

May the mutual love in the midst of our earthly families
also be for us a path to your Kingdom
where all together we will form the family
of all those who love you and bless you
through your Son Jesus Christ, in the joy of
the Holy Spirit. Amen.

HOMILY

Today we are celebrating a marvel. God offers the holy family of Nazareth for our admiration and as a model of all Christian families.

The biblical readings are very rich. In addition, the feast itself offers many themes for reflection, admiration and praise. Since one cannot say everything, I made choices; therefore, I eliminated some themes. Nevertheless, I hope that what I have chosen will please you.

1. Sense of God in the Holy Family

Twice Luke notes the human progress of the child Jesus. After the episode of the Presentation in the Temple, he writes:

The little child grew and became strong,
filled with wisdom.
And the grace of God rested upon him.   Lk 2, 40

And after the episode when Jesus remained in the Temple, Luke notes:

Jesus grew in wisdom and stature, and in grace
before God and people.   Lk 2, 52

Jesus grew in stature. At first, he resembled all newborns. From infancy he progressed to a toddler, to a child, and then to an adolescent. He passed through the crisis of puberty. He noticed that Rebecca or Judith, girls of the neighborhood, seemed to surround him; then he became an adult man. We understand these developments easily. They are a normal part of the path of every human "born of woman," as Scripture says.

Luke affirms that Jesus also grew in wisdom. He gradually discovered his mother and his father. He identified himself progressively with his body, sucked his thumb and grabbed his toes. He learned his first Aramaic words: *Imma,* mama. The day that he said *Abba,* papa, for the first time, Joseph felt his heart melt with tenderness. He sang throughout that day while working with his wood.

Jesus also learned the elements of human wisdom, the rules of good behavior, what was proper for him to do, what he had to avoid. He was not a child with a "swelled head," I mean with a body of a child and the head of an adult. Luke says that he grew in wisdom.

Now the flower of wisdom and its crown is what Scripture calls "the fear of God,"[1] what we call today "religion." It expresses itself principally in praise and adoration.

Of course, this religion flourished already, on the marvelous stem of Jesse. But in the chosen people, multiple were the dwellings, multiple the spiritualities. Jeremiah's was distinguishable from Isaiah's; the Yahwist course differed from the Elohist's course. The priestly ideal did not get into the Deuteronomic ideal.

Now Jesus, true son of Israel, has a unique and personal way of standing before God. He inherited it from the tradition of Israel, most certainly, but possesses it also from his own personality. And that personality also comes from the education that he received and especially from his earthly father and mother.

It is marvelous to try to venture through the path that goes from Mary and Joseph to Jesus and to see how the two of them brought up their child.

A Certain Taste for Paradox

In Jesus, true son of the East, there is a certain taste for hyperbole or exaggeration which incites smiles and impels reflection.

Jesus knows how to speak delightfully about swallowers of camels and strainers of gnats. He sees professors of ethics who walk solemnly with a beam in their eye and lay blame on those who only have a little straw in theirs. He also imagines camels that strain to pass through the eye of a needle. He points at "doctors'-old-goatskins" who cannot hold the new wine of the Good News; that would make them crack, he said smiling.

A Certain Sense of Poverty

This taste for paradox leads him to present affirmations which would not be supportable if good sense did not correct them. But they make a sharp impression on the imagination. When one hears them a single time, one can never forget them. He proclaims:

> Happy are you the poor,
> for the Kingdom of God is yours!　　　　　　　Lk 6, 20
> But woe to the rich,
> for you have your consolation!　　　　　　　Lk 6, 24

The affirmation is incorrect on the theological level. For there are some rich to whom the Kingdom of God belongs, such as Joseph of Arimathea, such as the "holy women" who helped Jesus with their goods, such as Mary the gentle, Martha the needy, and Lazarus the friend whose hospitality Jesus loved. It is a question then of an affirmation which lacks any nuance in the theology of poverty, in one word, an undue generalization.

Matthew saw it well, for he corrects the formula "Happy the poor" by adding "Happy the poor *in spirit.*" For material poverty is nothing if it does not open itself upon spiritual poverty. In the same way, Matthew corrects the formula of Jesus: "Happy are those who hunger and thirst," by adding to it "for justice." For it serves no purpose to be hungry if one does not also hunger for justice.[2]

Now it is precisely this lack of nuance that we find in you, kind and gentle Virgin Mary. Like Jesus, you also lack accuracy, you exaggerate, you generalize. You affirm in fact in the Magnificat:

> The hungry, God fills with good things, and the rich,
> he sends away empty (handed).   Lk 1, 53

You should have stated precisely in your song:

> The hungry for justice, he fills with good things,
> and the evil rich, he sends away empty (handed).

There existed in Nazareth a very sharp sense of poverty; better yet, a loving and marvelous adoration of this God who loves the poor and neglects the rich. The words of Jesus imitate those of Mary, and the two together seem to say: "All the rich are evil. All the poor are dear to the heart of God. And if there are any exceptions, they are so rare that one may avoid speaking about them." That which signifies also, in a more positive way: "Take care, take extreme care to remain poor before God. Do not be proud before him! Otherwise, you risk losing yourself." This is really what Jesus will say:

> How difficult it is for those who are rich
> to enter into the Kingdom of God!   Lk 18, 24

A Certain Sense of Humility

The spirituality of poverty is very close to that of humility. The words of the Magnificat:

> The Lord has cast his eyes
> upon the humility of his servant.   Lk 1, 48

permeated the dwelling of Nazareth like a perfume from heaven. In the home of Joseph and Mary, pride was not welcome. One said:

> Deploying the strength of his arm,
> the Lord scattered those with proud hearts.   Lk 1, 51

Jesus will remember the song from Nazareth. He will teach:

> Whoever exalts himself will be humbled,
> but the one who humbles himself will be exalted.   Lk 18, 14

The altar where this religion of the God who loves the humble is celebrated is the heart of the faithful. If the heart is rotted with pride, the Lord deserts the altar and scatters its stones. "He scatters those with proud hearts," said Mary. If the heart is meek and humble, God establishes his dwelling there.

> "Learn from me," taught Jesus,
> "for I am meek and humble in heart."   Mt 11, 29

Here then is the heart of Jesus, which is similar to your heart, Mary, pretty and humble princess of Nazareth. Here is Jesus, the servant, who comes not to be served, but to imitate you, Mary, who glorify yourself in being the servant of the Lord! Here is the Messiah meek and humble in heart who imitates you, Mary, the Lady of humility. You have succeeded in Nazareth in forming your child! Please, would you not like to form the children that we are today so that we may be like our firstborn Brother?

Blessed be you also, Joseph, for it is said that if a man and a woman love each other with tenderness—as in your case!—they receive their heart from each other. "They are a real pair," it is said. Your heart had to be quite beautiful to bring so much splendor and humility to your wife, Mary! Yes, blessed be you, Joseph, Mary, and Jesus!

2. Childhood Memories

Everyone likes to bring into their adult life their childhood memories as unchangeable treasures. These memories rise quite naturally to the surface of our hearts on difficult days, when we run the risk of getting stuck in the hard anxieties of daily life. This spiritual pilgrimage to the "golden age" of childhood—which is quite the opposite of infantilism—is, according to Jesus, a necessary condition for entrance into the Kingdom.

> Amen, I say to you:
> If you do not change
> and do not become like little children,
> you will not enter into the Kingdom of heaven   Mt 18, 3

At the age of thirty, at the full maturity of his intelligence and will, Jesus had kept the soul of a child. His memory led him often to Nazareth, near to Mary and Joseph.

The Lesson of Mending

When a tunic or cloak had a tear, Mary mended it. She sat down on the mat, took the garment in her hands, and checked it. The child Jesus approached the mat and checked on mama. What was she going to do? Grown-ups—in the judgment of children—sometimes have unforeseeable, strange behavior. To repair the old cloak, why does she take this old and used piece of cloth which will not hold up very long? Why does she not take this much newer and prettier piece?

Then mama explained:

> No one sews a piece of unshrunk cloth to an old cloak. Otherwise, the added piece pulls away from the cloak, the new from the old. And the tear becomes worse.   Mk 2, 21

Later, Jesus will remember the lesson of the mended cloak. Between the aging Pharisaism and the newness of the Gospel there is not a difficulty of adaptation, but there is total incompatibility. The Good News cannot be a patching of dying Judaism. The new wine of the Gospel cannot be poured into the old wineskins of human traditions. And Jesus added smiling:

> New wine in new wineskins!   Mk 2, 22

Mary looked after the clothes regularly. She took them out of the hutch that Joseph had made, examined them carefully to see if the moths had made holes, then spread them out in the sun to air.

Later, the Lord will say:

> Store up treasures in heaven
> where neither moth nor worm destroy.   Mt 6, 20

Joseph's Bushel

Joseph made doors, windows, partitions, and ploughs. When people came to take delivery of an order, they asked: "How much is it?" Joseph would answer: "A bushel of wheat." Now there are bushels, and there are bushels. There is the bushel that one measures stingily. And there is the bushel that one heaps up, that one shakes, that overflows.

The Lord will remember the bushels that Joseph of Nazareth earned. He will say:

Give, and it will be given to you.
A good measure, compressed, shaken, overflowing,
will be given into your lap.
For with the measure that you have measured,
one will measure for you in return. Lk 6, 38

The Baker of Nazareth

Bread was the fundamental food in Israel. To say "have a meal," one simply said "eat some bread." Mark tells us in this way that Jesus and his disciples were harassed by the crowd "to the point that they could not even eat any bread."[3]

The preparation of the bread was an important task in the daily life of Mary. One had to begin by grinding the grain. Mary sat on her heels, facing the millstone.

This millstone consisted of two superimposed stones, the bottom stone in the form of an upside down cone with an opening in the bottom to allow the flour to filter through, the stone on top in the form of a point adjusted into the cone. To turn the millstone it was better for two to work together, providing that they worked well together. Jesus will remember a familiar scene in Nazareth when, to evoke the suddenness of the coming of judgment, he will say:

Two women will be grinding together:
one will be taken, the other will be left. Lk 17, 35

The preparation of dough is always an operation that children love to watch, especially while trying to put their hands into it. One buried the yeast in the dough, and everything went into fermentation. The Lord seems to speak about his mother when he says:

To what can I compare the Kingdom of God?
It is like yeast
that a woman took and hid
in three measures of flour
until everything had risen. Lk 13, 20-21

If one prepared the bread too much in advance, it became sour and covered with mold. Mary baked it every day. She taught the child Jesus that it was necessary to ask God for bread day after day:

Give us this day
our daily bread. Mt 6, 11

The Little Ravens

Children—it must be in their genes—are attracted by bird's nests. This fascination grows in the spring when the nests are elated with the chirping of the young birds.

In Nazareth one liked to pray with the Psalm:

Sing to the Lord thanksgiving…
He bestows food to the cattle
and to the young of the ravens who cry out. Ps 147, 7-9

To celebrate the restoration of his love with his people, had the Lord not promised to make a covenant "with the birds of the sky?"[4]

Like all the boys of the world, the child Jesus liked to climb trees to celebrate the truth of the words of the Psalm about the birds.

The Lord will remember later the little ravens of Nazareth. He will make them enter triumphantly into his Gospel, in the Sermon on the Mount:

Consider the ravens:
They do not sow or reap,
have neither storeroom or loft,
and God feeds them!
How much more are you worth than birds? Lk 12, 24

The Dens of Foxes

On the day of the Sabbath, Joseph, Mary and the little one went for a walk, which was called at that time "the Sabbath journey."[5]

Jesus loved to accompany his father on his walks. Sometimes, in the neighboring countryside, Joseph would show him the den of a fox under a scraggly bush, or the nest of a bird on the top of a poplar. Can you imagine a bird without a nest? Can you imagine a man without a home? Such will be, however, the condition of the Son of man. The Lord will remember the dens and the nests of the country of Nazareth. He will say:

The foxes have dens,
and the birds of the sky have nests.
But the Son of man has no place
to rest his head. Lk 9, 58

Where Do Babies Come From?

One day, Jesus asked Mary: "Imma, where do babies come from?" Mary answered: "Go ask your father." "Abba, tell me, where do babies come from?" Joseph reflected a moment, then answered (fathers today still do the same!): "Go ask your mother. You see that I am busy working on this table!"

Mary explained the best that she could. Is she not the most simple of mothers? "Babies are born in the heart of their mother. You see Rebecca, our neighbor; she is large because she is carrying a baby in her heart."

Jesus asked: "When I was born, were you in pain?" Mary answered: "The mother who loves her child is full of joy to give birth to the child she loves."

And the Lord will explain later to his disciples:

A woman, when she is going to give birth, is sad,
because her hour has come.
But when she has given birth to the child,
she no longer remembers her sadness
in the joy that a child has come into the world.   Jn 16, 21

3. A Model Love

To conclude, let us say a word about the family ideal.

Sometimes one thinks that the ideal Christian family is a large family (the more children there are, the more it is Christian). That can be true. That can also be completely incorrect. The most holy family that the earth knows is a family with one child.

That which makes the quality of a family, its "goodness," its "excellence," is the quality of the love that unites a man and a woman. Not the number of children begotten. But the quality of the love which begot them. Let us examine ourselves on the quality of our love. Toward our wife, toward our husband, toward our children.

Joseph and Mary loved each other with the true love of a man and a woman. A love which had the savor of the first love in paradise, which was not riveted to those crutches that are carnal tendernesses because it was stronger and more gentle than flesh. Not because it ignored or despised the flesh—it was rooted in it!—but because it was all illuminated, all inflamed by the Spirit.

For Paul, family life develops "in the Lord." Husbands and wives must make themselves known in their love, as a manifestation of Jesus Christ. They must also discover their children—who do not cease to become "different" each day—as revelations of Christ. And they must cherish each other in that discovery. Naturally, if that discovery is one of a new goodness, of a new grandeur, they must give thanks for it to God the Father. If it is the discovery of a weakness, they must forgive each other. Paul sums this up wonderfully:

Make for yourselves a heart full of tenderness
and goodness, of humility, gentleness and patience.
Bear with each other and forgive...
Above all that, let there be love:
that is what makes unity in perfection.
And may the peace of Christ reign in your hearts.   Col 3, 12-15

Let us each examine ourselves on the quality of our love for God. The quality of a family is not measured by the number of children begotten. In the same way the quality of our love toward God is not measured by the number of prayers recited, of Masses attended, but rather by the quality of our service to our brothers and sisters through love for God.

Familial love is more noble because it participates in the beauty of the love of God. It is here that Joseph, Mary, and Jesus form the most fulfilled family since their mutual love is identified with their love of God.

Blessed be the Lord Jesus! He, the God of infinite joy, who does not need the service of any creature, wanted to need the love of a father, the tenderness of a mother.

Blessed be he because he also accepts the service of our love. To him glory forever and ever!

CONCLUDING PRAYER

For the father that you gave to us
and because you are our Father in heaven,
we bless you.
Help the men that you call to fatherhood
to be the reflection on earth of your fatherly love,
we pray to you.

You are our Father.
Hear our prayer!

For the mother who carried us
and because the Virgin Mary is our Mother in heaven,
we bless you.

Holy Family

Help each woman that you call to motherhood
be for her child the sign of your tenderness,
we pray to you.

> *You are our Father.*
> *Hear our prayer!*

For the husband or the wife that you gave to us
and who is flesh of our flesh and sign of your love,
we bless you.
Help each family to recognize that their tenderness is a path to
heaven,
we pray to you.

> *You are our Father.*
> *Hear our prayer!*

For the children that you gave to us
and because they are your adopted children
in your only Son,
we bless you.
Help us to recognize in each person
the image of Jesus, your firstborn Son,
we pray to you.

> *You are our Father.*
> *Hear our prayer!*

For those who live in solitude
and because you are their family in heaven,
we bless you.
Help them to feel that you love them
as no one could ever love them on earth,
we pray to you.

> *You are our Father.*
> *Hear our prayer!*

Hear us, God our Father,
in the name of the love that you bear for Jesus,
the Child of the Virgin Mary, and our brother
forever and ever. Amen.

NOTES TO HOLY FAMILY
1. Sir 1, 18.
2. Compare Lk 6, 20, 21 with Mt 5, 3 and 6.
3. Mk 3, 20.
4. Hos 2, 20.
5. Acts 1, 12.

SOLEMNITY OF MARY, MOTHER OF GOD

JANUARY 1—OCTAVE OF CHRISTMAS

READING I   NUM 6, 22-27

A reading from the book of Numbers

The Lord said to Moses: "Speak to Aaron and his sons and tell them:
This is how you shall bless the Israelites. Say to them:

The Lord bless you and keep you!
The Lord let his face shine upon you,
    and be gracious to you!
The Lord look upon you kindly
    and give you peace!
So shall they invoke my name upon the Israelites,
    and I will bless them."
The Word of the Lord.

RESPONSORIAL PSALM   Ps 67, 2-3. 5. 6. 8

R/. (2) May God bless us in his mercy.

May God have pity on us and bless us;
    may he let his face shine upon us.
So may your way be known upon earth;
    among all nations, your salvation.
R/. May God bless us in his mercy.

May the nations be glad and exult
    because you rule the peoples in equity;
    the nations on the earth you guide.
R/. May God bless us in his mercy.

May the peoples praise you, O God;
    may all the peoples praise you!
May God bless us,
    and may all the ends of the earth fear him!
R/. May God bless us in his mercy.

READING II   GAL 4,4-7

A reading from the letter of Paul to the Galatians

When the designated time had come, God sent forth his Son born of a woman, born under the law, to deliver from the law those who were subjected to it, so that we might receive our status as adopted sons. The proof that you are sons is the fact that God has sent forth into our hearts the spirit of his Son which cries out "Abba!" ("Father!"). You are no longer a slave but a son! And the fact that you are a son makes you an heir, by God's design.

The Word of the Lord.

GOSPEL   LK 2, 16-21

A reading from the holy gospel according to Luke

The shepherds went in haste to Bethlehem and found Mary and Joseph, and the baby lying in the manger; once they saw, they understood what had been told them concerning this child. All who heard of it were astonished at the report given them by the shepherds.

Mary treasured all these things and reflected on them in her heart. The shepherds returned, glorifying and praising God for all they had heard and seen, in accord with what had been told them.

When the eighth day arrived for his circumcision, the name Jesus was given the child, the name the angel had given him before he was conceived.

The gospel of the Lord.

INTRODUCTORY PRAYER

On the threshold of this new year
we want to bless you, God our Father,
Master of time and Lord of eternity.

Each new day that you create
you renew your love for us,
and each moment that you invent
you fill with the smile of your Son Jesus.

Day after day, in our joys and in our pains,
help us to advance on the path which is your Son Jesus;
help us to sing the songs of love of your Holy Spirit.

And when the river of time empties into the ocean of
your eternity,
when the darkest hour of our night breaks forth
into the dawn of your eternal Day,
welcome us into your arms, our Father,
for the eternal feast in your house,
forever and ever. Amen.

HOMILY

1. The Feast of Jesus and Mary

According to the liturgical calendar, today we celebrate the feast of Mary,
Mother of God. But according to the Gospel, we celebrate the feast of the
holy name of Jesus. Today, in fact, eight days after Christmas, Joseph gave
to his child the name Jesus, as the angel had commanded.

There is not, however, any contention between the two feasts. For just as
each child is a feast for its mother, Jesus is the feast for Mary. The whole
long story of Our Lady is summed up in this: She is the mother of Jesus.
She is the only woman who could say to her God and Savior, "*Tinoki*, my
little one!"

May each child be in the same way the feast for its mother! Scripture
affirms:

The woman will be saved through childbearing.   1 Tm 2, 15

She is saved not by the simple fact of transmitting life to a little one, but
by the vocation of "raising" that little one according to the fullest meaning
of this beautiful word. Helped by her husband, she "raises" her child, that
is, she lifts it from her womb to the heart of God, from earth to heaven.

All through this new year, may Jesus also be our feast. Paul says to us:

Everything that you say and do,
may it always be in the name of the Lord Jesus,
giving thanks through him to God the Father.   Col 3, 17

It is with much suitability that the entrance song of the Mass of the day
began formerly with these words: "*In nomine Jesu*, in the name of Jesus."

May all this new year, with its unknown joys and its pains that we are going
to discover, begin and end always *In nomine Jesu*, in the name of Jesus.

2. The New Year: Our Life, A Gift From God

An old Jewish legend believed that on the day of the New Year—*Rosh ha-Shana*—the heavenly tribunal decides who will die that year and who will live, who will be raised up to God and who will be humbled. That is to say that there is not, in the New Year, any implicit renewal of existence. Life is an agreement that God has established, and that agreement is brought into question each year. Each day of this new year appears as a new gift from God. It was also thought that on this day the just were inscribed in the Book of Life, and the unrepentant who refused to convert themselves were abandoned to death. As for those in the middle, who were neither consecrated saints nor unrepentant sinner, God granted them a supplementary delay, the time of repentance, according to these marvelous words from the Book of Wisdom:

> You give to your children sweet hope
> that after sin you leave time for repentance. Wis 12, 19

But what is a person in the middle?

To that question, an old sage answered: "It is a person like me."

The time of our life, the time of this new year is the time in which God deploys his mercy. God is tenderness. Time is like the house of our life that Jesus fills with his tenderness.

Each day of our life, each moment of our existence is also solemn and irreplaceable. For it is the unique moment for us when God offers us a new fervor, a new love, so that we can cry to him with the Spirit in our heart: "Abba, Father!"

Cyclical Religion and Historical Religion

This year, which today we wish to be a "Happy New Year" is also, in a certain way, a lie that we fashion for ourselves to soothe our own anguish before time and our distress before the days that slip away from us. It is said:

> Time skillfully assumes the appearance of eternity by subtly giving us each morning a day quite like the one that it stole from us the day before. Time slips away from us always without ceasing to present the same face so that the year that has passed seems to rise again in the year that is beginning.[1]

Sometimes we live as though we never have to die. It seems to us naively that everyone is aging around us except ourselves. In meeting a friend whom we have not seen for a long time, we say to ourselves: "My! How you have aged!" And our friend likewise thinks secretly: "My! How you have aged!"

In reality, time pursues its solemn and merciless course which congeals all things in their eternity. What is wasted is wasted. Forever! What is saved is saved. Forever.

The religions of the ancient East—and the pagan religions of our time—are all cyclical religions. They are built upon the rhythms of nature and the alternation of the seasons. They sacralize; that is, they make sacred the cycle included between one spring and another, between one autumn and another. Once the cycle is completed, everything begins again at its starting point. The years come together and pile up upon the airs of time, closed upon themselves, prisoners of each other. History does not progress.

Thus on the Babylonian New Year, the *akitu*, one solemnly recited the poem of creation—*Enuma Elish*—in the temple of the god Marduk. Two groups of ballet dancers mimed the battle that had taken place "at that time" between the god Marduk and the marine monster, Tiamat. Marduk's victory signified the passage from Chaos to Cosmos. Each year, the same celebration would be played again. Each year, one would come back to the starting point.[2]

The Christian religion is entirely something else. It is historical. It has a beginning. For us, it is our birth; it is our baptism. It is leading to a future: to meet God, to see him face to face. Everything that stagnates on this road is lost. Forever. Everything that progresses, matures or excels is saved for eternity. No backward return is possible. When Abraham left Ur of Chaldea, it was to never come back again. When we begin on the road of Christ, it is to never look back again.

May we never have a cyclical religion! May we flee from Babylonian religions! Simply said: To have a cyclical religion is to turn in circles. May we never turn in circles! May each year bring us closer to God! May the light of His face shine on us each new day! May God smile upon us at each moment. And then, each day will be saved for eternity.

3. The Gospel

This gospel torments us with its beauty. Each word astonishes us with its splendor. It is written:

> The shepherds found Mary, Joseph,
> and the newborn baby lying in a manger.
> Having seen him, they understood the word
> that had been said to them about this little child.   Lk 2, 16-17

Whoever has met God in the mystery of Christmas can no longer keep quiet. He is never again at peace. Or rather, his peace will be to communicate his encounter with God to all his brothers and sisters.

Luke writes that "they understood the *word.*" In Hebrew, the word "word," *dabar,* also means event. That is to say that each event of our life is also a word of God. Each day, at each step, if we want it, the angels say to us: "I announce to you a great joy…Christ the Savior!"

It is written then:

> Mary remembered all these words with care
> and meditated upon them in her heart.   Lk 2, 19

The verb used by Luke that we translate as "meditate" *(symballousa)* is very suggestive. It literally means to throw *(ballein)* together *(syn).* Mary confronts, brings together, juxtaposes, and links together the different "words" of her history. Often a fact, taken separately, seems without great meaning. Sometimes even without logic. It surprises and astonishes. It is only later, when we replace it in the long chain of love through which God binds us to himself and leads us, that it bursts into light. We could also say: A word taken separately hardly has any meaning. Several words "thrown together" can construct a poem. That is the way in which God changes the mystery of our life into a great poem of love. In directing our life day after day, event after event, God is always right. And we are always right to trust in him.

It is written further:

> And the shepherds returned,
> glorifying and praising God
> for all that they had seen and heard.   Lk 2, 20

All who have met Mary, Joseph, and the newborn baby, with the shepherds, make their lives praise and glorification of God.

It is written finally:

When the eight days were fulfilled
for the circumcision,
he was then called by the name Jesus,
the name by which he had been called by the angel
before his conception in the womb (of his mother).   Lk 2, 21

Here is the most stupefying fact.

Jesus receives in his flesh the sign that indicates that he too belongs to the people of God while he is the Son of God! He receives the wound that signifies he participates in the promise made to Israel while he himself is the promise! He is integrated into the people of Abraham while he will affirm, in John's Gospel: "Before Abraham was, I am!"[3]

Blessed be you, Lord Jesus, God of eternity, who for us became a small child in the arms of Mary, the Daughter of David!

4. New Year's Wishes

Without prayers, New Year's wishes are merely testimonies of friendship. Often, they are only simple courtesies. Of course, courtesies are always precious, and it is expected that we Christians always be conspicuous for politeness. But we know well that even the most exquisite politeness can change nothing in our health— that one wishes us good or, in our situation, that one wishes us full of happiness. Even less can it change anything in our heart.

That is why we accompany our wishes with our prayers. Otherwise, they are only simple dreams of love for those whom we love. But with prayer, the dream of love can become the reality of the love of God.

I wish then that, with the grace of God, the new year may be kind to you, and the tenderness of Jesus may accompany you day after day on the path of your life.

On this path that we are taking together through these homilies, I do not know how far you will accompany me. I am not your guide; I do not want to be, in any way. In a session with priests that I was leading, a reporter came to me smiling and asked: "Are you the guru of the group?" Well, no, Christians do not have any guru! They cannot even have a teacher. "Do not call yourselves 'teachers'," said Jesus, "for you have only one Teacher, Christ."[4] I am simply seeking with you. I travel with you. The path is Christ. The joy of the road is the Holy Spirit. And the house is the Father.

Mary, Mother of God

As a wish, I take the prayer that Paul formulated for the Philippians, for whom he had a special love:

> May God the Father fulfill all your desires
> according to his riches, with magnificence,
> in Christ Jesus.   Phil 4, 19

To him love and glory each day of this new year and forever and ever.

CONCLUDING PRAYER

On this first day of the year,
the day of the feast of your name,
we present to you, Lord Jesus, our wishes
and we pray to you.

Let your Kingdom come; let your love be near!

Like the snowflake prepares itself to welcome
the first kiss of the sun,
may your faithful prepare themselves to welcome
the sweetness of your love.

Let your Kingdom come; let your love be near!

Like the dawn of spring prepares itself
to vanquish the night of winter,
may the light of your truth prepare itself
to triumph over our mistakes.

Let your Kingdom come; let your love be near!

Like the meadows prepare themselves to find again
the joy of their jonquils,
may sinners prepare themselves to find again
the joy of your forgiveness.

Let your Kingdom come; let your love be near!

Like the buds prepare themselves under the winter frost
to celebrate the ecstacy of spring,
may we prepare ourselves, in the winter of our life,
to bless you during eternity.

Let your Kingdom come; let your love be near!

Like the fiancée adorns herself with jewels
to please her betrothed,
may your Church adorn herself with holiness
to please your love.

>*Let your Kingdom come; let your love be near!*

Like Mary who kept all the words
and meditated upon them in her heart,
all through this new year
may we keep in our hearts
the memory of your love.

>*Let your Kingdom come; let your love be near!*

We pray to you, Lord Jesus:
May each day of this new year
be saved for eternity
and bless your love. Amen.

NOTES TO SOLEMNITY OF MARY, MOTHER OF GOD

1. P. J. Houyvet, "En l'an de grace…", in *Assemblées du Seigneur,* 11 (Paris: Editions du Cerf, 1970), p. 82.
2. Cf. L. Deiss, *God's Word and God's People* (Collegeville, MN: The Liturgical Press, 1976), pp. 117.
3. Jn 8, 58.
4. Mt. 23, 10.

EPIPHANY

READING I   **Is 60, 1-6**

A reading from the book of the prophet Isaiah

Rise up in splendor, Jerusalem! Your light has come,
  the glory of the Lord shines upon you.
See, darkness covers the earth,
  and thick clouds cover the peoples;
But upon you the Lord shines,
  and over you appears his glory.
Nations shall walk by your light,
  and kings by your shining radiance.
Raise your eyes and look about;
  they all gather and come to you:
Your sons come from afar,
  and your daughters in the arms of their nurses.
Then you shall be radiant at what you see,
  your heart shall throb and overflow,
For the riches of the sea shall be emptied out before you,
  the wealth of nations shall be brought to you.
Caravans of camels shall fill you,
  dromedaries from Midian and Ephah;
All from Sheba shall come
  bearing gold and frankincense,
  and proclaiming the praises of the Lord.
The Word of the Lord.

RESPONSORIAL PSALM   **Ps 72, 1-2. 7-8. 10-11. 12-13**

R/. (11) Lord, every nation on earth will adore you.

O God, with your judgment endow the king,
  and with your justice, the king's son;
He shall govern your people with justice
  and your afflicted ones with judgment.

R/. Lord, every nation on earth will adore you.

Justice shall flower in his days,
  and profound peace, till the moon be no more.
May he rule from sea to sea,
  and from the River to the ends of the earth.

R/. Lord, every nation on earth will adore you.

The kings of Tarshish and the Isles shall offer gifts;
   the kings of Arabia and Sheba shall bring tribute.
All kings shall pay him homage,
   all nations shall serve him.

R/. Lord, every nation on earth will adore you.

For he shall rescue the poor man when he cries out,
   and the afflicted when he has no one to help him.
He shall have pity for the lowly and the poor;
   the lives of the poor he shall save.

R/. Lord, every nation on earth will adore you.

READING II   EPH 3, 2-3. 5-6

A reading from the letter of Paul to the Ephesians

I am sure you have heard of the ministry which God in his goodness gave me in your regard. God's secret plan, as I have briefly described it, was revealed to me, unknown to people in former ages but now revealed by the Spirit to the holy apostles and prophets. It is no less than this: in Christ Jesus the Gentiles are now co-heirs with the Jews, members of the same body and sharers of the promise through the preaching of the gospel.

The Word of the Lord.

GOSPEL   MT 2, 1-12

A reading from the holy gospel according to Matthew

After Jesus' birth in Bethlehem of Judea during the reign of King Herod, astrologers from the east arrived one day in Jerusalem inquiring, "Where is the newborn king of the Jews? We observed his star at its rising and have come to pay him homage." At this news King Herod became greatly disturbed, and with him all Jerusalem. Summoning all of the chief priests and scribes of the people, he inquired of them where the Messiah was to be born. "In Bethlehem of Judea," they informed him. "Here is what the prophet has written:

   'And you, Bethlehem, land of Judah,
   are by no means least among the princes of Judah,
   since from you shall come a ruler
   who is to shepherd my people Israel.'"

Herod called the astrologers aside and found out from them the exact time of the star's appearance. Then he sent them to Bethlehem, after having instructed them: "Go and get detailed information about the child. When you have discovered something, your findings report to me so that I may go and offer him homage too."

After their audience with the king, they set out. The star which they had observed at its rising went ahead of them until it came to a standstill over the place where the child was. They were overjoyed at seeing the star, and on entering the house, found the child with Mary his mother. They prostrated themselves and did him homage. Then they opened their coffers and presented him with gifts of gold, frankincense, and myrrh.

They received a message in a dream not to return to Herod, so they went back to their own country by another route.

The gospel of the Lord.

INTRODUCTORY PRAYER

We bless you, God our Father.
In guiding the Magi to the manger of the infant Jesus,
you open a path of hope for the nations.
In lighting the light of faith on their way,
you make the morning star rise in our hearts.
In receiving their offering of gold, frankincense,
and myrrh,
you accept the homage of our love.

We pray to you:
To all those who seek you with uprightness, send a star—
a reason to hope and love—
which will guide them toward your house of light
where we will celebrate together your love of a Father
through your Son Jesus, in the joy of the Holy Spirit,
forever and ever. Amen.

HOMILY

1. The Mystery of Epiphany

Matthew's Gospel presents to us a passage full of poetry, the poetry of a newborn child, of a star, and of Magi, gold, frankincense, and myrrh. It is the popular theme of a child predestined and unjustly persecuted by an evil king but escaping miraculously from his persecutors and then becoming savior of his people.

This theme we have already met in the life of Moses. When the Angel of the Lord asks Joseph to come back to the land of Israel, he takes up word-for-word the invitation made by God to Moses to come back to Egypt. By translating the biblical texts literally, we obtain the following parallel:

Mt 2, 20	Ex 4, 19
For they are dead	For they are dead
those who sought	those who sought
the soul (life) of the	your soul (life).
child.	

Matthew also relies upon Isaiah 60 (from which the First Reading gives us an extract):

> The people from Sheba will come
> bearing gold and frankincense
> and proclaiming the praises of the Lord.   Is 60, 6

Finally, it is written in Psalm 72 (which is the Responsorial Psalm of this feast):

> The kings of Tarshish and of the Isles
> will bring presents.
> The kings of Arabia and of Sheba
> will make offerings.   Ps. 72, 10

On the historical level, Matthew's text does not allow us to seek exactly what happened. It would be as imprudent to deny the historicity of the whole account as it would be to admit the historicity of each detail. In return, it is possible to understand the message of the Gospel, that is, what Matthew wanted to present to us as the Good News.

Epiphany and the Search for God

In Luke's Gospel, Jesus reveals himself to the shepherds, to Simeon, to Anna, in short to the "little ones" of Israel, to the humble and to the poor. Everyone—Zachariah, Mary, the angels, Simeon, Anna—begins to sing the praises of the Lord.

In Matthew's Gospel, Jerusalem and its king are not aware of Jesus. Little children are slaughtered and lamentation rises in Bethlehem. But strangers and pagans seek him, find him, and worship him. Jesus, ignored and refused by Jerusalem, is welcomed and worshiped by the nations.

God is present in the world, even if the world is not aware of him. He is present in Jerusalem, even if Jerusalem is not aware of him. He is present in his Church, even if the people sometimes forget him or ignore him. His presence is as real as that of spring in the heart of a little grain of wheat buried in the frozen earth. God is present in your heart, even if your heart is in darkness or in the frozen ground. But you must seek him. "Epiphany" means "manifestion." But there is no epiphany of God without passionate seeking for his face. There is no revelation without quest for his love; there is no star to rise and shine in our darkness if we do not raise our eyes to heaven.

Thus, if the essence of the mystery of Epiphany is the manifestation of Jesus to the Magi and through them to all nations, the essence of our response is seeking God. The prayer of the epiphany is the cry of the Psalm:

It is your face, O Lord, that I seek!   Ps 27, 8

How strange then is our God! How marvelous is his epiphany! We wait for him on a great feast day, and he comes to us in the banality of daily life. We wait for him in great discourses of the pope, the bishops, of priests, and he comes to us in the very simple words of our brothers and sisters! We wait for him on a sunny day, and he comes to us on a gray, rainy sometimes dark, foggy day! We wait for him in sublime events and yet, the truly sublime is to recognize him in daily life. It is in the least of our brothers and sisters— and in what we have done for them—that the epiphany of Christ is realized. If we want it, each day can become a feast of the epiphany.

Yes, our God is strange! Even for Mary, the little Galilean who clasps the baby in her arms! The angel had said to her: "He will be great!"
And here in the epiphany he appears quite modest, quite insignificant!

The angel had said to her: "He will be called Son of the Most High." And here they said of him: "It is the little son of the carpenter."

The angel had said to her: "The Lord God will give him the throne of his father David." And here his throne is a manger in a stable!

The angel had said to her: "He will reign over the house of Jacob forever, and his reign will have no end." And here he is persecuted by a stupid and greedy Herod.

In winter, two branches of a tree, one dried out and the other living, look alike. One would say: "Here are two dead branches." But in the spring, life bursts forth in one and death reveals itself in the other. In the winter of our life, this desire for God, this quest for his face, is our life:

> You who seek God,
> may your hearts live long!   Ps 22, 27

It does not say: "You who find God," or even "You who have already found God," but "You who seek God..." When in a hundred years, when in a thousand years, when in a billion years...when we will no longer be anything but a little dust on this ball that is called earth, which dances around the sun, when the angel will sound the trumpet, when all the angels will cry out: "Wake up! It is the epiphany! Wake up! It is eternity!". Then God our Father will gather our heart from the dust; only then, will we have found God for eternity. Like the Magi, we will see the Infant with Mary his mother. And eye to eye, we will discover the splendor of his love.

2. Following Matthew's Text

Matthew gives us precious historical information when he writes:

> Jesus was born in Bethlehem
> in the days of King Herod.   Mt. 2, 1

We know through the historian Josephus that Herod died around Passover 750 according to the Roman calendar, which is the year 4 of our era.[1] Now, he became gravely ill in September-October 749 and definitely left Jerusalem for Jericho on that date. Since the Magi met him in Jerusalem, Jesus was therefore surely born before that date, therefore before September 749.

The Magi

Who were these good Magi? Kings? But Matthew says nothing about kings. How many were they? Three? But the Gospel says nothing about three.[2] What were their names? Gaspar, Milchior and Balthasar? But these names appear only in a pretty poem invented in the seventh century. From where did they come? From the East? But that is hardly enlightening. It is just more poetic to say that they came from the East. They came from the place where the sun rises; they came from the region where light dwells. They were seekers of God.

The Star

Having arrived in Jerusalem, the Magi inquired:

> Where is the king of the Jews who has just been born?
> We have seen his star in the east
> and have come to worship him. Mt 2, 2

And later, the evangelist writes further:

> Behold, the star that they had seen in the east
> went before them.
> It came to a stop above the place where the little child was.
> When they saw the star,
> they rejoiced with great joy. Mt 2, 9-10

This star is the most popular and the most marvelous element of the account. It poses a problem. And we ask ourselves: Is it true or legendary? Must we then disconnect the star from the crèche or must we keep it?

In itself, I do not see any difficulty for God, who created millions of stars, to create also a miracle of light that Matthew calls star and which would have guided the Magi. But it is not a marvel that we must seek, but the message that Matthew wants to give to us.

A prophecy which was very popular in the time of Christ—it is even cited in the literature of the monks of Qumran—announced that a star, that is, a king, would rise over Jacob:

> Oracle of Balaam, son of Beor,
> oracle of the man with a penetrating look...
> I see him...I perceive him:
> A star issued from Jacob becomes chief,
> a sceptre rises, issued from Israel. Nm 24, 15, 17

The star of Bethlehem reveals the royalty of the child. It is really this royalty that the Magi come to worship when they ask: "Where is the king of the Jews?"

This manifestation of the royalty of Jesus preludes in some way the eschatological manifestation of the sign of the Son of man on the last day:

Then will appear in heaven
the sign of the Son of man...
coming on the clouds of heaven
with power and great glory.   Mt 24, 30

On that blessed day, the morning star, it is said, will rise in the heart of those
who have sought God.[3] That morning star is none other than Christ himself
according to the last words of the Book of Revelation:

I Jesus...
I am the offspring of David,
the morning star, the radiant.   Rv 22, 16

The star that guided the Magi, the star that guides us day after day, the star
that we carry as the most precious treasure in our heart, that star is the light
of God in us. Each human heart was wanted, loved, created to be the
receptacle of that star. Guided by that radiant star, we walk towards Christ
Jesus. "To the conqueror," says Jesus, "I will give the Morning Star."[4]

The Child with Mary, His Mother

After their interview with Herod, the star appeared again to the Magi. Such
a wonderful star can only lead to a wonderful king, reigning in a wonderful
palace, surrounded by a wonderful court. But the star goes straight to the
field of shepherds, to one of those caves where one can take refuge in
winter, where one can encamp if absolutely necessary. And the Magi
discover a little king, a king all confined and shrunken. A king in a decor
of a lowly cow stable surrounded by a donkey and sheep.

Yes, how strange then is our God! Truly, he judges us only by our hearts.
To the robes set with gold of Herod's court, he prefers Mary, the little
Galilean with the heart of gold, with her husband Joseph, the carpenter who
has big calloused hands filled with straw, and with the little child placed
in a manger who is the God of eternity. Mary who tries in the homeliness
of the cave to make herself pretty, or at least presentable for her husband.
And for the Magi, what an epiphany! She gives them the little one to touch,
to carry, to embrace while she arranges her hair and straightens her robe,
and the "little one" suddenly must be cared for! There is what Matthew's
text means:

Entering into the house,
they saw the child with Mary, his mother.   Mt 2, 11

3. Called to Share in the Same Promise

The epiphany, the manifestation of Jesus to the Magi, preludes his manifestation to all the nations. It is the feast of hope for all the people who have not yet seen the star. Paul affirms:

> Such is the mystery of Christ...
> The nations are associated to the same heritage,
> to the same body, to share in the same promise
> in Christ Jesus, through the Gospel.　　　　　　Eph 3, 3, 6

How may we realize the mystery of Jesus? How can we work for its fulfillment?

If the Magi come to Bethlehem, it is because the star shone upon Bethlehem. If the nations come to the Church, it is because they have seen the light of God shine upon the Church.

Each heart has been created to be like a monstrance of a star, light for our brothers and sisters. The Church herself is the communion of all those who carry the light of God in their heart. They are light for their brothers and sisters; they guide them to Christ.

We must come back to the marvelous prophecy of the Book of Isaiah from where the First Reading is taken. The prophet announces the jubilant pilgrimage of the nations to Jerusalem. And why do the nations want to go there? Because they saw the light of God shine upon the Holy City:

> Arise! Shine, for here is your light,
> and the glory of the Lord has shone upon you...
> Nations shall walk toward your light,
> and kings, towards the brightness of your dawn.　　　　Is 60, 1, 3

On the historical level, the prophecy refers to the return from captivity after the edict of Cyrus in 538. Like a light, the mercy of God shone upon the exiles of Babylon. Their return put into motion the pilgrimage of the peoples to Jerusalem.

In reality, the return of the exiles was less lyrical than the prophecy had foretold. The light had shone, indeed, upon Jerusalem, but the plenitude of its brightness still remained an object of hope. As for the nations, we cannot pretend that they had jostled each other at the doors of the Holy City.

A second fulfillment of the prophecy took place at the time of the coming of Christ. John writes:

> The Word became flesh.
> He pitched his tent among us
> and we saw his glory.   Jn 1, 14

This glory, in Jesus, was made light of the world; it shines in the heart of the Church.

But this shining splendor in the heart of the Church, of which we are witnesses, also remains a hope. That is why the fulfillment in plenitude of the prophecy of the Book of Isaiah is reserved for the end of time, or better yet, for the beginning of eternity. Then the Church here below will be transfigured into the New Jerusalem, the one that comes from heaven and about which it is said:

> The glory of God illuminated it,
> and the Lamb was its lamp.
> The nations shall walk by its light.   Rv 21, 23-24

We are situated between the second and the third—the last—fulfillment. We are called to carry the prophecy to its full realization. What a marvelous vocation is ours! But also, what a responsibility!

Sometimes we get tired of crying to the nations: "Come to us! Come into our Church!" They could well answer us sometimes: "Where is your star? Where is your light? Your prophecy affirms that the glory of the Lord has shone upon you. Where then is that glory that we may admire it? Your prophecy speaks about the brightness of his dawn. Where then is your dawn? Where then is his brightness? If we are to see among you the same fog that exists among us, then is it worth it to change our place?"

This is true; sometimes we have much grayness. That comes from our mediocrity. Sometimes we also have much brightness. That comes from Christ.

One can say that the greatest obstacle to the evangelization of the world today, to the actual diffusion of the Gospel of Christ, to the shining of the star upon the world is the life of Christians. And the greatest cause of the actual diffusion of the Gospel and the shining of the star is also the life of Christians.

A Jubilant Procession

How joyous and jubilant is this procession that the prophet evokes. Everyone will celebrate there the praises of the Lord. It is written:

> Your sons arrive from far
> and your daughters are carried in arms...
> They sing the praises of the Lord.   Is 60, 6

Perhaps you know the song "Sion, sing, break into song," with this text from the Book of Isaiah: "Arise, shine, for here is your light!" The first time that we sang it in our major seminary, an aged Father, who was a professor with me, waited for me at the end of the celebration, at the bottom of the steps of the organ loft. He said to me: "The melody of this new song is beautiful. But the words are absolutely not suitable!" I did not understand. He said to me: "You see, in a seminary, one should never sing: 'The daughters are carried in arms.'" I answered: "Father, it is not I who dared to say that; it is the prophet; it is the Holy Spirit."

Oh! If all our celebrations could be filled with the jubilation of the Holy Spirit! Without it being necessary to carry daughters in arms, could we not render our liturgies more worthy of the prophecy of the Book of Isaiah and of the joy of the Holy Spirit!

Prayer

We shall pray for all those who have stopped along the way for want of looking at the star. In the Gospel, they are still in Jerusalem. I want to speak especially about a part of Israel which has not yet discovered its Messiah in Bethlehem. It was not always their fault. For Christians, in the course of the ages, have sometimes so beaten them down that they no longer had the time to seek the star.

We shall also pray for all people, those whom the Church calls "the nations." The star is what gives to each life its most profound meaning. The one who does not have the star is dead.

We Christians should not pretend that we possess the star in our heart. Rather it is the star that lives in and possesses our heart. In the same way that when the sun gives light to your face, we do not say that your face possesses the sun, but that the sun visits your face. May our hearts become, then, transparent to the light of God.

The star can also live in any other heart, whatever its belief may be. How many belong to the Church, said Saint Augustine, who do not belong to Christ! And how many belong to Christ who do not belong to the Church!

We have spoken at length about the Epiphany. We must not forget the essential: to make the mystery ours by celebrating it. Here is how Gregory Nazianzen invited his faithful to celebrate it in the fourth century:

Christ is born: glorify him!
Christ comes from heaven: go to meet him!
Christ descends upon our earth: exalt him to the heavens!...

Respect the census of Herod:
thanks to it, you have been registered in heaven.
Venerate this birth: it broke the chains
in which you were born.
Honor little Bethlehem: she led you to paradise.
Adore the manger: while you were without speech,
thanks to it, you were nourished by the Word...

With the star, hasten; with the Magi, offer your gifts:
gold as to the King, incense as to God,
and myrrh as to the man who died for you.

With the shepherds, give glory!
With the angels, sing hymns!
With the archangels, dance with joy!
Let one joy unite heaven and earth![5]

To Christ Jesus, born of the Virgin Mary, who revealed himself to the shepherds, to the Magi and to us, to him glory and love for ever and ever.

CONCLUDING PRAYER

Entering into the house,
they saw the Child with Mary, his mother.

Let us pray now for the salvation of all people.
With the Magi, may we all find
the Child with Mary, his Mother.

Give us, O Lord, the Morningstar!

Epiphany

We pray to you, Lord, for our beloved Church.
May she be the epiphany of your beauty on the world.

May she announce to all people the tenderness
of the child with Mary, his Mother.

Give us, O Lord, the Morningstar!

We pray to you for those who, following the Magi,
went to seek your light.
Make rise in the heaven of their hearts
a star of love which will lead them
to the child with Mary, his Mother.

Give us, O Lord, the Morningstar!

We pray to you for the astronomers who scrutinize heaven
and help us discover the splendor of your universe.
Make them read in the infinity of the stars
the infinitely greater marvels of the love
of the child with Mary, his Mother.

Give us, O Lord, the Morningstar!

We pray to you for those who joyously offer to you
the gold of their love, the frankincense of their prayer,
and the myrrh of their sacrifice.
Increase in them, day after day, the joy of serving
the child with Mary, his Mother.

Give us, O Lord, the Morningstar!

We pray to you for those who walk in darkness,
who have allowed the brightness of your star,
their reason to hope and love

to be extinguished in their heart.
Awaken in them the flame of hope,
put them back on the path
of the child with Mary, his Mother.

Give us, O Lord, the Morningstar!

We pray to you for the Herods
who, even today, seek to kill Christ.
Break the pride of the powerful who persecute the poor.
Make them discover the justice and love
of the child with Mary, his Mother.

Give us, O Lord, the Morningstar!

We, too, Lord, have seen your star,
and we are coming into your house
to worship the child with Mary, his Mother.
When the dawn of the eternal Day rises,
give us the Morningstar, your Son Jesus,
the child of Mary
and our brother for eternity. Amen.

NOTES TO EPIPHANY

1. The Christian era has been calculated by Dionysius Exiguus (around 500-550). It takes the year 754 as year one of the Christian era. There is, therefore, an error of four or five years at least.
2. In antiquity, like in the catacombs of Domitille in Rome, four of them were represented, two on each side with the Virgin in the middle, which gave a good arrangement. The Syrian and Armenian traditions counted up to twelve of them, which seems to be a very generous calculation.
3. Cf. 2 Pt 1, 19.
4. Rv 2, 28.
5. Gregory Nazianzen (329/330-390). *Sermo 38*. 1.17-18. Transl. L. Deiss. Cf. Pg 36, 312A 333A.

BAPTISM OF THE LORD

READING I   Is 42, 1-4. 6-7

A reading from the book of the prophet Isaiah

Here is my servant whom I uphold,
  my chosen one with whom I am pleased,
Upon whom I have put my spirit;
  he shall bring forth justice to the nations,
Not crying out, not shouting,
  not making his voice heard in the street.
A bruised reed he shall not break,
  and a smoldering wick he shall not quench,
Until he establishes justice on the earth;
  the coastlands will wait for his teaching.
I, the Lord, have called you for the victory of justice,
  I have grasped you by the hand;
I formed you, and set you
    as a covenant of the people,
    a light for the nations,
To open the eyes of the blind,
    to bring out prisoners from confinement,
    and from the dungeon, those who live in darkness.

The Word of the Lord.

RESPONSORIAL PSALM   Ps 29, 1-2. 3-4. 3. 9-10

R/. (11) The Lord will bless his people with peace.

Give to the Lord, you sons of God,
  give to the Lord glory and praise,
Give to the Lord the glory due his name;
  adore the Lord in holy attire.

R/. The Lord will bless his people with peace.

The voice of the Lord is over the waters,
  the Lord, over vast waters.
The voice of the Lord is mighty;
  the voice of the Lord is majestic.

R/. The Lord will bless his people with peace.

The God of glory thunders,
    and in his temple all say, "Glory!"
The Lord is enthroned above the flood;
    the Lord is enthroned as king forever.

R/. The Lord will bless his people with peace.

READING II   ACTS 10, 34-38

A reading from the Acts of the Apostles

Peter addressed Cornelius and the people assembled at his house in
these words: "I begin to see how true it is that God shows no partiality.
Rather, the man of any nation who fears God and acts uprightly is
acceptable to him. This is the message he has sent to the sons of Israel,
'the good news of peace' proclaimed through Jesus Christ who is Lord
of all. I take it you know what has been reported all over Judea about
Jesus of Nazareth, beginning in Galilee with the baptism John
preached; of the way God anointed him with the Holy Spirit and power.
He went about doing good works and healing all who were in the grip
of the devil, and God was with him."

The Word of the Lord.

GOSPEL   LK 3, 15-16. 21-22

A reading from the holy gospel according to Luke

The people were full of anticipation, wondering in their hearts whether
John might be the Messiah. John answered them all by saying: "I am
baptizing you in water, but there is one to come who is mightier than I.
I am not fit to loosen his sandal strap. He will baptize you in the Holy
Spirit and in fire.

When all the people were baptized, and Jesus was at prayer after
likewise being baptized, the skies opened and the Holy Spirit descended on him in visible form like a dove. A voice from heaven was
heard to say, "You are my beloved Son. On you my favor rests."

The gospel of the Lord.

INTRODUCTORY PRAYER

We bless you, Lord Jesus,
on this day when we celebrate your baptism.
You, the Lord, submitted yourself
to the baptism of John, the servant.
You, the Holy One, the immaculate, implored forgiveness
for the sins of your human family.
You, the Covenant for the people and light of the nations,
became the Lamb who takes away the sin of the world.

We pray to you:
May the voice of your Father come also upon us,
may it say to each one of us:
"You also are my child
in whom I have placed all my love!"
Then our lives will be changed into your eternity,
and we will celebrate your love forever and ever. Amen.

HOMILY

1. Jesus and the Baptism from John

John the Baptist had proclaimed the proximity of the Kingdom of God and the urgent necessity of doing penance for one's sins. He had said: Prepare yourselves to meet God. Do penance for your sins; convert yourselves. That is, turn to God, come back to your Father in heaven.

In receiving baptism from John, Jesus says: "Yes, this preaching comes authentically from God. Yes, you must stop on the road of evil and turn to God. Come back to your Father." And he, Jesus, does not present himself as our judge. He places himself on our side; he walks with his brothers and sisters. He does penance with us for mistakes that he did not commit but which are mistakes of the human family of which he is a part. He purifies himself from impurities whose stain he does not bear, but which tarnish the human family to which he belongs.

This mystery touches us directly today. By being baptized, Jesus makes our baptism possible. Even more, it is only with him that we can be purified. Without him we cannot convert ourselves or come back to God. He alone can take us by the hand. Little does the density of the darkness matter, for we do not even have the eyes to see! Little does the length of the road matter, for we do not even have the feet to walk! Little does the height of heaven matter, for we do not even have the hands to scale the heavenly wall!

Christ saves us. He says to us: You do not know the way? You do not have feet? It matters little! Come with me; I am your way.

You are groping in the darkness? You don't have good eyes? You don't even have eyes? It matters little! Come with me; I am your light, the light of the world.

You do not know how to love God? You have a heart that is sick, numb in indifference? It matters little! Come with me; I am your heart for loving the Father!

Let us live in your love, Lord Jesus. Let the heavens be torn open above each of us! Let the hope of God's voice come upon us! "You also are my beloved child. In you I have placed all my love!"

2. Gospel and History

During the baptism of Jesus, God suddenly invaded history and revealed himself to Jesus. Nothing indicates that Jesus foresaw that manifestation; nothing indicates that he sought it. Luke writes simply:

> While Jesus was praying...
> the heavens were torn open.   Lk 3, 21

It is in this moment that the prayer of the Old Testament is granted:

> Oh, if you would tear open the heavens
> and come down!   Is 63, 19

The Mystery and its Expression

What really took place at the baptism of Jesus? We Christians believe marvelous things happened. However, our interest in them is not because they are marvelous, but rather because these events are recorded in the Gospels, and they are proclaiming the Good News. Is it necessary then to believe that the heavens were torn apart (like a sheet) and that a dove came out of heaven?

On the one hand there is a spiritual mystery. It took place in the soul of Jesus. This mystery is made known to us both by images and by biblical citations.

As for images, they are true, not in their very literalness, but in the meaning that they express. When I say: "That man is a lion," I do not mean that he has a mane and that he leaps in the savannah like a lion. I mean that he is courageous and strong like lions are said to be.

Here likewise, in the text that we are considering, there are images also: the rending of heaven, the heavenly voice, the dove. I must interpret them, that is, decipher their message.

What about the biblical citations? They relate principally to the Servant of Yahweh according to the Book of Isaiah. The First Reading of this feast refers to this servant. The parallel between Isaiah and Mark is the following:

Is 42, 1	Mk 1, 10-11
Here is my servant	You are my Son
(son)	(servant)
whom I uphold,	
my chosen one.	the beloved (chosen) one;
whom my soul prefers.	in you I am pleased.
I put upon him	He saw
my spirit.	the Spirit descend upon him.

The expression *beloved Son*[1] is important to note. It does not occur in any other part of the Bible except in the episode of the sacrifice of Isaac, whom his father Abraham, on the order of God, prepares to sacrifice. This text suggests, then, that Jesus is the new Isaac, the lamb of the sacrifice of the New Covenant.

It is enlightening to understand the allusion to the figure of Moses in this text. It is written in the Book of Isaiah 63, 11 that God made him *go up from the sea and placed in him his Spirit.* This calls to mind that the Spirit came upon Jesus precisely when he came forth from the waters of the Jordan.

It is very evident that one cannot, in the framework of a homily, exploit all these allusions. They show at least the riches—if not the complexity—of the evangelic text.

A Naïve Reading?

One could ask: Can we not be content with an entirely naïve reading of the Word and believe quite simply what is written?

Of course, the Bible is the book for simple hearts, and the Spirit never faults those who venerate the Word with uprightness. But the Spirit also enlightens those who seek God's message with humility and accuracy.[2]

We are forced to ask questions. Here is the problem. In Mark the heavenly voice says:

| You are my Son, the beloved. | Mk 1, 11 |

But in Matthew, it says:

| This is my Son, the beloved. | Mt 3, 17 |

In Luke, on the contrary, it proclaims:

You are my Son.

| Today I have begotten you. | Lk 3, 22 |

If we were satisfied with a naïve reading, we would then be obliged to conclude: Either Mark is true and Matthew and Luke are not, or else the voice spoke three times, since the accounts do not agree.

We would also be obliged to admit that Jesus instituted the Eucharist four times (once according to Matthew, once according to Mark, once according to Luke and once according to the tradition of Paul in 1 Cor 11, 23-26). We would also be obliged to admit that Peter denied his Master nine times (three times according to each Evangelist: Matthew, Mark, and Luke) for there also, as in so many other places, the traditions do not overlap. We are therefore invited to seek in the diversity of the traditions—which is their very richness and almost the seal of their authenticity—the message of the Spirit.

And this message is exciting.

3. Riches of the Evangelic Text: You Are My Son

In its early form, the heavenly voice conveyed no doubt: "You are my servant." This title of "servant," Jesus bore in fact in the most archaic texts. Thus Peter, before the Sanhedrin,[3] speaks about the "holy servant Jesus."

Later on, the community replaced the title of "servant" with the title of "Son" which expressed better the dignity of Christ after his Resurrection. Paul writes in fact:

Jesus, son of David according to the flesh,

has been established Son of God with power

| through his resurrection from the dead. | Rom 1, 4 |

The replacement of "servant" by "son" is quite easy for the word servant, *èbed* in Hebrew, *pais* in Greek,[4] can mean at the same time "son" and "boy" or "servant."

This title of son is not in itself anything exceptional. It was the privilege of every pious Israelite living in the Covenant. Everything depends on the quality of the sonship which is signified.

In Mark, the heavenly voice addresses itself directly to Jesus:

> You are my Son, the beloved.   Mk, 1, 11

Matthew undoubtedly thought that Jesus knew well that he was the beloved Son. But the Christian community had to learn about it and know it. The voice addresses itself therefore to the community:

> This is my Son, the beloved.   Mt 3, 17

This theophany can be considered as the inaugural vision of the prophetic vocation of Jesus. Just as Isaiah sees the heavens open and to the Lord's question: "Whom shall I send, who will be my messenger?" answers: "Here I am, send me!". Just as Jeremiah, Ezekiel, and Paul receive their prophetic investiture in an inaugural vision,[5] thus is Jesus established servant of God in his baptismal vision. His baptism represents his consecration as servant-son and his being sent into mission.

As for the depth of this relation of love between the carpenter of Nazareth and the God of Israel, between Jesus and his Father, it is impenetrable for us. It remains their secret. We can simply suppose that thirty years of hidden life, which were so many years of prayer, worship, and humble submission, made their relationship an unfathomable depth of intimacy.

In You I Have Placed All My Love

There is nothing servile about the title of servant. Quite the contrary, in relationship to God it is the most noble title that a creature can bear. Our most sublime vocation is to be allowed to serve God. For this title is a title of love. The more we serve God, the more he makes us enter into his tenderness. The more we humble ourselves in his service, the more he exalts us.

Now the service of Jesus was total. That is why he is also the beloved Son.

In biblical vocabulary, the title of *beloved* son is practically the equivalent of *only* Son. Now it is precisely about this son that it is said:

> In you I have placed all my love.   Mk 1, 11

That is, all the infinite love of which the Father is capable—if one can speak in this way!—he made rest on the Only One. Or further: God cannot love anyone outside of this Son who has all his love. There is no portion of his love that does not go to his Son.

And what about us? What remains for us then? Are we not loved? Yes, infinitely. How then? In Jesus. Clearly, we are loved in the same measure that we make ourselves one with Christ, in the same measure that our face reproduces the features of the Beloved, in the same measure that our voice sings in unison with the Only One, in the same measure that our heart loves with the one of Jesus.

But then, this love that is given to us is not measured. It is the infinite love with which the Father loves Christ that comes upon us. The Father has only one love: the Son. In him, he places all his kindness. Such is the love which is given to us; in us also he places all his kindness. This is what Paul affirms, a statement which makes our mind reel in the emptiness of infinity and makes us tremble with joy: "The Father loved us in his Son Jesus even before the creation of the world."[6]

Blessed be you, God our Father, for loving us thus in your Son Jesus.

The Holy Spirit

It is written moreover:

> The Holy Spirit descended upon Jesus...
> like a dove.   Lk 3, 22

When God chooses a prophet to carry his word, he gives him the Spirit, his very "breath." By making a play on the words, we could say that God gives his breath to someone who would risk "running out of breath" for the work to be accomplished.

That is why Luke likes to associate spirit and power. It is said about John the Baptist:

> He will walk before the Lord
> with the breath (or spirit) and power of Elijah.   Lk 1, 17

In the announcement to Mary, the angel Gabriel says to the Virgin:

> Holy Breath (or Spirit) will come upon you
> and power from the Most High will cover you
> with his shadow.   Lk 1, 35

It is precisely this association of Spirit and power that we find again in Peter's discourse which alludes to the baptism of Jesus:

> Jesus of Nazareth:
> God anointed him with the Holy Spirit and power.   Acts 10, 38

It is under the movement of this Spirit and strengthened by his unction that Jesus will proclaim the Good News to the poor.[7]

Even today, no one can pretend to announce the Good News of the Kingdom if he has not received, like Jesus, the anointing of the Spirit.

In saying that, we tremble. Is our heart sufficiently filled with the Spirit so that our poor human words might become authentic words of God? Pray for us priests, for your bishops, for your catechists. Pray also for yourselves: That we may all together form the prophetic people, the people bearing the Spirit, the people of the baptism of Christ.

The Dove

This dove that descends upon Jesus is a lovely image. It is as lovely as it is difficult to interpret. Mark writes:

> (Jesus) saw the heavens torn open
> and the Spirit, like a dove,
> descending upon him.   Mk 1, 10

Matthew's text comes close to Mark's without reproducing it, but Luke strays considerably from Mark's tradition:

> The heaven was opened
> and the Holy Spirit, in a bodily form,
> descended upon him.   Lk 3, 22

Through these three traditions, one can reasonably know the following: The Gospels, witnesses of the faith of the early community, teach that Jesus was consecrated by the Spirit of God. This Spirit descends upon him as a dove would hover and descend. The point of comparison bears, not upon the dove, but upon the descent of the Spirit.

The closest biblical text is the one of the account of creation. It is written there:

> The Spirit of God hovered over the waters.   Gn 1, 2

One could propose the following comparison: Just as the Spirit of God hovered over the original waters to make them fruitful, in the same way the Spirit of the Father hovered over the waters of the baptism to make the ministry of Jesus fruitful in view of the new creation.

At any rate, no visual representation is possible. If the dove had been visible upon the waters of the Jordan; if the voice from heaven, on the other hand, had resounded in the silence of the desert, how are we to understand that John the Baptist seemed to doubt later the mission of Jesus to the point of asking him: "Are you the one who must come?"[8] The coming of the Spirit is a mystery which takes place in the soul of Jesus; the voice of the Father resounds in the silence of his conscience.

While He Was Praying

According to Luke, the theophany took place after the baptism, while Jesus was praying. He writes:

> When Jesus had been baptized,
> while he was praying,
> heaven was opened.   Lk 3, 21

We know that Luke likes to mention the prayer of Jesus. He notes it before the choice of the Twelve, before Peter's profession of faith, before the Transfiguration, before the teaching of the "Our Father."[9] There is little chance that if the early source mentioned this prayer of Jesus at the baptism, Matthew and Mark would have dared to omit it. There is every chance that Luke inserted it. Could we not consider the whole life of Jesus as a single and unique prayer?

This prayer, here, is tied to the effusion of the Spirit. We could establish the following parallel: In the same way that Jesus, at the dawn of his public life, receives in prayer the Spirit who guides him in his messianic vocation, thus the early community, at the dawn of the Church, that is, on the day of Pentecost, receives in prayer the Spirit who guides it in its vocation in the service of the nations.

Among the "children of the woman," as Scripture says, Jesus was certainly the one who had the least need of prayer since his heart dwelled near the heart of God at all times. And yet he was the one who prayed the most. His prayer is his dialogue with the Father. Our prayer is the look of a child toward the Father, in the light of the Holy Spirit. Are we conscious enough of the necessity of prayer? Is each one of our decisions the result of a dialogue with the Spirit, of a look toward the Father?

For when we pray, heaven is opened to the eyes of our heart as it was for Jesus. When we pray, the Spirit of God rests upon us as he did upon Jesus. When we pray, we receive our vocation and the Father says to us, as he did to Jesus: "You also are my beloved child." When we pray the voice also says to us, as it did to Jesus: "In you I have placed all my love."

The Witness of the Father According to Luke

Luke's version of the witness of the Father differs from Matthew's and Mark's. It declares:

> You are my Son.
> Today I have begotten you. Lk 3, 22

This is a citation from Psalm 2. In the early Church, this Psalm was applied to the Resurrection of Jesus. In his homily at Antioch of Pisidia, Paul argues in this way:

> We announce to you this Good News: the promise made to our fathers, God has fulfilled in our favor for us, their children, by raising Jesus, as it is written in the [second] psalm:
> "You are my Son.
> Today I have begotten you." Acts 12, 32-33

The divine sonship of Jesus, which breaks forth in the mystery of the Resurrection, Luke anticipates then in some way by placing it already at the baptism. He will be able to connect then upon the genealogy of Jesus by affirming that he is at the same time "son of Adam and Son of God."[10]

The mystery of Jesus illuminates our own Christian condition. Jesus is proclaimed Son of God at the time of his baptism, but the plenitude of his mystery will not burst forth until the time of his Resurrection. In the same way, we become children of God at the time of our baptism, but the total plenitude of our sonship will not burst forth until the time of our own resurrection. This will then be the eternal marvel. John writes:

> From now we are children of God.
> But what we shall be has not yet been made known.
> We know that when that will be made known
> we shall be like him
> because we shall see him just as he is. 1 Jn 3, 2

Then we also shall live in his light; we shall dress ourselves in his joy. Eye to eye we shall see this eternal love that he has given us!

The Mission of Jesus

In the homily that he gives in the synagogue of his village in Nazareth, Jesus applied the words of the Book of Isaiah to himself:

The Holy Spirit is upon me, for he has anointed me
to preach the Good News to the poor.
He has sent me to proclaim freedom to the prisoners,
the return of sight to the blind,
to announce freedom to the oppressed,
to proclaim a year of the Lord's grace. **Lk 4, 18-19**

Peter will sum up this ministry of Jesus to the poor in a superb way:

He went around doing good. **Acts 10, 38**

Now the vocation of Jesus is also that of the Christian. According to Paul, the Christian is baptized, that is, plunged into the mystery of Christ Jesus.

It is said about Jesus: "The Spirit has sent me to take Good News to the poor." Is our life an announcement of this Gospel of grace? Lord, make your Good News reveal itself in our life for all the poor who walk with us toward your Kingdom.

It is said about Jesus: "Here is my servant." Sometimes we are content to serve God from time to time when we have the time to think about it. Are we full-time servants in the depths of our soul, placing ourselves day after day in the service of the Kingdom? Or do we sometimes work like slaves bound to the task? Lord, make us faithful servants.

It is said: "I make my Spirit rest upon him." What spirit inhabits us? What spirit makes us live? Lord, make us bearers of your Holy Spirit.

It is said: "He will not crush the bruised reed; he will not extinguish the flickering wick." From a reed that was already bruised by the wind of evil, Jesus made a shoot of hope. From a smoldering wick, he made a light of joy. Are we like a winter wind that bruises the reeds, or like a spring that makes the flowers bloom for our brothers and sisters? Are we smoke that reddens the eyes, or a fire of joy? Lord, make us the light of the world!

It is said: "He will not cry out, will not raise the tone." It is useless to cry. The voice of God is heard in silence. And the voices of our brothers and sisters are only understood in love. Lord, make us the epiphany of your love, the revelation of your tenderness.

It is said further: "I have taken you by the hand." Are we happy that God has placed his hand upon us? Do we walk in God's footsteps, without preceding him and advising him about what he should or should not do, without following too far behind him and dawdling on the path of his holy will? Help us, Lord, to walk in your rhythm, putting our steps in your steps. Help us also to take our brother and sister by the hand to lead them to you!

It is said finally: "In you I have placed all my joy." What a marvel! God places all his joy in us because he looks at us in Jesus, the Son of his love! Do we place all our joy in God? Are we fountains of happiness for our brothers and sisters? Or better, do we make them cry sometimes? Give us the grace, Lord, to imitate your Son Jesus. Let it be said of us also: "Wherever they went, they did good." With Christ we also want to be this Covenant of the peoples. And on the day of your love, you will say to us also, as you did to Jesus: "You also are my beloved child. In you I have placed all my love."

CONCLUDING PRAYER

While Jesus was praying,
the heavens were opened.
When we pray to you, God our Father,
for us, too, let your heaven open
and reveal to us your love of a Father.

> *You are our Father.*
> *Hear our prayer!*

While Jesus was praying,
the Holy Spirit descended upon him.
When we pray to you, God our Father,
send your Holy Spirit upon us as well
and pour out into our hearts your love.

> *You are our Father.*
> *Hear our prayer!*

While Jesus was praying,
a voice came from heaven saying:
"You are my beloved Son."
When we pray to you, God our Father,
reveal in the secret of our heart as well
that we are the children of your love.

> *You are our Father.*
> *Hear our prayer!*

While Jesus was praying,
the voice from heaven also said to him:
"In you I have placed all my love."
When we pray to you, God our Father,
make the plenitude of your love rest upon us.

> *You are our Father.*
> *Hear our prayer!*

God, our Father in heaven,
you who have only one beloved Son
in whom you have placed all your love,
we pray to you:
Send upon us your Holy Spirit.
May he fashion in us your face of eternity.
Recognize in our praise the voice of your beloved,
and in our heart, the heart of your firstborn Son.
We are his brothers and sisters, and you are our Father
forever and ever. Amen.

NOTES TO THE BAPTISM OF THE LORD

1. Cf. Gn 22, 2, 12, 16.
2. Luke says, in the prologue of his Gospel (1, 3), that he has made his inquiries with accuracy *(akribôs)*.
3. Acts 4, 27-30.
4. We have the same equivalences in the French *garçon* and in the English *boy*.
5. Is 6, 8; Jer 1, 4-10; Ez 1, 1-3; Acts 9, 3-6.
6. Eph 1, 4.
7. Cf. Lk 4, 18-10 citing Is 61, 1-2.
8. Cf. Mt 11, 3.
9. Cf. Lk 6, 12; 9, 18, 28; 11, 1. The parallels of Mark and of Matthew do not mention the prayer of Jesus.
10. Lk 3, 38.

Seasons of Lent and Easter

ASH WEDNESDAY

READING I   JL 2, 12-18

A reading from the book of the prophet Joel

Even now, says the Lord,
  return to me with your whole heart,
  with fasting, and weeping, and mourning;
Rend your hearts, not your garments,
  and return to the Lord, your God.
For gracious and merciful is he,
  slow to anger, rich in kindness,
  and relenting in punishment.
Perhaps he will again relent
  and leave behind him a blessing,
Offerings and libations
  for the Lord, your God.
Blow the trumpet in Zion!
Proclaim a fast,
  call an assembly;
Gather the people,
  notify the congregation;
Assemble the elders,
  gather the children
  and the infants at the breast;
Let the bridegroom quit his room,
  and the bride her chamber.
Between the porch and the altar
  let the priests, the ministers of the Lord, weep,
And say, "Spare, O Lord, your people,
  and make not your heritage a reproach,
  with the nations ruling over them!
Why should they say among the peoples,
  'Where is their God?'"
Then the Lord was stirred to concern for his land and took pity on
  his people.
The Word of the Lord.

RESPONSORIAL PSALM   Ps 51, 3-4. 5-6. 12-13. 14, 17

R/. (3) Be merciful, O Lord, for we have sinned.

Have mercy on me, O God, in your goodness;
   in the greatness of your compassion wipe out my offense.
Thoroughly wash me from my guilt
   and of my sin cleanse me.

R/. Be merciful, O Lord, for we have sinned.

For I acknowledge my offense,
   and my sin is before me always:
"Against you only have I sinned,
   and done what is evil in your sight."

R/. Be merciful, O Lord, for we have sinned.

A clean heart create for me, O God,
   and a steadfast spirit renew within me.
Cast me not out from your presence,
   and your holy spirit take not from me.

R/. Be merciful, O Lord, for we have sinned.

Give me back the joy of your salvation,
   and a willing spirit sustain in me.
O Lord, open my lips,
   and my mouth shall proclaim your praise.

R/. Be merciful, O Lord, for we have sinned.

READING II   2 COR 5, 20—6, 2

A reading from the second letter of Paul to the Corinthians

We are ambassadors for Christ, God as it were appealing through us.
We implore you, in Christ's name: be reconciled to God! For our sakes
God made him who did not know sin to be sin, so that in him we might
become the very holiness of God.

As your fellow workers we beg you not to receive the grace of God in
vain. For he says, "In an acceptable time I have heard you; on a day of
salvation I have helped you." Now is the acceptable time! Now is the
day of salvation!

The Word of the Lord.

GOSPEL   MT 6, 1-6. 16-18

A reading from the holy gospel according to Matthew

Jesus said to his disciples: "Be on guard against performing religious acts for people to see. Otherwise expect no recompense from your heavenly Father. When you give alms, for example, do not blow a horn before you in synagogues and streets like hypocrites looking for applause. You can be sure of this much, they are already repaid. In giving alms you are not to let your left hand know what your right hand is doing. Keep your deeds of mercy secret, and your Father who sees in secret will repay you.

"When you are praying, do not behave like the hypocrites who love to stand and pray in synagogues or on street corners in order to be noticed. I give you my word, they are already repaid. Whenever you pray, go to your room, close your door, and pray to your Father in private. Then your Father, who sees what no man sees, will repay you.

"When you fast, you are not to look glum as the hypocrites do. They change the appearance of their faces so that others may see they are fasting. I assure you, they are already repaid. When you fast, see to it that you groom your hair and wash your face. In that way no one can see you are fasting but your Father who is hidden; and your Father who sees what is hidden will repay you."

The gospel of the Lord.

INTRODUCTORY PRAYER

On this day the Church invites us
to begin our Lenten pilgrimage.
Through the voice of our friend, the prophet Joel,
the Lord calls to us today:
"Come back to me with all your heart...
Come back to the Lord your God,
for he is tender and merciful,
slow to anger and full of love."

Our path of Lent is a path of return,
this return is an encounter
with the tenderness of God.
Who in exile would not rejoice to return home?
What prisoner would not rejoice to come back ?

Who among us would not rejoice to encounter
the tenderness and the mercy of God?

Blessed then be our Father in heaven!
He offers us this opportunity
to discover once again his mercy.
He grants us this Ash Wednesday
as a door of hope on the path of return.
To God be the glory forever and ever. Amen.

HOMILY

Each time Jesus speaks to us, joy rises up in our lives like the morning sun, making our hearts rejoice.

The Good News that God gives us today is the following: We are dust, and we are sinners. But God is seeking us. He loves us. He says to us today:

Return to the Lord your God,
for he is tender and merciful,
slow to anger and full of love.   Jl 2, 13

For this road of return, Jesus offers to us three paths of joy: prayer, almsgiving and fasting. In the days of Jesus, these were important works of piety and Jewish observance. These three works invite all Christians to the joy of the gospel.

Prayer

This Good News first concerns prayer.

To pray to God is a feast. But for this feast to succeed, Jesus tells us: withdraw into your room. Close the door of your heart, and there you will find your Father. With him, close to him, you will rejoice. Like a bird close to its nest. Like a lover close to the beloved. Like a child close to its Father. A thousand difficulties can await you on the path of your Lent, of your life, in your walk toward the Lord's Passover. A thousand waves of sadness or discouragement can threaten to engulf your boat. But prayer will keep you in peace close to your Father. As the psalm says:

I keep my soul in peace and silence
like a weaned child close to its mother.
My soul is within me like a weaned child.   Ps 131, 2

A longer time of prayer is suggested during Lent. How long? We must all decide according to our own hearts and according to the feast that we wish to offer our hearts. We are all so busy! We sometimes think we are indispensable. And yet, look at our cemeteries. They are filled with people who were very busy, who sometimes thought they were indispensable! I am not a prophet but a simple priest. However, I can assure you of this before God: When you finally lay aside your "indispensable" occupations, terminate the Lent of your life and present yourself before your Father in heaven to take part in the Resurrection of Jesus. You will not regret the time that you will have dedicated to prayer.

Starting today, prayer can be the joy of your life. It is a feast with your Father! Do not deprive yourself of the joy of this feast!

Almsgiving

Secondly, this Good News concerns almsgiving.

To give alms for the love of God is a feast.

Share with your brothers and sisters. Do not give them something useless that you do not want but give them something that you like and that will make them happy.

We live in times of inflation. Therefore, save your money by investing it where it will not lose its value. Jesus says to us: "Make for yourselves purses that will not wear out; make a treasure in heaven."[1]

Above all, share the bread of love with your brothers and sisters. Give the alms of a smile to one who is grumpy. Give the alms of joy to one who is sad.

For your feast of almsgiving to be successful, Jesus tells you, do not look at what you give. Look only at your Father, and you will rejoice with him.

Fasting

To fast for the love of God is a feast! Jesus says to you: "Anoint yourself!" Let your assembly be fragrant. For when you fast, when you deprive yourself for your brothers and sisters, you enrich your heart.

If there are some among you who want to acquire a youthful figure, if there are pounds to be lost, the liturgy says to you today: "Now is the acceptable time!" It is now that the diet must begin.

Once, when I was in Morocco, I traveled on the road that leads to the holy city of Fez. My Muslim driver was a very holy man, with a faith as solid as granite. Along the way we discussed everything and nothing. I asked him: "Is it hard for you to fast during Ramadan?" Ramadan is the ninth month of the Moslem year, spent in fasting from sunrise to sunset. He answered me: "Yes, sometimes very hard. Every Ramadan I lose eleven pounds." Then he asked me: "And you Christians, when you fast during the forty days of Lent, how many pounds do you lose?" I did not dare to answer him.

And you, would you have dared?

Let us not disregard the humble practice of fasting. Of course, as in all things, one must use moderation and common sense. Saint Francis de Sales, who was not only a great saint but also a man full of humor, said that the deer of the forest run badly in two seasons: the season when they are too fat and the season when they are too thin. Therefore, to run briskly in the forest of the Lord, do not be too fat or too thin. Do what is necessary to fill your Lent with the joy of the Lord.

Now is the Acceptable Time

To conclude, I would like you to hear a voice that resounded in Jerusalem toward the middle of the fourth century, in the Church of Anastasis where the Tomb of the Resurrection is found. This text comes to us from the mystagogic catechism attributed to Cyril of Jerusalem (314-387). He is addressing himself to candidates for baptism and, through this marvelous voice, he speaks to us:

As ministers of Christ we have welcomed each of you and, as though we were filling the office of porter, we have left the door open. Perhaps you entered with a soul stained by sin, with a perverse intention.

If you are wearing the garment of greed, get other clothes and come back. Rid yourself of lust and impurity and put on the sparkling garment of purity.

I admonish you about this before Jesus, the Spouse of souls, makes his entrance and notices your clothing. A long reprieve is accorded to you: you have forty days to repent; you have ample time to divest yourself of your clothes, to wash, to get dressed again, then to return…

Perhaps you came for another reason? It happens that a man wants to please a woman and comes for that reason. Moreover, one can say the same thing concerning women. It also happens that a slave wants to please his master, or a friend a friend.

. I take what is on the hook; I take you, you who came with a bad intention but who will be saved by a good hope. Doubtless, you do not know where you are going and you do not know the net that has caught you? You have fallen into the net of the Church! Allow yourself to be taken alive, do not flee! Jesus hooks you not to make you die, but to make you live after having made you die. For you must die and rise again. Indeed, you have heard the words of the Apostle: "Dead to sin, but alive for God in Christ Jesus" (Rom 6, 11). Begin to live from today!

God has made the call: It is you whom he has called! It is of one mother that you have become the sons and daughters, you who have been registered.[2]

"Now is the acceptable time," Paul affirms. To tell the truth, it is always the "time" *(kairos)* of God. But some times are more decisive than others. What would you do if this Lent were the last one that the patience of God offered to you?

Now, if this were truly your last Lent, this time would no longer be feast days that the Father would be offering to you. It would truly be the threshold of the feast, the feast where your misery will meet his mercy, the feast where the Lent of your life will meet his eternal Passover.

Blessed be you, Father, for that day when the dust that we are, on this Ash Wednesday, will meet your eternity on the day of Resurrection.

CONCLUDING PRAYER

Now is the acceptable time;
Now is the day of salvation.
Let us then pray that our lives
will be worthy of the Gospel of Christ.
Remember us, O Lord, in your loving care.

For the prayers on our lips
while our hearts are far from you
and for all our vain celebrations
when we make a spectacle of your Church,
forgive us, Lord.
For our secret prayers, filled by your Spirit,
offered in living praise to your glory,
thank you, Lord.
Teach us to pray according to your gospel.
Remember us, O Lord, in your loving care.

For the alms we give with ostentation,
when we make a spectacle of your Church,
forgive us, Lord.
For our secret almsgiving transfigured by your love,
offered in living praise to your glory,
thank you, Lord.
Teach us to give according to your gospel.
Remember us, O Lord, in your loving care.

For our works of piety and our fasting like the Pharisees,
when we make a spectacle of your Church,
forgive us, Lord.
For our secret sacrifices joined to your sacrifice,
offered in living praise to your glory,
thank you, Lord.
Teach us to fast according to your gospel.
Remember us, O Lord, in your loving care.

Look, O Lord, at the dust
that marks our foreheads
and recognize us as your children.
From the clay of the earth
you fashioned the earthly Adam
and the beautiful Eve, his companion.
From the dust of our earth you raised
the blessed body of your Son, Jesus.
You took him from the dust of the grave;
you made him rise in the glory of the Resurrection.
When the day comes that we will sleep in the land of dust
and you will make the eternal Day dawn,
recognize then on our foreheads
the sign of your Son Jesus,
and awaken us for the eternal feast. Amen.

NOTES TO ASH WEDNESDAY
1. Lk 12, 33.
2. *Procatéchèse aux candidats au Baptéme,* trans. L. Deiss, *Printemps de la Liturgie* (Paris: Edition du Levain, 1979), pp. 258-259.

FIRST SUNDAY OF LENT

READING I   DT 26, 4-10

A reading from the book of Deuteronomy

Moses told the people: "The priest shall then receive the basket from
you and shall set it in front of the altar of the Lord, your God. Then you
shall declare before the Lord, your God, 'My father was a wandering
Aramean who went down to Egypt with a small household and lived
there as an alien. But there he became a nation great, strong, and
numerous. When the Egyptians maltreated and oppressed us, imposing
hard labor upon us, we cried to the Lord, the God of our fathers, and he
heard our cry and saw our affliction, our toil and our oppression. He
brought us out of Egypt with his strong hand and outstretched arm, with
terrifying power, with signs and wonders; and bringing us into this
country, he gave us this land flowing with milk and honey. Therefore, I
have now brought you the first fruits of the products of the soil which
you, O Lord, have given me. And having set them before the Lord,
your God, you shall bow down in his presence. Then you and your
family, together with the Levite and the aliens who live among you,
shall make merry over all these good things which the Lord, your God,
has given you.

The Word of the Lord.

RESPONSORIAL PSALM   Ps 91, 1-2, 10-11. 12-13. 14-15

R/. (15) Be with me, Lord, when I am in trouble.

You who dwell in the shelter of the Most High,
  who abide in the shadow of the Almighty,
Say to the Lord, "My refuge and my fortress,
  my God, in whom I trust."

R/. Be with me, Lord, when I am in trouble.

No evil shall befall you,
  nor shall affliction come near your tent,
For to his angels he has given command about you,
  that they guard you in all your ways.

R/. Be with me, Lord, when I am in trouble.

Upon their hands they shall bear you up,
  lest you dash your foot against a stone.

You shall tread upon the asp and the viper:
  you shall trample down the lion and the dragon.

R/. Be with me, Lord, when I am in trouble.

Because he clings to me, I will deliver him;
  I will set him on high because he acknowledges my name.
He shall call upon me, and I will answer him;
  I will be with him in distress;
  I will deliver him and glorify him.

R/. Be with me, Lord, when I am in trouble.

READING II.   ROM 10, 8-13

A reading from the letter of Paul to the Romans

What does Scripture say? "The word is near you, on your lips and in
your heart (that is, the word of faith which we preach)." For if you
confess with your lips that Jesus is Lord, and believe in your heart that
God raised him from the dead, you will be saved. Faith in the heart
leads to justification, confession on the lips to salvation. Scripture says,
"No one who believes in him will be put to shame." Here there is no
difference between Jew and Greek; all have the same Lord, rich in
mercy toward all who call upon him. "Everyone who calls on the name
of the Lord will be saved."

The Word of the Lord.

GOSPEL   LK 4, 1-13

A reading from the holy gospel according to Luke

Jesus, full of the Holy Spirit, returned from the Jordan and was led by
the Spirit into the desert for forty days, where he was tempted by the
devil. During that time he ate nothing, and at the end of it he was
hungry. The devil said to him, "If you are the Son of God, command
this stone to turn into bread." Jesus answered him, "Scripture has it,
'Not on bread alone shall man live.'"

Then the devil took him up higher and showed him all the kingdoms of
the world in a single instant. He said to him, "I will give you all this
power and the glory of these kingdoms; the power has been given to me
and I give it to whomever I wish. Prostrate yourself in homage before
me, and it shall all be yours." In reply, Jesus said to him, "Scripture
has it,

'You shall do homage to the Lord your God;
him alone shall you adore.'"

Then the devil led him to Jerusalem, set him on the parapet of the temple, and said to him, "If you are the Son of God, throw yourself down from here, for Scripture has it,

'He will bade his angels watch over you';
and again,
'With their hands they will support you, that you may never stumble on a stone.'"

Jesus said to him in reply. "It also says, 'You shall not put the Lord your God to the test.'"

When the devil had finished all this tempting he left him, to await another opportunity.

The gospel of the Lord.

INTRODUCTORY PRAYER

We bless you, God our Father,
refuge in all our grief,
relief in all our trials.
Help us to live according to your grace
during these days of Lent
that your patience offers to us
so we may come back to you with all our heart.
Send us your holy angels.
May they accompany us and protect us
as they protected your Son Jesus.
May they lead us to your house
where we will celebrate you, with the Holy Spirit,
forever and ever. Amen.

HOMILY

1. The Profession of Faith According to Deuteronomy

On this first Sunday of Lent, the holy liturgy offers as the First Reading the profession of faith according to Deuteronomy. This profession of faith is expressed in the recitation of a story. When one presented the first fruits, one said: "My father was a wandering Aramean," and then one recounted the descent into Egypt, the transformation of the clan of Abraham into a great nation, the merciless bondage, the cry toward the God of the fathers, the deliverance from Egypt, and the entrance into the Promised Land flowing with milk and honey.

What is the significance of such a profession of faith? It is immense. In the Christian religion, history appears as the place where God reveals himself. History is not a conglomerate of senseless deeds glued together under the pressure of centuries, but a succession of events that are linked together and manifest God.

This dignity of history, the place where God reveals himself, does not infringe upon the dignity of the Word of God, but it affirms the priority of the event over the Word. Thus, before being recorded in the Bible, the Exodus and the entrance into the Promised Land were lived by the chosen people. This is why Vatican II rightly affirms that Revelation is manifested (first) by events and (then) by writings.[1]

These realities bear great importance for our lives. When we say history is the place where God is revealed, we mean the history of our life is the place where God is revealed to us. Each event of our life is a word of God. Each day manifests the Law and the Prophets. Each moment is Gospel. By reciting the history of our life, we proclaim our profession of faith. It is in this history that we must discover God, recognize his tenderness, and worship his love.

The dignity of the Word of God in Scripture is not diminished by the fact that events precede Scripture. For it is the Word of God that allows us to understand the meaning of the events which form the course of our existence. The more we know the Bible, the more we understand the meaning of our life, the more we come near to God.

In the darling book *Children's Letters to God*, Emily writes:

> Dear God,
> Could you write more stories? We have already read all the ones you have written and are starting over again.
>
> Gratefully,
> Emily[2]

The new stories in God's new book are those that we are writing today in the book of our life.

2. The Temptation of Jesus

By placing the account of the temptation of Jesus on the First Sunday of Lent, the holy liturgy reminds us that this time of return to God is consecrated especially to fighting against the powers of evil. By "powers of evil" we do not mean the horned and cloven-hoofed little devils who would be in conflict with us, but the evil which lives in our hearts and hinders us in our return to God. Jesus overcame the powers of darkness through his cross of light. "He disarmed the powers and principalities,"[3] says Paul, by dragging them in his triumphal procession. We are invited to take part in this triumph. Lent is a time of victory.

Historicity of the Account

In the face of such a strange and marvelous account, where folklore joins hands with the supernatural, the first question that comes to mind concerning the temptation is its historicity. Is it really true?

We do not hesitate to say that on the historical level, it is perfectly true that Jesus made a retreat in the desert and that he was tempted. But the rest —the way in which the temptations unfolded—remains the mystery of Christ. The temptations are true according to the truth given to us by the evangelists.

We can think that these temptations were completely real even if they were interior. They ripped open his soul; they flogged his imagination. In the lugubrious chaos of the desert, in the anguish of the frightful solitude, in the hunger that tortures and the thirst that hallucinates, Jesus felt the weight of his mission as the Servant of Yahweh, as he had been proclaimed at baptism, and the temptation of an easy messianism that would attract crowds eager for signs and wonders but would separate him from his Father. Indeed, later on he will accomplish the messianic works about which Satan speaks, but it will never be at the instigation of the devil. Jesus will feed the crowds with miraculous bread, but will flee the crowd that wants to make him king. He will accomplish the miracles signifying the coming of the messianic era, but never by conjuring tricks intended for a crowd longing for a "sign from heaven." He will receive all power in heaven and on earth, but that will be after the mystery of his Passion.[4]

Over and against a Christian community that tends to be scandalized by the humility of the Messiah, the Gospels affirm that an earthly messianism, with a great show of miracles or egoistic use of power, would have been only a diabolic messianism, a temptation coming straight from the devil. By submitting to these, the "Servant of Yahweh" would have become the valet of Satan!

Biblical Signification of Temptations

In biblical vocabulary, the meaning of the verb "to tempt" is rather fluid, and this diversity of meaning can bring about difficulties of interpretation. "To tempt" can mean to propose trials to the faithful in order to allow them to affirm their attachment to God. In this sense, God tempted Abraham. "To tempt" can also mean to incite to evil. In this sense, God does not tempt anyone. The first kind of temptation is a privilege of the chosen people. It is a gift of grace; it leads to life. The second temptation brings forth death. "To tempt" finally can mean to address a type of provocation to God in order to force his intervention. In this sense, the children of Israel tempted God in the desert of the Exodus.[5]

The account of the temptations of Jesus plays upon these different meanings. After the last temptation, Luke can write that Jesus had "exhausted all the forms of temptation."

What is the purpose of the temptations that God gives to us? Deuteronomy explains to us with all desirable clarity, almost with a certain naïvete:

It is the Lord your God who is tempting you to find out if you truly love the Lord your God with all your heart and with all your soul.

Temptations, therefore, are the proof of faithfulness and love. They reveal to us whether we love our God "with all our heart and with all our soul." They are not anomalies or whims to panic us or terrorize us on our path toward the Promised Land. On the contrary, they are the normal way through which the Holy Spirit leads us. Luke writes:

Jesus, full of the Holy Spirit, left the banks of the Jordan. And he was led by the Holy Spirit into the desert where for forty days he was tempted by the devil.   Lk 4, 1-2

Matthew is even more explicit:

Jesus was led into the desert by the Holy Spirit to be tempted by the devil.   Mt 4, 1

Forty Days

The forty days of Jesus' temptations in the desert bring to mind the forty years of Israel's temptations in the desert of the Exodus.

> Remember how the Lord your God made you walk in the desert for forty years to humble you, to test you, to know the depths of your heart: whether or not you would keep his commandments. Dt 8, 2

Jesus appears now as the new Moses, the leader of the people of the New Covenant. In fact, Moses spent '"forty days and forty nights" on the holy mountain "in the presence of Yahweh" before receiving ''the tablets of the words of the Covenant'' and transmitting them to the people.[6] Jesus spent '"forty days and forty nights'' (Mt) in the desert in the presence of his Father before transmitting the law of the Gospel to the community of the New Covenant.[7]

The Temptations of the Exodus

The Exodus serves as a biblical framework for the account of the temptations of Jesus. The following parallel can be established: Just as Israel, the firstborn of Yahweh,[8] was led into the desert to be tempted for forty years, thus Christ, proclaimed beloved Son of the Father at baptism, was driven into the desert by the Spirit of God to be tempted for forty days, and his temptations were precisely the same as those of Israel.

- The first temptation recalls the episode of the manna.
- The second temptation (according to Luke; the third according to Matthew) recalls the episode of the golden calf.
- The third temptation (according to Luke; the second according to Matthew) goes back to the episode of Massah and Meribah.

What is the significance of these comparisons? Jesus relives in his soul the temptations of the people of the Exodus. Today the people of the Exodus is the Christian community. By studying the temptations of Jesus, we look at our own temptations. By seeing how Jesus triumphed over them, we learn how to overcome our own. It is our salvation that is involved in this part of the Gospel. It is not a simple question of exegesis, but a problem of life. Origen (+253/254) explains:

All the temptations that we must undergo, the Lord experienced first, in the flesh that he had assumed. But he was tempted precisely in order that we too might be able to conquer through his victory.

First Temptation

The first temptation is the one of bread. What a marvel to change the gravelly pebbles or stones of the desert into a miraculous bread! Messianic success would be assured. It is a miracle more desirable than they ever dreamed that Jesus, for the benefit of all the chosen people, would become the baker who furnishes free bread.

The ironic tone of the devil: "If you are the Son of God" calls to mind the sarcasm of the Pharisees at the foot of the cross: "Let him come down from the cross... for he said: I am the Son of God."[10]

If Jesus had yielded, he would have appeared Messiah and "Son of God" not according to the will of his Father, but according to the manner proposed by Satan. The Servant of Yahweh would have become the slave of the devil.

Jesus' answer is a quotation from Deuteronomy. It goes back to the episode of the manna in the desert. Here is the text as it is presented in Deuteronomy:

> God gave you manna to eat...to show that you do not live by
> bread alone, but by every word that comes from the mouth
> of God.   Dt 8, 3

The manna, nourishment for the body, was also a teaching for the heart. As true "bread from heaven," it satisfied the pilgrims of the Exodus. At the same time, it created a hunger for the Word of God in their souls.[11]

What was the manna of Jesus? What was his food, that is, what gave him the spiritual strength to cross the desert of his Exodus? He made it clearly known:

> My food is to do the will of him who sent me.   Jn 4, 34

The people of the Exodus had often neglected to obey the Lord. The manna was to be a test of obedience. God had said:

> I am going to put them on to the test to see whether or not they
> will obey my commands.   Ex 16, 4

Why did God test them? Surely they would not obey his commands. God concluded sadly:

> Forty years that generation has disgusted me, and I said:
> People with hearts led astray!   Ps 95, 10

Jesus on the contrary, as he advanced in the Exodus of his life, would continuously discover God's will of love and humbly fulfill it. He would be able to say those unheard- of words that no one will ever be able to repeat after him and which are the most beautiful homage to his Father:

147

I always do what pleases him. Jn 29

What is our food? Do we eat the bread of pride that we bake in the oven of vanity? the bread of riches? the bread of sensuality? If only this time of Lent could incite us to satisfy ourselves with that manna which is the Word of God, if it could convince us to bow our rebellious heads and submit ourselves to that word of love that God speaks to us day after day in the depths of our heart.

Let us ask another question: What do we know about the Bible? What are we intending to do in order to enter into a better knowledge of the Word? What are we going to do? We must stay alive. But how will we stay alive if we do not nourish ourselves with that Word which is Christ Jesus?

Second Temptation

In Luke, the second temptation is the one in which the devil lays claim to worship; in Matthew, it is the one where he urges Jesus to throw himself down from the pinnacle of the Temple. It is generally admitted that it is Luke who changed the early order of the temptations to end with the mention of Jerusalem in third place. We know that this theme is very dear to Luke since he begins his Gospel with the service of Zachariah in the Temple of Jerusalem and ends it with the mention of the community reunited in the Temple and blessing God.

A mountain so high that one can contemplate from its summit "all the kingdoms of the world with their glory"[12] does not exist. But the temptation to run after glory and power does exist, and a thousand golden calves solicit our worship every day.

And what is the answer of Jesus?

You shall worship the Lord your God
and serve him only. Dt 6, 13

Jesus again quotes from Deuteronomy and evokes the episode of the golden calf in the desert of the Exodus.[13]

Israel carried in its heart the hope of dominating the nations and feasting on their riches.[14] It is this earthly messianism that the devil proposes to Jesus. But the messianism according to the heart of God is a messianism of humility which announces the Good News to the poor, a messianism where the nations, instead of being stripped of their riches, are on the contrary invited to share the spiritual vocation of Israel, a messianism which finally will pass through the mystery of the cross.

One day Jesus will receive all the kingdoms of the earth with their glory. But this will be after his Passion and Resurrection:

All power has been given to me in heaven and on earth.   Mt 28, 18

That power he will receive from his Father, by reason of his obedience. He does not receive it from the devil.

Every day the duty of worship and praise is proposed to us as well as to Israel. To worship God is to recognize that he is the Master of our destiny; it is to affirm that he is the Lord of love and tenderness even if that love and tenderness are concealed from the eyes of our heart. Finally, it is to put that love in the service of our brothers and sisters. Then, by working with all our strength for the Kingdom while recognizing ourselves as useless servants, we will become coheirs of the glory of Christ. The Book of Revelation states the following:

You made of them, for our God, a kingdom and priests. And they will reign on earth!   Rv 5, 10

Third Temptation

For the third temptation the devil "leads" Jesus to Jerusalem and places him at the top of the Temple. It is useless to ask ourselves how he did it. We have said that all these temptations take place in the soul of Jesus and the dialogues with the devil resemble a rabbinical discussion on the personality of the Messiah.

Jerusalem is the place of the Passion and the Resurrection of Jesus, then of the outpouring of the Spirit upon the early community. Therefore it is there that Luke places the decisive confrontation of Jesus with the devil.

An old tradition taught:

When the king, the Messiah, will reveal himself, he will come and place himself on the roof of the sanctuary. Then he will preach to the Israelites; he will say to them: 'You, the poor, the time of your redemption is here![15]

The demonstration proposed by the devil came therefore directly from the purest tradition. The people see themselves called to a captivating spectacle. Jesus, leaping into the dizzy emptiness, what a spectacle! What a demonstration! The devil had said to him, "If you are the son of God, throw yourself down!" And suddenly becoming a Scripture scholar and devotee of the Bible, the devil quotes the wonderful Ninety-first Psalm: Whoever trusts in the Lord is sure to be protected. If necessary, the angels will carry him in their arms lest his foot strike a stone. But the devil is a bad Scripture scholar; his interpretation of the Psalm is fundamentalist. Jesus answers him:

> You shall not put God to the test. Lk 4, 12

Once again Jesus takes a quotation from Exodus, which goes back to the episode of Massah and Meribah. The whole community of the children of Israel, wandering in the desert, arrived at Rephidim where there was no water. Tortured by thirst, the people grumbled against Moses. On the order of Yahweh, Moses struck the rock with his staff. Water gushed forth and the people were able to quench their thirst. The text of Exodus explains:

> This place received the name of Massah (which means test) and Meribah (which means contestation) by reason of the quarrel sought by the children of Israel and of the test to which they had submitted Yahweh by saying: "Is the Lord with us or not?" Ex 17, 7

Is God with us or not? What a question! How many times have we heard: "If God existed, would that have happened?" Also how many times have we not set ourselves up as advisors of the Most High when we told him what he ought to do? How many times have we thought: "We have prayed and we have not been heard; God was not with us."?

This supreme temptation, this essential question of existence: "Is God with us or not?", Jesus asked on the cross when he implored: "My God, my God, why have you forsaken me?" Mindful of the love of the Father, he also added: "Into your hands I commend my spirit."

The temptation of Massah-Meribah is always present. The Psalm affirms it quite clearly:

> Today, if you hear his voice,
> do not harden your heart as you did at Meribah,
> as you did on the day of Massah in the desert. Ps 95, 7-8

And the Letter to the Hebrews beseeches us: As long as this "today" lasts, let no one allow his heart to be hardened by the seduction of sin![16]

To the question: "Is God with us or not," God answered. He answered us by giving us Emmanuel, that is, God-with-us. His answer is Jesus.

It is precisely when we are in the depths of distress and temptation that the presence of Jesus is guaranteed to us. In this marvelous Psalm of the angels, the Lord affirms to us:

> He calls me and I answer him. I am with him in distress. Ps 91, 15

Thus each one of our troubles is at the same time a song of hope. Each one of our temptations proclaims to us that God is with us, in our distress. At the end of the account of the temptation, Matthew notes very nicely:

> Then the devil departed. And the angels approached and
> served him.   Mt 4, 11

This ending is consistent with the hope of Israel as it is revealed in an apocryphal writing from the first or second century before the Christian era. It is said:

If you do good, men and angels will bless you. God will be glorified by you among the nations, the devil will flee far from you, the savage beasts will fear you, the Lord will love you, and the angels will cling to you.[17]

Instead of the bread of the devil, Jesus now has the service of angels. They will serve him until his Passion and will comfort him.[18] They will surround him in the mystery of his Resurrection; they will be an escort of glory for him when he rises into the heaven of his Ascension.

Emmanuel

May the temptations of the devil, I mean of the evil that seeks to dominate us, not frighten us at all. Rather may they make a dawn of confidence rise on the path of our Exodus. The Psalm of the angels tells us this in a wonderful way: A thousand fall on your right, ten thousand or more, if necessary, on your left; you remain out of reach; the Lord stays with you "in distress." He is Emmanuel at the very heart of your temptations, Emmanuel also at the heart of your joys, Emmanuel for eternity.

To him glory forever and ever.

PRAYER

Like Abraham, we are vagabond refugees;
we wander in a land of exile.
Let us pray to our Father, the God of love:
may he open for us the door of the true Promised Land,
the heaven of his Son Jesus Christ.

When we are weak and discouraged
in the midst of the temptations of this life,
be our strength and our victory.
Are you not the God of love?

Have mercy on us

When we are seduced
by the bread of pride and falsehood,
put in our heart hunger for your Word.
Are you not the God of love?

Have mercy on us

When we are tempted to bow down
before the idols of riches and pleasure,
be our defense.
Are you not the God of love?

Have mercy on us

When we are tempted to put to the test
by demanding of you signs and wonders,
keep us in the simplicity of trust.
Are you not the God of love?

Have mercy on us

When we wander alone in the desert of this life
in the midst of scorpions and serpents,
send us your holy angels to protect us.
Are you not the God of love?

Have mercy on us

You have assured us, Lord,
that all those who call upon your name will be saved.
We have presented to you our prayer:
hear us, stay with us in our trials,
and we will bless you, God of love,
forever and ever. Amen.

NOTES TO FIRST SUNDAY OF LENT

1. *Constitution Det Verbum.* See my work *God's Word and God's People* (Collegeville, Minnesota: The Liturgical Press, 1976), pp. 273-283.
2. *Children's Letters to God.* (New York: Essandres Special Edition, 1967).
3. Col 2, 15.
4. Cf. Jn 6, 15 and Mt 28, 18.
5. Cf. Gn 22, 1. Jas 1, 13. Ex 17, 7.
6. Ex 34, 28. Cf. Dt 9, 9.
7. One can also note that these forty days which preface the public life of Jesus make a counterpart to the forty days which precede the Ascension.
8. Cf. Ex 4, 22.
9. *Homilies on Saint Luke,* XXIX, 3.
10. Mt. 27, 42-43.
11. Cf. Wis 10, 20, 26.
12. Mt 4, 8; cf. Lk 4, 5.
13. Mt 4, 8. Moses (Dt 34, 1-4) and Baruch (*Apocalypse of Baruch,* 73, 3) are also supposed to see the whole earth from a very high mountain.
14. See for example Is 60, 12-16.
15. Cg. Strack-Billerbeck, *Kommentar zum Neuen Testament aus Talmud und Midrasch,* vol. 1 (Munich: C. H. Beck, 1961), p. 151.
16. Heb 3, 13.
17. *Testament of the Patriarchs, Testament of Nephtali,* VII. Cf. Daniel-Rops, *La Bible Aprocryphe* (Ccrf-Fayard, 1953), p. 144.
18. Cf. Lk 23, 43.

SECOND SUNDAY OF LENT

READING I   GN 15, 5-12. 17-18

A reading from the book of Genesis

God took Abram outside and said: "Look up at the sky and count the stars, if you can. Just so," he added, "shall your descendants be." Abram put his faith in the Lord, who credited it to him as an act of righteousness.

He then said to him, "I am the Lord who brought you from Ur of the Chaldeans to give you this land as a possession." "O Lord God," he asked, "how am I to know that I shall possess it?" He answered him, "Bring me a three-year-old heifer, a three-year-old she-goat, a three-year-old ram, a turtledove, and a young pigeon." He brought him all these, split them in two, and placed each half opposite the other; but the birds he did not cut up. Birds of prey swooped down on the carcasses, but Abram stayed with them. As the sun was about to set, a trance fell upon Abram, and a deep, terrifying darkness enveloped him.

When the sun had set and it was dark, there appeared a smoking brazier and a flaming torch, which passed between those pieces. It was on that occasion that the Lord made a covenant with Abram, saying: "To your descendants I give this land from the Wadi of Egypt to the Great River [the Euphrates].

The Word of the Lord.

RESPONSORIAL PSALM   Ps 27, 1. 7-8. 8-9. 13-14

R/. (1) The Lord is my light and my salvation.

The Lord is my light and my salvation;
   whom should I fear?
The Lord is my life's refuge;
   of whom should I be afraid?

R/. The Lord is my light and my salvation.

Hear, O Lord, the sound of my call;
   have pity on me, and answer me.
Of you my heart speaks; you my glance seeks.

R/. The Lord is my light and my salvation.

Your presence, O Lord, I seek.
   Hide not your face from me;

Do not in anger repel your servant.
   You are my helper: cast me not off.

R/. The Lord is my light and my salvation.

I believe that I shall see the bounty of the Lord
   in the land of the living.
Wait for the Lord with courage;
   be stouthearted, and wait for the Lord.

R/. The Lord is my light and my salvation.

READING II   PHIL 3, 17-4, 1

A reading from the letter of Paul to the Philippians

Be imitators of me, my brothers. Take as your guide those who follow
the example that we set. Unfortunately, many go about in a way which
shows them to be enemies of the cross of Christ. I have often said this
to you before; this time I say it with tears. Such as these will end in
disaster! Their god is their belly and their glory is in their shame. I am
talking about those who are set upon the things of this world. As you
well know, we have our citizenship in heaven; it is from there that we
eagerly await the coming of our savior, the Lord Jesus Christ. He will
give a new form to this lowly body of ours and remake it according to
the pattern of his glorified body, by his power to subject everything to
himself.

For these reasons, my brothers, you whom I so love and long for, you
who are my joy and my crown, continue, my dear ones, to stand firm in
the Lord.

The Word of the Lord.

GOSPEL   LK 9, 28-36

A reading from the holy gospel according to Luke

Jesus took Peter, John and James, and went up onto a mountain to pray.
While he was praying, his face changed in appearance and his clothes
became dazzlingly white. Suddenly two men were talking with him—
Moses and Elijah. They appeared in glory and spoke of his passage
which he was about to fulfill in Jerusalem. Peter and those with him
had fallen into a deep sleep; but awakening, they saw his glory and
likewise saw the two men who were standing with him. When these
were leaving, Peter said to Jesus, "Master, how good it is for us to be

here. Let us set up three booths, one for you, one for Moses, one for Elijah." (He did not really know what he was saying.) While he was speaking, a cloud came and overshadowed them, and the disciples grew fearful as the others entered it. Then from the cloud came a voice which said, "This is my Son, my Chosen One. Listen to him." When the voice fell silent, Jesus was there alone. The disciples kept quiet, telling nothing of what they had seen at that time to anyone.

The gospel of the Lord.

INTRODUCTORY PRAYER

On this day we celebrate your radiant Transfiguration,
and we want to praise you and bless you, Lord Jesus.
Your face shines like the sun,
and your clothes are woven of light and glory.

With the Apostles Peter, James, and John,
lead us upon the mountain to pray,
and we also will be able to contemplate your splendor,
O transfigured Christ!

With Moses and Elijah, welcome us into your glory
and speak to us of your Father.

With the Apostles, upon awakening from our dreams,
may we be able to lift our eyes toward your splendor
and see nothing but you alone, Jesus.

Only Son, full of grace and truth,
may we be able one day to hear
the voice from the Father say to us from heaven!
"You also are my beloved Son!
In you I have placed all my love."
Then our life will be transfigured into your eternity. Amen.

HOMILY

1. The Covenant with Abraham

What a feast it was when Abraham left Ur of Chaldea! And what audacity it took to announce to Sarah; "Pack up. We are leaving. I am going to saddle the camels." He was seventy-five years old! An age long beyond retirement! He was at an age when the majority of our population today relies on Social Security and on the pension they have carefully accrued throughout their life (one is never prudent enough; one does not know what can happen). What youth Abraham displays! True faith, the audacity to believe, laughs at age. God can invade the soul of a little boy or girl and make it a heaven of springtime; he can transform a dying old man into a threshold of paradise.

Faith is a walk toward a goal that God alone knows. It is not a vision of something clear, but a trust, an attachment to Someone who sees.

This promise of God was the joy and light of Abraham in his wandering, like a "vagabond Aramean." It was also his hope and his tedious pain. For a man who was seventy-five years old, with a wife of sixty-five, it was urgent, indeed, to have a child as soon as possible—at least one—in whom the promise would be fulfilled. Abraham had to wait another twenty-five years before having Isaac. Twenty-five years of pure faith! It is this time of waiting that the Liturgy invites us to celebrate today. We contemplate Abraham between seventy-five and one hundred years of age.

The Sacrifice of Abraham

The text reveals a not very homogeneous editing, with repetitions and discordances. Thus, in verse six, Abraham is invited to contemplate heaven in order to count the stars: therefore we think that we are in the middle of the night. Then, in verse twelve, we attend the setting of the sun. The distinction of the sources—Yahwist and Elohist—is uncertain. In spite of this conglomeration of writings coming from different sources, the text is of incomparable splendor.

One day when the waiting had become too heavy to bear, Abraham dialogued with God. His question sounds like a complaint:

> O Lord God, what will you give me?
> I go on childless.
> You have not given me any descendants.   Gn 15, 2-3

The ways of God are always strange. He rarely seems to answer our questions. Or he answers in obscure ways. Here he answers by demanding a new sacrifice.

Abraham obeys. He carefully prepares the victims, immolates them, and waits for the fire from heaven to come consume them.

Here is an offering acceptable to God since it is God who asked for it, and fire from heaven will surely descend upon it. Alas! It is birds of prey that come down instead:

> As the birds of prey came down on the pieces,
> Abraham drove them away.   Gn 15, 11

We think about the old patriarch seated next to that slaughter which, in spite of its insignificance—what value do pieces of meat have for God?—is just the same a sign of his love and his hope, and there he is obliged to chase away carrion eaters!

God remains a difficult friend. He loves you more than you can possibly imagine. But he tests your love. Not because he needs to know its strength, but because you need to know its weakness. We are great when our sacrifice seems useless to God.

The sacrifice that you present to God you must defend and keep yourself. You offer a present to God. He accepts it from your hands; then he places it back in your hands for you to keep.

You offer him your good will. He accepts it; then he places it back in your hands for you to defend all the temptations of discouragement.

You offer him your conversion. He accepts it; then he places it back in your hands for you to defend against all the seductions of sin.

You offer him your love. He accepts it; then he places it back in your hands for you to defend against the fascinations of the world.

Conclusion of the Covenant

The rite of the conclusion of the Covenant is archaic. We labor to understand it. The smoking fire pot and the blazing torch symbolize the presence of God who will manifest himself to Moses in a parallel way in the burning bush and in the devouring flame which crowned Sinai. The sleep of Abraham signifies the passivity of the creature in the face of the work of God: When God works, we sleep. The Greek translation underlines well the marvelous character of this rest: "At the setting of the sun," it is written, "an ecstacy *(ekstasis)* fell upon Abraham." The thick darkness that fell at the setting of the sun preserved Abraham from seeing God, therefore from dying, for we cannot see God without dying. The passing of the fire pot and the torch between the quarters of the victims is difficult to interpret for our modern mentality.[1] But the editor of Genesis seems perfectly at ease to conclude:

> That day, the Lord made a Covenant with Abraham.   Gn 15, 18

Father of the Faith

Abraham is the father of the faith. This faith is not expressed in a Creed that Abraham would have recited, but in a total trust in the God of the Covenant who made his life pass on strange and mysterious paths.

Our Covenant today is Christ Jesus himself. Our faith in that Covenant is our total trust in Jesus Christ who makes our life pass on mysterious paths. But all our paths are paths of his love.

2. The Transfiguration

The baptism of Jesus rises like a royal portico at the entrance of his public life. The Transfiguration, where the voice from heaven repeats the words of the baptism, opens a new door of glory on the path of Christ at the moment when he definitively sets out toward the Passion.

Mystery of glory, source of our joy! We are delighted for Jesus. In his Incarnation, he took the form of a slave; he is proclaimed today by the voice from heaven, "beloved son of the Father."

We are full of joy that the Lord, who in his Passion will appear like a criminal, abandoned by God and despised by people—"I am a worm, not a man,"[2] says the Psalm—is at this moment clothed with radiant light as with a garment of glory.

We are full of joy that Jesus who "was of divine nature," but who "made himself nothing" in human distress,[3] is recognized on this day as belonging to the world of God.

The Transfiguration, one might say, ought to be the usual state of Jesus. What is marvelous is not that he was transfigured, but that during all the other days of his life among us, the divinity that dwelled in him did not split the human envelope that imprisoned it. Should he not have been a continual theophany, a continual manifestation of God?

The transfiguration of Jesus is the pledge of our own future glorification:

> The Lord Jesus will transform our poor bodies into the image of
> his glorious body.   Phil 3, 21

Happy are those to whom God will say, when he welcomes them into his arms at the hour of their Passover, when the long and agonizing exodus of their life will be finished: "You also are my beloved children!" In each one of us, even an old grandmother whose mind already wanders a little, there is the yearning for lost youth, the nostalgia of a childhood to be found again. This desire will be heard when our Father in heaven will say to us: "You are my child, you are my daughter, I love you. Your life has not been useless for me. You have the same face as my Son. Your voice is similar to his. Your eyes resemble his eyes. You have the same heart." Then he will transfigure our life into his eternity.

The Holy Mountain

Cyril of Jerusalem (+387) identified the mountain of the Transfiguration as Tabor (588 m). It could also possibly be Mount Hermon (2.814 m) or one of the neighboring summits near Cesarea of Philippi. Psalm 89 gives these two mountains a good biblical recommendation:

Tabor and Hermon
cry for joy at your name. Ps 89, 13

In any case, this "high mountain" has a religious significance. In fact, since the revelation at Sinai, Yahweh was venerated as the "God of mountains and eternal hills."[4] The Gospels are inspired by this tradition. The Sermon on the new Law takes place on a mountain. It is also on a mountain that Jesus chooses and gathers together the Twelve, representing the new people of God. Finally it is on the Mount of Olives that he is carried off to heaven. In the Second Letter of Peter, the mountain of the Transfiguration is called "the holy mountain," and this title goes directly back to Sinai, "the mountain of God." What Scripture affirms in this way is that the mountain of the Transfiguration became the new Sinai of the New Covenant.

The Evangelists' Account of the Transfiguration

Mark describes the Transfiguration in popular, almost naïve terms. His tradition is undoubtedly the earliest.

And he was transfigured before them.
And his clothing became dazzling,
so white that a fuller on earth
cannot whiten in that way. Mk 9, 2-3

Matthew undoubtedly found the comparison with the fuller a little shallow, not solemn or biblical enough. His description goes back rather to the heavenly man written about in the Book of Daniel:

His face had the look of lightning;
his eyes, like flaming torches. Dn 10, 6

It is to be noted that Revelation uses this same prophecy from Daniel to present the risen Christ. He is the Son of man. "His hand holds seven stars and his face is like the sun which shines in all its brilliance."[7] Clearly, according to Matthew, the Transfiguration is an anticipation of the Resurrection.

Luke thinks that his Greek readers, who are less familiar with Daniel, would hardly be moved by the prophetic argument. He prefers to come back to his beloved theme of prayer:

> He climbed the mountain to pray.
> And while he was praying,
> his face appeared quite different
> and his clothes shone like lightning. Lk 9, 29

Therefore, it is under the intensity of his prayer that Jesus is transfigured. It is in the dazzling light of his dialogue with his Father that he is declared "beloved Son."

The Witnesses

Luke mentions twice the presence of "two men" (9, 30 and 32) meaning angels. We likewise find again two men "in resplendent clothes" at the Resurrection and "two men dressed in white" at the Ascension.[8] Later these angels were identified as Moses and Elijah.

Their presence affirms the presence of the Law and the Prophets next to Jesus. Thus it is the whole of the Word of God that authenticates the mission of Jesus. Moses is the man of the Exodus who met God at Sinai and transmitted the Law and the Covenant to the people. Elijah is the prophet who made the pilgrimage to the sources; he walked for forty days in the desert of the Exodus, was nourished with a miraculous bread that the angels served him, and met God on the mountain of Horeb, that is, Sinai. The other witnesses were Peter, James, and John. Their behavior seems strange to us.

> Peter and his companions were overcome with sleep. Lk 9, 32

We truly ask ourselves if these three privileged people did not have anything better to do than sleep during such a marvelous spectacle to which they could have been witnesses.

Let us not incriminate the three sleepers too quickly. This sleep must be understood here as a religious attitude. In theophanies, God accomplished his purposes while people are at rest. Adam is asleep, in ecstacy *(exstasis)* when God creates Eve. Abraham is in ecstacy when God concludes the Covenant.[9] In our visions, we are drawn out of ourselves and attracted to God. This is the point: We cannot enter into the mystery of God if God does not draw us to it, does not take us out of our human prison, does not raise us above our earthly condition.

With Moses and Elijah, with Peter, James and John, it is heaven and earth that venerate Jesus, the Messiah.

The Exodus of Jesus

Whereas Mark and Matthew simply note that Moses and Elijah talked with Jesus, Luke indicates to us the very subject of their conversation:

> They spoke about his "exodus."   Lk 9, 31

The word *exodus* is used in biblical vocabulary either to designate the going out of Egypt or to designate death.[10] By employing this term, Luke uses it in all its biblical richness. To translate this word as "death" seems discordant with the context of glory and light of the Transfiguration, also with Moses and Elijah whose vocation is linked to the Exodus. The exodus of Jesus is his going out of this world of pain and his entrance into the light of heaven. His life, most certainly, passes through death, but it is in order to empty into the eternity of resurrection. His is not a death alone, but at the same time a resurrection from the dead.

It is precisely through this resurrection from death that he becomes our Passover,[11] that is, our own exodus, the passage from this world to the Father, the passage of which the first Exodus had been the symbol.

The Intervention of Peter

The intervention of Peter is delightful in its simplicity and in its inappropriateness. In the solemn and theological framework of the evangelic account, it brings a very human note, touching in its tactlessness. Translating Mark's text literally, we have:

> And answering,
> Peter says to Jesus:
> "Rabbi, it is good for us to be here.
> Let us make three tents, one for you,
> and one for Moses and one for Elijah."
> He hardly knew what to say,
> for they were seized by fear.   Mk 9, 5-6

"And answering": In fact, no one had asked Peter anything. But it is characteristic of rich and exuberant natures to intervene at every turn and even out of turn. Nevertheless, in spite of its tactlessness, Peter's intervention is very precious to us.

The Feast of Tents

The tents Peter speaks about evoke very clearly the Feast of Tents.[12] During the week of this feast, the Israelites lived under tents in memory of the forty years of sojourn in the desert of the Exodus. It was a feast populated with common joy and filled with processions and dances. People came to draw water from the fountain of Shiloh to pour it in libation on the altar of the Temple, and they said: "Whoever has never seen the rejoicing of the 'drawing of water' has never seen joy in his life." They also celebrated the "cloud" of the Exodus, the sign of the protective presence of Yahweh and his glory throughout the Exodus. Thus, to live under the tents signified reliving the experience of their ancestors, entering into special communion with God, and living in his presence. Such is precisely the experience that the three privileged disciples had:

> While he was saying that, a cloud appeared.
> And it covered them with its shadow.
> And they were seized by fear
> upon entering into the cloud. Lk 9, 34

The celebration of light was also very significant: Four candelabras were placed in the Temple, in the pavilion of women. Their light was so intense, it was said, that it illuminated all the courtyards of the houses of Jerusalem. Jesus, resplendent with the glory of the Father,[13] his face shining like the sun and his clothes scintillating with the brightness of lightning, appeared to the Apostles true "light of the world."[14]

The high point of the feast took place on the seventh day. Now it is precisely on the seventh day that the Gospels place the Transfiguration. It is placed "after six days" in Matthew and Mark or "about eight days later" in Luke, that is, after Jesus was recognized as the Messiah by Peter. We find ourselves therefore in a celebration of Jesus' messianity, whose beginning takes place at Cesarea of Philippi, at the time of Peter's confession, and whose summit is the Transfiguration.

Now we understand Peter's reflection better:

> Master, it is good for us to be here. Lk 9, 33

"It is nice here. It is better than on the dusty roads of Galilee or in the midst of the traps of the Pharisees. Let us stay here. Let us prolong these moments of happiness!"

Later, when Peter tells us what happened, he will avow, smiling I suppose, that he did not know what he was saying.

The Voice from Heaven

That was true. For this messianism of tranquil happiness was not the one that the Father had arranged for Jesus. His vocation was to be the Servant of Yahweh. This vocation was renewed again in these words from heaven:

> This is my beloved Son,
> in whom I am well pleased.   Mt 17, 5

or further, according to Luke:

> This is my Son, whom I have chosen.   Lk 9, 35

We already heard these words at the baptism. We explained that they come from the Book of Isaiah:

> Here is my servant whom I uphold,
> my chosen one whom my soul prefers.   Is 42, 1

In Hebrew as in Greek, the word *servant* can also mean *son*. Now, according to Paul, Jesus had been established "Son of God by his Resurrection from the dead."[15] Therefore it was quite normal that the early community, in its reading and in its understanding of the text of the Book of Isaiah, replaced *servant* with *son*.

We cannot enter into the intimacy of love which bound Jesus to his Father. This intimacy remains his secret and his mystery. However, we can try to picture the essential aspects of the Transfiguration.

Jesus has gone up on the mountain with his three disciples to pray. At that time of his ministry, he had become conscious that he no longer had any chance of escaping persecution and death (as the first announcement of the Passion that he had just made shows). In the course of his prayer, he receives the revelation that his vocation, filled with the love of his Father, remains that of the Servant of Yahweh. He will accomplish the deliverance of Israel, not according to an earthly messianism, but according to the messianism forecast by the Scriptures, that is, through his suffering and through his death.

Conclusions

The mystery of the Transfiguration is very rich, and many conclusions can be reached. For the sake of brevity, let us consider the following two reflections:

Disfigurement—Transfiguration

It was good for Christ to know the joy of the Transfiguration before having to undergo the disfigurement of his Passion.

It was good for the Apostles to see their Master transfigured before seeing him disfigured. The three privileged witness of the Transfiguration are also the three witnesses at Gethsemane.

It is also good for us who are going to be disfigured by death to know that we are called to enter into the light of transfiguration.

> The righteous will shine like the sun
> in the Kingdom of their Father.   Mt 13, 43

To Live Transfigured

The Transfiguration of Jesus answers the essential questions of our existence.

Can the glory of heaven irrupt in our time of misery? Can the children of this earth be transfigured into children of heaven? Can a "son of man" become son of God? Yes, because through faith in Christ Jesus, we become children of God.[16]

Can the bread of the earth be transfigured into the bread of heaven? Can our miserable human prayer become divine praise? Yes, for the power of the Holy Spirit can transform our earthly bread into Eucharist, into a song of praise to the glory of the Father.

Can those who already belong to the Kingdom of heavenly light enter into dialogue with those who are still groping in the darkness of this life? Yes, for the words of Moses, Elijah, and all the other prophets, transfigured into the Word of God, come to us and continue to speak to us.

Does the Father himself still speak to us today in the mystery of the Transfiguration of Jesus? Yes, for he says to us: "Listen to him!"

Like the Apostles, may we be able to awaken from our sleep and see only Jesus. Then our lives with all their joys, pains and loves, will be transfigured into eternity.

CONCLUDING PRAYER

With Abraham, our father in faith,
with Moses, Elijah, Peter, James, and John,
let us pray to Christ Jesus:
may he intercede for us next to his Father

> *Christ, be our light of glory.*

We were children of this earth.
You transfigured us into the children of God.
Thank you, Lord.
Gather us together in your house next to your Father.

> *Christ, be our light of glory.*

We heard the words of the earth.
You gave us the words of heaven.
Thank you, Lord.
Open our hearts to your Gospel of glory.

> *Christ, be our light of glory.*

We ate the stale bread of the earth.
You transfigured it into bread of heaven.
Thank you, Lord.
Satisfy us with the joy of your Eucharist.

> *Christ, be our light of glory.*

We were a community of sinners on earth.
You transfigured us into the Church of the saints of heaven.
Thank you, Lord.
Keep us in the unity of your Church.

> *Christ, be our light of glory.*

Everything that you touch, Lord of glory,
you transfigure through your divinity.
We pray to you:
Transfigure our darkness into your light,
our sadness into your joy,
our ugliness into your beauty,
our body of misery into your body of glory,
our earth into your paradise,
our mortal life into your eternity.
And we will bless you forever and ever. Amen.

NOTES TO SECOND SUNDAY OF LENT

1. In an ordinary covenant (cf. Jer 34, 18-20) the contracting parties who pass between the pieces of the victims signify that they accept, in case of perjury, to undergo the fate of the victims.

2. Ps 22, 7.

3. Cf. Phil 2, 6-7.

4. 1 Kgs 20, 23.

5. Cf. 2 Pt 1, 18 and 1 Kgs 20, 23.

6. Compare Mt 10, 6 with Dn 10, 9-10.

7. Rv 1, 16. Some exegetes think that the Transfiguration is a paschal apparition of the Risen One which took place in the public life. The Evangelists do not experience any difficulty in working with such displacements.

   The problem arises from the fact that the Apostles, by fleeing at the time of the Passion, show that they did not keep any remembrance of the divine glory that they had seen at the Transfiguration (cf. Lk 9, 32). This causes one to think either that the Transfiguration really takes place after the Resurrection, or that it takes place before the Resurrection, after the confession of Cesarea Phillipi, and that it was enriched with elements coming from the accounts of the Resurrection.

8. Lk 24, 4; Acts 1, 10.

9. Cf. Gn 2, 21 and 15, 12.

10. Exit from Egypt: Ex 19, 1; Heb 11, 22. Death: 2 Pt 1, 15.

11. Cf. 1 Cor 5, 7.

12. See R. Martin-Archard, *Essai biblique sur les Fêtes d'Israel* (Geneva: Ed. Labor et Fides, 1974).

13. Heb 1, 3.

14. Jn 8, 12. It is probable that Jesus pronounced these words on the occasion of this feast.

15. Rom 1, 4.

THIRD SUNDAY OF LENT

READING I   Ex 3, 1-8, 13-15

A reading from the book of Exodus

Moses was tending the flock of his father-in-law Jethro, the priest of Midian. Leading the flock across the desert, he came to Horeb, the mountain of God. There an angel of the Lord appeared to him in fire flaming out of a bush. As he looked on, he was surprised to see that the bush, though on fire, was not consumed. So Moses decided, "I must go over to look at this remarkable sight, and see why the bush is not burned."

When the Lord saw him coming over to look at it more closely, God called out to him from the bush, "Moses! Moses!" He answered, "Here I am." God said, "Come no nearer! Remove the sandals from your feet, for the place where you stand is holy ground. I am the God of your father," he continued, "the God of Abraham, the God of Isaac, the God of Jacob." Moses hid his face, for he was afraid to look at God. But the Lord said, "I have witnessed the affliction of my people in Egypt and have heard their cry of complaint against their slave drivers, so I know well what they are suffering. Therefore I have come down to rescue them from the hands of the Egyptians and lead them out of that land into a good and spacious land, a land flowing with milk and honey."

"But," said Moses to God, "when I go to the Israelites and say to them, 'The God of your fathers has sent me to you,' if they ask me, 'What is his name?' What am I to tell them?" God replied, "I am who am." Then he added, "This is what you shall tell the Israelites: I AM sent me to you."

God spoke further to Moses, "Thus shall you say to the Israelites: The Lord, the God of your fathers, the God of Abraham, the God of Isaac, the God of Jacob, has sent me to you.

"This is my name forever;
this is my title for all generations."

The Word of the Lord.

RESPONSORIAL PSALM   Ps 103. 1-2, 3-4. 6-7. 8. 1.

R/. (8) The Lord is kind and merciful.

Bless the Lord, O my soul;
   and all my being, bless his holy name.
Bless the Lord, O my soul,
   and forget not all his benefits.

R/. The Lord is kind and merciful.

He pardons all your iniquities,
   he heals all your ills.
He redeems your life from destruction,
   he crowns you with kindness and compassion.

R/. The Lord is kind and merciful.

The Lord secures justice
   and the rights of all the oppressed.
He has made known his ways to Moses,
   and his deeds to the children of Israel.

R/. The Lord is kind and merciful.

Merciful and gracious is the Lord,
   slow to anger and abounding in kindness.
For as the heavens are high above the earth,
   so surpassing is his kindness toward those who fear him.

R/. The Lord is kind and merciful.

READING II   1 Cor 10, 1-6. 10-12

A reading from the first letter of Paul to the Corinthians

I want you to remember this: our fathers were all under the cloud and all passed through the sea; by the cloud and the sea all of them were baptized into Moses. All ate the same spiritual food. All drank the same spiritual drink (they drank from the spiritual rock that was following them, and the rock was Christ), yet we know that God was not pleased with most of them, for "they were struck down in the desert."

These things happened as an example to keep us from wicked desires such as theirs. Nor are you to grumble as some of them did, to be killed by the destroying angel. The things that happened to them serve as an example. They have been written as a warning to us, upon whom the

169

end of the ages has come. For all these reasons, let anyone who thinks he is standing upright watch out lest he fall!

The Word of the Lord.

GOSPEL   LK 13, 1-9

A reading from the holy gospel according to Luke

At that time some were present who told Jesus about the Galileans whose blood Pilate had mixed with their sacrifices. He said in reply: "Do you think that these Galileans were the greatest sinners in Galilee just because they suffered this? By no means! But I tell you, you will all come to the same end unless you reform. Or take those eighteen who were killed by a falling tower in Siloam. Do you think they were more guilty than anyone else who lived in Jerusalem? Certainly not! But I tell you, you will all come to the same end unless you begin to reform."

Jesus spoke this parable: "A man had a fig tree growing in his vineyard, and he came out looking for fruit on it but did not find any. He said to the vinedresser, 'Look here! For three years now I have come in search of fruit on this fig tree and found none. Cut it down. Why should it clutter up the ground?' In answer, the man said, 'Sir, leave it another year while I hoe around it and manure it; then perhaps it will bear fruit. If not, it shall be cut down.'"

The gospel of the Lord.

INTRODUCTORY PRAYER

We bless you, God of our ancestors,
of Abraham and Sarah, Isaac and Rebekah, and Jacob and Rachel.
On Sinai you revealed yourself to your servant Moses
as the God of compassion and mercy,
the God rich in grace and faithfulness.
You granted us the plenitude of that love
when you gave us your Son Jesus.

We pray to you:
Fill each moment of our life with your presence
so that it may be for all our brothers and sisters—
those who do not know you, those who do not love you—

a revelation of your compassion and mercy.
May the whole earth bless your love
through your Son Jesus, in the joy of the Holy Spirit,
forever and ever. Amen.

HOMILY

1. God Reveals His Name to Moses

Moses in the Land of Midian

"At that time," says the Bible, "Moses, having grown up, visits his people."[1] They had been condemned to hard labor in the immense stone-yards of the Pharaoh. Moses sees an Egyptian hit one of his people. He kills the Egyptian and hides his body in the desert sand. The police begin an investigation. "Pharaoh heard about this affair and sought to kill Moses."[2] Moses flees into the peninsula of Sinai, the length of the Red Sea, and arrives in the land of Midian, at the southeast of the Gulf of Agaba. He is welcomed by the priest Jethro. He marries one of Jethro's daughters, Zipporah, by whom he has a son, Gershom, and becomes a shepherd of the flocks of the father-in-law.

That is where his meeting with Yahweh takes place. It is one of the most beautiful scenes in the Bible.

The Burning Bush

Among the ancient people there were traditions concerning places that were believed to be sacred: springs inhabited by nymphs making "virgin" water spring forth, seed from heaven, sacred wells that one celebrated because they had been dug by princes with their sceptres,[3] sacred trees like the oak of Moreh "at the holy place of Shechem," or the oaks of the soothsayers which, it was said, produced oracles.[4]

Unaware of the Midianite traditions concerning the sacralization of places, Moses ventures inadvertently with his flock upon the "mountain of God," Horeb, which tradition identifies as Sinai. It is there that God will reveal himself to Moses.

> The angel of the Lord appeared to him in the midst
> of the fire which came from the bush.
> Moses looked at it: the bush burned
> without being consumed.   Ex 3, 2

171

This bush that burns without being consumed remains for us today just as mysterious as it was for Moses. No one hypothesis is certain. It was sometimes thought to be a shrub which had been struck by lightning. In fact, the word bush, *sené*, calls to mind the name of the mountain Sinai. Now the God of Sinai takes pleasure in manifesting himself in storms, in the midst of lightning and thunder.

In the biblical account, there are three important events: the revelations of Yahweh, the vocation of Moses, and finally the prophecy of the Covenant of Sinai.

Revelation and Vocation

At the burning bush, Moses receives the revelation of the name of God and his own vocation. In other words, upon discovering the name of God, he also discovers his own name. To the question: "Who am I to go find the Pharoah"[5] corresponds the question: "Who are you? What is your name?" God calls Moses by his name; Moses will be able to call upon God by the name above all blessing: "Yahweh!"

Every person's vocation is, in a certain way, incommunicable, that of Moses more than any other. But every vocation also reveals the mystery of our own vocation. Each time that God calls us and we respond like Moses: "Here I am," God reveals his name to us. The more we know God, the more we learn to know ourselves. God reveals himself so more intimately to us the more we entrust ourselves to him. May we be able to attain the supreme desire in our life, that which makes its riches and plunges us into an ocean of peace and joy: to know God! May we be able to obtain this by saying with Moses: "Here I am!"

Vocation and Covenant

The vocation of Moses is the service of his brothers and sisters to enable them to enter into the Covenant. This service begins with the liberation from Egypt: "You will bring my people out of Egypt."[6] Afterwards he will lead all the liberated people to Sinai for the conclusion of the Covenant, there also where Moses received his vocation.

Every vocation, following that of Moses, is a service of our brothers and sisters. Of course, it involves a certain distancing of oneself. But it is a question of a distancing from the banality of a life without ecstasy, sometimes even of a distancing away from sin. For the call of God, far from isolating us from our brothers and sisters, integrates us into the immensity of the people of God and makes us live at the same time in the presence of the One who says to us, as he did to Moses: "I will be with you."[7] Without his "Yes," Moses would have remained merely the husband of Zipporah, bound to the smile of his wife and his children, and his memory would have foundered in the sands of the desert of Aqaba. By accepting God, he became the father of an immense multitude—Jews, Christians, and Moslems celebrate his memory—while keeping the dark eyes of Zipporah. He would have remained Jethro's shepherd, and the Negeb Desert and his sheep would have been his horizon; whereas he became the shepherd of the people of the Exodus and of all those who call upon the God of Israel.

Our vocation does not take us away from our brothers and sisters, but only from our mediocrity. It places us at the heart of the Church, there where the heart of God is also found.

How many have remained attached to the dark eyes of their Zipporah while God wanted to make them contemplate the beauty of heaven and earth as well! How many have stayed dutiful to their father-in-law —or mother-in-law—while God wanted to make them shepherds in his Church! May we be able to fulfill our vocation completely, which is to exist in the sight of God just as he wanted us, just as he loves us.

Yahweh

The revelation of the divine name is at the heart of the account. But this heart remains mysterious. The richness of the name of God is at least as profound as his mystery.

Speaking about himself, God calls himself "I am":

> I am the one who is.

You will speak in this way to the children of Israel:

> The One who sent me to you is "I AM."

Speaking about God, we call him "Yahweh," which is translated: "He Is." *Yahweh* is the long form of the name. *Yah* is the short form. It is found in *Hallelu-Yah,* (praise Yah[weh]), and sometimes in poetry.

Pronunciation

Our pronunciation of "Yahweh" is probable but remains conjectural. It is based among others upon the Greek transcriptions *Iaoué* and *Iabé*. Here is something amazing: the most blessed name in heaven and on earth, the one which is the source of all blessing, and we do not know the exact way to pronounce it! It would not have been difficult, however, for God to teach us. It seems that God always keeps a part of his mystery, so infinite he is!

We know that after the Exile, the faithful, through respect and through piety, no longer pronounced the blessed name of God. They replaced it with *Adonai*, Lord. We Christians, who, as Paul says, have been freed from feasts of a New Moon and Sabbaths,[8] so much the more from purely human traditions, pronounce the name of Yahweh with love and at the same time with infinite respect. However, we should avoid doing it in the presence of our orthodox Jewish brothers and sisters out of respect for their sensibility.

Significance of the Name

Almost all recent authors attach the name *Yahweh* to the root of the Hebrew verb *to be*. Yahweh is an archaic verbal form. It is really the sense of *to be* that the text of Exodus gives to the divine name. Upon copying the Hebrew, one grasps the difficulty of translating: *Ehyen* (I Am), *asher* (The One), *ehyeh* (I Am). How can these be understood?

God the Ineffable

Properly speaking, "I Am" or "He Is" do not form a name. God's answer would therefore be evasive and would in fact mean the refusal to reveal himself clearly.[9]

This interpretation is valid in the sense that it insists upon the mystery of God and of his name. Among the Semites, in fact, the name can be identified with the person named. Sometimes even the Bible, instead of saying "God," says simply "Ha-Shem,"[10] that is, "The Name."

Indeed, if God reveals himself, it is in order that we might know him, love him, and enter into his intimacy. But he remains at the same time the Ineffable, the One whom we cannot fully name, so infinite is the richness of his splendor, so incomprehensible is the marvel of his love. Tradition loved to emphasize this ineffability of God. Gregory Nazianzen (+390) invokes God in these terms:

> O You, Beyond Everything!
>
> By what other name indeed to sing your praise?
> What hymn will celebrate you?
> For no word can express you!
> You alone are unknowable
> and all knowledge comes from you.

You alone are Ineffable
and everything that is said comes from you...
You are all names, but what shall I call you,
You alone who cannot be named?...

Have mercy, O You, Beyond Everything![11]

I Am the One Who Is

"I am the one who is" signifies first of all that Yahweh is *par excellence* the Existent, the One who rules the centuries, the God of eternity, the Eternal. The way in which the Hebrew is expressed adds a certain intensity, a totality. When God affirms: "I have mercy on whom I have mercy, and I have compassion on whom I have compassion,"[12] he signifies that he exists in plenitude. It is precisely this sense of intensity of existence that the New Testament underlines:

"I am the Alpha and the Omega,"
says the Lord God,
"the one who is, who was, and who is to come,
the Almighty." Rv 1, 8

It is also the meaning that John underlines in his Gospel when he makes Jesus say:

Before Abraham was, I Am. Jn 8, 58

This existence of the God of eternity must be understood here not as an existence in himself, in the infinite splendor of his divinity, but an existence which is a living and working presence in the service of his people. Idols are dead. They are nothing even before they exist; they lie like dead bodies of gold, wood, or metal next to those who worship them. But Yahweh is the God, the only one, who lives next to and with his own. At the very moment when he reveals himself as "I Am" to his people, he sees them, hears them, and knows them:

I see, yes I see the misery of my people...
I have heard their cries,
yes, I know their suffering.
I have come down to deliver them
from the hand of the Egyptians,
to bring them up to a spacious and fertile land,
to a land of milk and honey. Ex 3, 7-8

Throughout history, especially through the mouths of his friends the prophets, God will continue to manifest the infinite riches of his splendor by his various names. The day will come when he will say through the mouth of Jesus:

I Am the living bread come down from heaven.	Jn 6, 51
I Am the light of the world.	Jn 8, 12
I Am the gate for the sheep.	Jn 10, 7
I Am the Good Shepherd.	Jn 10, 11
I Am the resurrection.	Jn 11, 25
I Am the way, the truth, and the life.	Jn 14, 6
I Am the true vine.	Jn 15, 1

Yahweh, God of Compassion and Mercy

What is the name that expresses most intensely the nature of God?

God says it twice to Moses: once at the burning bush, as we have seen, and a second time in the context of the conclusion of the Covenant. This text is sublime:

> Moses called upon the name of Yahweh.
> Yahweh passed in front of him and cried out:
> Yahweh! Yahweh!
> God of compassion and mercy,
> slow to anger...
> rich in grace and faithfulness.   Ex 34, 5-6

It is this name that comes back throughout the Psalter as the refrain of the prayer of the people of God. Here it is in this Sunday's Responsorial Psalm, Psalm 103, unquestionably the most beautiful in the Psalter:

> The Lord is compassion and mercy,
> slow to anger and full of love.   Ps 103, 8

This revelation is the most sublime reality in the history of Israel. It is the foundation upon which its existence rests. The people of Moses are now ready to understand the marvelous journey that will lead them across the desert of Sinai to the Promised Land, to the crèche of Jesus. This revelation is so intense that the New Testament, by resuming it in the affirmation "God is love,"[13] will not be able to add anything to it. Nothing except this, which is also quite sublime: The love of God has taken for us the face of Jesus. He is the epiphany of the tenderness and mercy of God among us.

The God hidden in the burning bush and in the flames of Sinai, the One whose name, out of respect and piety, no one any longer dared to pronounce, became known in Jesus.

Today

We continue the journey undertaken by Moses. We walk in the light of the One who manifested himself as the only Existent, the only Love. We know the goal: to live in the eternity of Yahweh. It remains for us to walk toward that goal. Clearly, each one of us is called to verify that God is Existing-Love, the only Love; that he is Existing-Compassion, the only compassion; that he is Forgiving-Mercy, the plenitude of mercy.

We must discover that this word "God-Is-Love" is true, not because we read it in the Book of Exodus or in the Responsorial Psalm of the Mass of the Third Sunday of Lent; not because we heard it in a homily or discovered it in a book, but first of all because we discovered it in our heart, in the book of our life. It is in this discovery of the love of God at the heart of our life that we find the very reason of our existence and success of our life, along with the peace and joy of our heart.

It is thus that the revelation of the burning bush, which was at the heart of the story of Moses and his people, is at the heart of our life today.

2. Now Is The Time For Conversion

The Gospel alludes to two contemporary events that were topics of conversation of the time, but whose memory secular annals did not preserve.[14]

The first event is a slaughter perpetrated by Pilate. The procurator has massacred some Galileans in the courtyard of the Temple, undoubtedly at the time of the feast of Passover when they had come to offer sacrifices. Luke's text stigmatizes the horror perpetrated by Pilate: "He had mingled the blood (of the Galileans) with their sacrifices." Why had God allowed such an injustice by letting those who worshipped him be massacred? Among the people it was thought that surely those Galileans were sinners; God, therefore, had chastised their wickedness.

The second event is the fall of the tower of Siloam which killed eighteen people. Herod was a great builder. At the time of Jesus, Jerusalem resembled a vast construction site that the king had opened to embellish the city. The Jerusalem which Jesus knew was always encumbered with scaffolding, since the construction of the Temple had begun in 20-19 before the Christian era and was not finished until 62-64, six years before its final destruction.

Facing these two events, Jesus affirms two things:

These misfortunes are not a vengeance on the part of God. No one is authorized to speak in God's name while attributing these misfortunes to the account of his chastisements. We are all sinners, therefore spiritually insolvent. We are all debtors with respect to the mercy of God. These misfortunes are a call to conversion. The decisive time of our life is the present time, and the present time is the one of our conversion.

The Barren Fig Tree

Luke did not want to relate the story of the fig tree that Jesus had cursed for not having found any fruit on it and which had dried up in the field.[15] Undoubtedly he found it too sad. But he had his own story of the fig tree: the one which is offered another chance, a final chance.

There is always a last extension of time for conversion that God offers to us in our life. By making us read this story of hope in this time of Lent, the liturgy signifies to us that this last delay is this time of Lent in our life.

Blessed be the Lord! The God of compassion and mercy and also the God of patience. To him glory; to him our love forever and ever!

CONCLUDING PRAYER

Let us call upon the God of eternity,
the God of love.

Remember us, O Lord.

Blessed be you, Yahweh, God of eternity.
Your name is compassion.
For us also be compassion.

Remember us, O Lord.

Blessed be you, Lord, God of eternity.
Your name radiates mercy.
For us also be mercy.

Remember us, O Lord.

Blessed be you, Lord, God of eternity.
Your name is rich in kindness.
For us also be rich in kindness

Remember us, O Lord.

Blessed be you, Lord, God of eternity.
You keep your grace for Moses.
For us also keep your grace.

Remember us, O Lord.

Blessed be you, Lord, God of eternity.
Your name is resplendent with faithfulness.
For us also be faithful in your love.

Remember us, O Lord.

Blessed be you, Lord, God of eternity.
We bless you, Lord, God of eternity.
Your Holy Spirit says
that you crown us with love and compassion.
We pray to you:
Fulfill your promise to us;
give us your love and your compassion
in your Son Jesus, our Savior and our brother. Amen.

NOTES TO THIRD SUNDAY OF LENT

1. Ex 2, 11. See R. de Vaux, *Histoire ancienne d'Israel,* Coll. *"Etudes Bibliques"* (Paris: Ed. Gabalda et Cie, 1971), pp. 313-337. G. Michaeli, *Le livre de l'Exode* (Paris: Delachaux et Niestlé, Neuchâtel, 1974), pp. 46-58.

   The pericope proposed by the Lectionary, Ex 3, 1-8a, 10, 13-15, uses documents coming from Yahwist (verses 1-4a, 7, 8a) and Elohist (verses 4b, 6, 9-14) sources according to M. Noth, *Uberlieferungsgeschichte des Pentateuch* (Stuttgart: Kohlammer, 1948).

2. Ex 2, 15.

3. Cf. Nm 21, 17-18.

4. Cf. Gn 12, 6; Jgs 9, 37.

5. Ex 3, 11.

6. Ex 3, 10.

7. Ex 3, 12.

8. Cf. Col 2, 16. *Adon* signifies "Lord;" *Adoni* signifies "My Lord." *Adonai* is a plural of majesty. In the Greek translation of the Bible, *Yahweh* (about 6,350 times) and *Adonai* (about 500 times) are rendered as *Kyrios,* Lord.

9. In English we say in the same way: "Which is which?" Such ways of speaking are also found in Hebrew. Thus Moses says to the Lord: "Send whomever you sent," (Ex 4, 15) or to the Israelites: "Bake what you bake" (Ex 16, 23).

10. Lv 24, 11. All the references can be found in *Dictionnaire des Noms propres de la Bible* (Paris: Cerf-Desclée de Brouwer, 1978) art. "Yahvé."

11. Prayer attributed to Gregory Nazianzen, *Carminum Liber* I, 29. Cf. Pg 37, 507-508.

12. Ex 33, 19.

13. 1 Jn 4, 8, 16.

14. Lk 13, 1. The two pericopes which form this Gospel, that of Lk 13, 1-5 and 13, 6-9, are Luke's own; they come from particular sources impossible to specify.

15. Cf. Mt 21, 18-19 and Mk 11, 12-14.

FOURTH SUNDAY OF LENT

READING I   Jos 5, 9, 10-12

A reading from the book of Joshua

The Lord said to Joshua, "Today I have removed the reproach of Egypt from you."

While the Israelites were encamped at Gilgal on the plains of Jericho, they celebrated the Passover on the evening of the fourteenth of the month. On the day after the Passover they ate of the produce of the land in the form of unleavened cakes and parched grain. On that same day after the Passover on which they ate of the produce of the land, the manna ceased. No longer was there manna for the Israelites, who that year ate of the yield of the land of Canaan.

The Word of the Lord.

RESPONSORIAL PSALM   Ps 34, 2-3. 4-5. 6-7

R/. Taste and see the goodness of the Lord.

I will bless the Lord at all times;
  his praise shall be ever in my mouth.
Let my soul glory in the Lord;
  the lowly will hear me and be glad.

R/. Taste and see the goodness of the Lord.

Glorify the Lord with me,
  let us together extol his name.
I sought the Lord, and he answered me
  and delivered me from all my fears.

R/. Taste and see the goodness of the Lord.

Look to him that you may be radiant with joy,
  and your faces may not blush with shame.
When the afflicted man called out, the Lord heard,
  and from all his distress he saved him.

R/. Taste and see the goodness of the Lord.

READING II   2 COR 5, 17-21

A reading from the second letter of Paul to the Corinthians

If anyone is in Christ, he is a new creation. The old order has passed
away; now all is new! All this has been done by God, who has reconciled us to himself through Christ and has given us the ministry of
reconciliation. I mean that God, in Christ, was reconciling the world to
himself, not counting men's transgressions against them, and that he
has entrusted the message of reconciliation to us. This makes us
ambassadors for Christ, God as it were appealing through us. We
implore you, in Christ's name: be reconciled to God! For our sakes God
made him who did not know sin to be sin, so that in him we might
become the very holiness of God.

The Word of the Lord.

GOSPEL   LK 15, 1-3. 11-32

A reading from the holy gospel according to Luke

The tax collectors and the sinners were all gathering around Jesus to
hear him, at which the Pharisees and the scribes murmured, "This man
welcomes sinners and eats with them." Then he addressed this parable
to them: "A man had two sons. The younger of them said to his father,
'Father, give me the share of the estate that is coming to me.' So the
father divided up the property. Some days later this younger son
collected all his belongings and went off to a distant land, where he
squandered his money on dissolute living. After he had spent everything, a great famine broke out in that country and he was in dire need.
So he attached himself to one of the propertied class of the place, who
sent him to his farm to take care of the pigs. He longed to fill his belly
with the husks that were fodder for the pigs, but no one made a move to
give him anything. Coming to his senses at last, he said: 'How many
hired hands at my father's place have more than enough to eat, while
here I am starving! I will break away and return to my father, and say
to him, "Father, I have sinned against God and against you; I no longer
deserve to be called your son. Treat me like one of your hired hands."'
With that he set off for his father's house. While he was still a long way
off, his father caught sight of him and was deeply moved. He ran out to
meet him, threw his arms around his neck, and kissed him. The son said
to him, 'Father, I have sinned against God and against you; I no longer
deserve to be called your son.' The father said to his servants: 'Quick!

bring out the finest robe and put it on him; put a ring on his finger and shoes on his feet. Take the fatted calf and kill it. Let us eat and celebrate because this son of mine was dead and has come back to life. He was lost and is found.' Then the celebration began.

"Meanwhile the elder son was out on the land. As he neared the house on his way home, he heard the sound of music and dancing. He called one of the servants and asked him the reason for the dancing and the music. The servant answered, 'Your brother is home, and your father has killed the fatted calf because he has him back in good health.' The son grew angry at this and would not go in; but his father came out and began to plead with him.

"He said in reply to his father: 'For years now I have slaved for you. I never disobeyed one of your orders, yet you never gave me so much as a kid goat to celebrate with my friends. Then, when this son of yours returns after having gone through your property with loose women, you kill the fatted calf for him.'

"'My son,' replied the father, 'you are with me always, and everything I have is yours. But we had to celebrate and rejoice! This brother of yours was dead, and has come back to life. He was lost, and is found.'"

The gospel of the Lord.

INTRODUCTORY PRAYER

On this day we celebrate
the entrance of the people of the Exodus into the Promised Land
and the return of the prodigal son.

We praise you and bless you, God our Father,
for that day when you will welcome us into your Kingdom,
the true Promised Land, the heaven of Jesus Christ.
May each moment of our life prepare us for the day
when we will be able to truly say:
"Yes, I shall arise and go to my Father!"
Then will the eternal feast of your love begin
with your Son Jesus, in the joy of the Holy Spirit,
forever and ever. Amen.

HOMILY

1. Parable of the Father's Love (The Prodigal Son)

Luke is called the evangelist of mercy. He fully deserves that title. In the fifteenth chapter of his Gospel, he assembles three parables of mercy: the Parable of the Lost Sheep, the Parable of the Lost Coin, and the Parable of the Prodigal Son. Mark has none of these parables; Matthew only the one of the lost sheep.[1] In Luke, these three parables are joined by a kind of refrain, a refrain of joy:

> Rejoice with me,
> for I have found my sheep,
> the one which was lost.   Lk 15, 5

> Rejoice with me,
> for I have found the coin,
> the one that I had lost.   Lk 15, 9

> Rejoice with me,
> for my son was dead
> and has returned to life;
> he was lost and is found.   Lk 15, 24

The Parable of the Prodigal Son is not only the richest on the theological level, but also the most moving. Peguy, in his inimitable style, explains:

> All the parables are beautiful, my child,
> all the parables are great, all the parables are dear...
> But among all, among all three, it is the third parable which
> stands out...
> Unless one has a heart of stone, my child, who could hear it
> without weeping...
> For two thousand years, it has made innumerable people cry...
> It is famous even among the godless.
> It found even there a point of entry.
> Alone perhaps, it has remained planted in the heart of the godless
> Like a nail of tenderness.
> Now it says: A man had two sons.
> It is beautiful in Luke. It is beautiful everywhere.
> It is not only in Luke, it is everywhere.
> It is beautiful on earth and in heaven.
> It is beautiful everywhere.

Only thinking about it, a sob rises in your throat.
It is the word of Jesus which had the greatest reverberation...
In the world and in man.
In the heart of man.[2]

The poet speaks the truth. We fear to take the freshness off the parable by explaining it. But tears do not suffice to make a good commentary. We shall seek to limit ourselves to the essential points.

Introduction

The introduction bears the mark of Luke's hand. It prefaces the three parables:

Publicans and sinners
all came to see Jesus to hear him.
The Pharisees and the scribes recriminated against him:
"This man welcomes sinners
and eats with them!"
                                                              Lk 15, 2

The "non-conformism" of Jesus scandalizes the Pharisees. He welcomes sinners; he eats with them! His attitude toward "sinners" seems so shocking to the Pharisees who consider themselves righteous that they make it known by recriminating against him.

The Pharisees are present throughout the parable. It is necessary to keep an eye on them all the time and watch their reactions.

Structure

Like several other parables, the one of the Prodigal Son unfolds in two scenes. Obviously, Jesus likes this bipartite structure. He uses it in the Parables of the Pharisee and the Publican, the Two Sons, the Ten Virgins, and the Last Judgment.[3]

Three characters are in the scene and play in the game of God's mercy: the younger son, the older son, and the father. It is the father—and not the prodigal—who is the center of the account, to such a degree that it has been suggested to call this parable the Parable of the Father's Love.[4]

The Prodigal Son

The younger son claims his part of the inheritance: a third according to Jewish law.[5] In this case it had been a large sum since the father possessed fields and flocks and was surrounded by servants. The son goes abroad; in a pagan country—where pigs are found—he leads a life of perdition (*asôtôs,* literally: what one cannot save), and finally finds himself driven to feed swine, impure animals according to the Law.[6] He lost everything: the money of his inheritance, his honor as an Israelite, his dignity as a son, his religion that he is obliged to deny constantly because of his trade, and the Sabbath that he can no longer observe.

We can see that the portrait of the younger son is not flattering. It had to correspond a little to what the Pharisees thought about sinners.

The repentance of the prodigal touches us and fills us with joy. However, this repentance is far from being a model of conversion. What impels the prodigal to go back home is not regret for having hurt his father or the desire to make amends, or some other repentance worthy of the Kingdom, but his empty stomach that cries famine. He adds to it also the memory of servants who live at the paternal home in surroundings more agreeable than those of a pigsty.

Does Jesus exaggerate? Alas, no. He knows well the poor quality of our motives for conversion. When Gomer, the prostitute, the wife of the prophet Hosea and a symbol of Israel, decides to come back to her husband (that is, to God) she dreams first of all of recovering her bread, her water, her oil, and her wool; she expresses her conversion in this way:

> I am going to go back to my first husband,
> for I was happier then than I am today. Hos 2, 7

We might say, "Fortunately, the 'righteous' have a less down-to-earth piety." Alas, no. They also fly low. The Book of Jeremiah presents a wonderful song of return of the exiles to Zion; we read in it this affirmation that humbles our pride and our piety to the extreme.

> They will come shouting with joy to Zion;
> they will run to the good things of the Lord,
> to the wheat, the new wine and the fresh oil,
> to the sheep and the tenderest beef. Jer 31, 12

What attracts the righteous, then, are the tenderest steaks and the new wine. Their piety is attached to "the good things of the Lord" and not to the Lord of good things. How miserable we all are, true sinners or so-called righteous! Our love for God remains so venal! Jesus knows us well when he says: "No one is good except God alone."[7]

The Father and the Prodigal

What a wonderful father! What a delightful God! Here then in action is that forgiveness about which the prophet Micah dared to say:

> What God is like you
> who takes away sin,
> who forgives the transgression...
> who takes pleasure in showing mercy?   Mi 7, 18

No one can snatch his forgiveness from God. But it is God who takes pleasure in forgiving!

The father notices the son while he is still "far away," *makran*. Therefore, he was waiting for him; he loved him even when he was "far away," even when he was first with the prostitutes and then with the swine. This "far away" designates less material distance than spiritual estrangement. In biblical vocabulary, the expression "those who are far away" designates the pagans who have not yet entered into the Covenant.[8]

He is seized with pity *(esplagchnisthé)*, that is, with that love which seizes the bowels and makes the heart turn upside down. He runs to the prodigal. Most certainly, it is not the custom in the East for a father to run to his son, especially if the son left on an impulse and is coming back from a pigsty. Even in the West, we never see an employer run to an employee who offended him, to welcome him and forgive him. Only our God, Father of prodigals, as well as the "righteous," can have such habits. He is not content to wait for the prodigal; he runs to meet him. He throws himself on the prodigal's neck and embraces him not once, but fervently, tenderly *(katéphilèsen)*. In the biblical sphere, a kiss is the sign of forgiveness.[9]

The prodigal then recites his lesson, the one that he had prepared when he was in the pit of his misery:

> Father, I have sinned against heaven and against you.
> I am not worthy to be called your son...   Lk 15, 21

But just when he was going to add, "Treat me like one of your servants," the father interrupts him. He utters not a word of reproach but orders his servants; they will be the witnesses of his joy. Quick, take off his clothes of a swineherd; give him a festive robe,[10] "the most beautiful." Quick, put a ring on his finger, the ring with the stamp, to show that he has come back into his rights. Quick, put sandals on his feet so that he does not walk barefoot like the slaves. "Let us eat and be merry." And why this feast?

> For my son was dead
> and has returned to life;
> he was lost and is found.   Lk 15, 24

The prodigal had remained this father's son in spite of his sin. He was still his son upon his return not because he had become good again, but because his father was tenderness, not because he was without sin, but because his father was forgiveness.

The Older Son

What do the Pharisees think about all this forgiveness? We will know right away.

The older son is serious, obedient, and hard-working. He is just returning from work in the fields. He hears music and dances. He becomes angry. He is angry about his brother's conversion.

What the older son says about himself, about his years of service and obedience is not false. It calls to mind curiously the badge of self-satisfaction that the Pharisee in another parable had accorded himself.

> I fast twice a week;
> I give a tenth of all my income.   Lk 18, 12

The older son considers God not as a father, but rather as a patron to whom one renders services. It is up to him to remunerate justly: payment for services rendered.

After speaking first about himself, he then speaks about his brother. What he says about him is hateful, "That son of yours." He should have said, "My brother." Jesus had said that the prodigal son had spent his money in a life of perdition. The other brother specifies: "with prostitutes." Generally, in order not to scandalize our assemblies, the official Lectionaries slide over this term. But Luke's text says crudely: *Méta pornôn,* with "prostitutes."

The older son knows well that God forgives the sinner. It is written in the Bible; the prophets repeat it in emulation of one another. He likewise knows that the faithful must imitate God on this point. That the father welcomes the younger son, that he forgives him according to the Word of God, that he also gives him a good lesson in morals, eventually that he imposes a serious penance on him, that is well and good. (This is what good confessors still do today.) But to go from there to dancing and to killing the fatted calf for someone coming back from a pigsty is a step that no faithful would want to make, especially if he pretends to be a prophet.

Such is the opinion of the Pharisees. Clearly, by warmly welcoming sinners and feasting with them, Jesus is going too far. Forgiveness, yes. Dances and the fatted calf, no.

The Father and the Older Son

The Father who was all welcoming tenderness for the younger son, who was a sinner but repentant, is also that tenderness for the older son, who was "righteous" but grumbling. What a marvelous father! Who could be "father" in the same way as God?

He had run to meet the prodigal; he also goes out to meet the older son. It is always the father who runs to meet his children!

He had called the prodigal "my son." He calls the other son, with even more affection: "Child" *(teknon).*

He had invited the prodigal to come back home. He likewise invites the older son; even more, he begs him *(parekalei).*

The older son had said: "That son of yours." The father corrects him: "Your brother."

The father also reminds the older son, who had to know well the legalities about this, that all the family wealth one day would go to him. Everything—fields, flocks, servants—would be given to him and not only a calf to celebrate with his friends.

In a word, the father sums up the grace of the older son in these terms:

You, my child, are always with me.   Lk 15, 31

How, then, could his continual presence next to the father make him jealous of the forgiveness granted his brother?

The parable stops here. The outcome remains in suspense, open to further speculation: Did the Pharisees understand the story of God's tenderness? Do we understand it today?

Conclusion

Jesus was a marvelous storyteller. The dazzling images and the words of fire fuse like fireworks. From whom does he acquire this art? From Joseph? From Mary? From whom does he acquire this knowledge of the tenderness of God, this conviction in the innermost part of his being that God is love? Could it have been from the one who sang that the mercy of God extends from generation to generation over those who worship him?[11]

2. Jesus Justifies His Conduct

Jesus justifies his conduct first with the Pharisees. Their scandal did not come from the forgiveness accorded to repentant sinners, but from the excessive goodness that Jesus manifested to them: "That one welcomes sinners and eats with them." They criticized, in fact, the music, the dances, and the feast. For they knew their theology well. To forgive sinners, agreed. To feast with them, no. That was too much.

The accusation also contained an insinuation: If God welcomed sinners with orchestras and dances, why should the Pharisees take so much trouble to observe the works of the Law and to live as "righteous?" "We obey in every respect," they thought to themselves, "we live like saints, and that does not profit us..."

It is that question that the parable answers. The Pharisees must not take offense at the conduct of Jesus, for it imitates the conduct of God. And if the joy of the celebration of forgiveness seems odd to them, it is because the ministry of Jesus is also odd. If the joy that he creates in the midst of sinners seems excessive to the Pharisees, would this not be precisely because the light of the Kingdom of God has shown upon the poor, the humble, and the sinners?

This principal lesson is inscribed in the context in which Luke placed the parable, that is, in the conflict of Jesus with the Pharisees. If we read the parable in an broader context, we can discover yet other teachings in it.

Who is God?

Our God is a God of tenderness and mercy; He is not a master who keeps an account of our faults, but a love who forgives. God is not a lord who waits for the return of a slave, but a father who runs to meet his son while he is still far away.

Our God is also a God of joy, an organizer of feasts with dances, music, and celebration. He forgives not by reproaching us for our faults—there is not a single word of reproach in the whole parable—but by welcoming us into his arms, by embracing us tenderly.

Who is Righteous?

The "righteous one" is the one who welcomes his brother, who rejoices in his return to the Father. He is the son of God in the very measure that he imitates and shares the love of the Father from his brother. His covenant with God is expressed and lived in his fraternity with all people, with all sinners. If he refuses to welcome his brother, he excludes himself from the joy and the feast of God.

The righteous one does not prevail upon his obedience to his Father; he does not count his years of service. He is of course happy to obey and to serve, but he only counts on the love of God.

Does such a righteous person exist? Is there a righteous person who would not need to be converted? The parable seems to think that there is not.

Who is a Sinner?

The younger son is a sinner, certainly, but the older son is one also, he who has such a good opinion of himself but who becomes angry at his brother and at the feast of forgiveness. "All have sinned," says Paul, "and have fallen short of the glory of God."[12]

According to the parable, to be a sinner is to live far from the Father, to serve like a slave, to be dead.

But whatever may be the shame in which the sinner fell, he remains loved by God who comes to meet him in order to save him.

The Definitive Return to the Father

By having us hear the Parable of the Prodigal Son today, the Church reminds us that our whole life, and especially this time of Lent, is the time of our return to the Father. For the prodigal son about whom Jesus speaks is also each one of us. We are all far from the paternal home, the heaven of Jesus Christ, even if it is only through the poverty of our human condition. Whereas we are called to the royal condition of children of God, we are far from home because of the radical impossibility of finding by ourselves the path of return.

Jesus came into the midst of our human misery. He is taking you by the hand. He is leading you to his Father. He asks you also to take the hand of your brother and sister, especially the one who is in the greatest misery. Is there a heavier misery than the misery of sin? Is there a greater joy than the joy of helping your brother or sister travel with you to your Father?

A day will come when you will be able to say, in the amazement of truth, "Yes, I shall arise and go to my Father!" At the hour of your death, Someone, radiating joy and light, will come before you. Your Father, who has waited for you throughout your foolish and marvelous, shabby and grandiose life will run to meet you. Then, if the words of Luke have meaning and if what Jesus says is true, God will take you in his arms. He will embrace you tenderly. How? I do not know; I know so little about the ways of God. I am simply sure about the parable. Someone waits for you as no one in the world has ever waited for you, Someone who cherishes you as no one in the world has ever cherished you; Someone wants to inundate you with his love and transfigure you through his joy. He will say to His servants: "Quick, put gold sandals on his feet so that he may dance with the angels, for here is the land of freedom! Quick, take off his rough pilgrim's cloak, that "body of misery" (as Paul says);[13] clothe him in the "most beautiful garment," that is, his body of glory, that body transfigured by the Resurrection of my Son. Quick, let the music sing, let the feast for eternity begin."

> For my son was dead
> and has returned to life.
> He was lost and is found. Lk 15, 24

Blessed be you, Father, for that day when you will gather together the prodigals that we are into your Kingdom, with your Son Jesus, in the joy of the Holy Spirit, for the eternal feast!

CONCLUDING PRAYER

> We are your prodigal children.
> We left your house.
> But your forgiveness opens for us
> the path of return;
> your love welcomes us like your children.
>
> > Thank you, O Father of Jesus.
> > *Keep us in your love.*
>
> We are your prodigal children.
> We fled far from your tenderness.
> But you run to meet us;
> you clasp us in your arms; you embrace us.
>
> > *Thank you, O Father of Jesus.*
> > *Keep us in your love.*
>
> We are your prodigal children.
> We had put on the worn clothes of sin.
> You clothe us in the splendor of your grace.
>
> > *Thank you, O Father of Jesus.*
> > *Keep us in your love.*

We are your prodigal children.
We were living in the bonds of sin.
You break the chains of our slavery;
you put on our finger the ring
of the New Covenant.

Thank you, O Father of Jesus.
Keep us in your love.

We are your prodigal children.
We were dying of hunger in a faraway country of misery.
You prepare for us a festive banquet;
you satisfy us in your Eucharist.

Thank you, O Father of Jesus.
Keep us in your love.

We are your prodigal children.

We were singing the old songs of captivity.
You put on our lips and in our heart
the new canticle of freedom.

Thank you, O Father of Jesus.
Keep us in your love.

We want to bless you eternally,
Father of Jesus and source of the Holy Spirit.
We were dead
and you made us come back to life.
We were lost
and you found us again.
Keep us in your love forever and ever. Amen.

NOTES TO FOURTH SUNDAY OF LENT
1. Cf. Mt 18, 12-14.
2. Ch. Peguy, *Oeuvres poétiques complètes* (Paris: Ed. Gallimard, 1957), pp. 622-624.
3. Cf. Lk 18, 9-14. Mt 21, 28-31; 25, 1-12; 25, 31-46.
4. Cf. Joachim Jeremias, *The Parables of Jesus,* trans. S. H. Hooke, rev. ed. (New York: Charles Scribner's Sons, 1963), p. 128.
5. Cf. Dt 21, 17.
6. Cf. Lv 11, 7-8.
7. Mk 10, 18.
8. Cf. Is 57, 19, cited in Acts 3, 29 and cultivated in Eph 2, 13-17.
9. Cf. 2 Sm 14, 33.
10. As the Pharaoh did for Joseph, Gn 41, 42.
11. Lk 1, 50.
12. Rom 3, 23.
13. Phil 3, 21.

FIFTH SUNDAY OF LENT

READING I   Is 43, 16-21

A reading from the book of the prophet Isaiah

Thus says the Lord,
who opens a way in the sea
and a path in the mighty waters,
Who leads out chariots and horsemen,
a powerful army,
Till they lie prostrate together, never to rise,
snuffed out and quenched like a wick.
Remember not the events of the past,
the things of long ago consider not;
See, I am doing something new!
Now it springs forth, do you not perceive it?
In the desert I make a way,
in the wasteland, rivers.
Wild beasts honor me,
jackals and ostriches,
For I put water in the desert
and rivers in the wasteland
for my chosen people to drink,
The people whom I formed for myself,
that they might announce my praise.

The Word of the Lord.

RESPONSORIAL PSALM   Ps 126, 1-2. 2-3. 4-5. 6

R/. (3) The Lord has done great things for us;
we are filled with joy.

When the Lord brought back the
captives of Zion,
we were like men dreaming.
Then our mouth was filled with laughter,
and our tongue with rejoicing.

R/. The Lord has done great things for us;
we are filled with joy.

Then they said among the nations,
   "The Lord has done great things for them."
The Lord has done great things for us;
   we are glad indeed.

R/. The Lord has done great things for us;
   we are filled with joy.

Restore our fortunes, O Lord,
   like the torrents in the southern desert.
Those that sow in tears
   shall reap rejoicing.

R/. The Lord has done great things for us;
   we are filled with joy.

Although they go forth weeping,
   carrying the seed to be sown,
They shall come back rejoicing,
   carrying their sheaves.

R/. The Lord has done great things for us;
   we are filled with joy.

READING II   PHIL 3, 8-14

A reading from the letter of Paul to the Philippians

I have come to rate all as loss in the light of the surpassing knowledge
of my Lord Jesus Christ. For his sake I have forfeited everything; I
have accounted all else rubbish so that Christ may be my wealth and I
may be in him, not having any justice of my own based on observance
of the law. The justice I possess is that which comes through faith in
Christ. It has its origin in God and is based on faith. I wish to know
Christ and the power flowing from his Resurrection; likewise to know
how to share in his sufferings by being formed into the pattern of his
death. Thus do I hope that I may arrive at resurrection from the dead.

It is not that I have reached it yet, or have already finished my course;
but I am racing to grasp the prize if possible, since I have been grasped
by Christ [Jesus]. Brothers, I do not think of myself as having reached
the finish line. I give no thought to what lies behind but push on to
what is ahead. My entire attention is on the finish line as I run toward
the prize to which God calls me—life on high in Christ Jesus.

The Word of the Lord.

GOSPEL   JN 8, 1-11

A reading from the holy gospel according to John

Jesus went out to the Mount of Olives. At daybreak he reappeared in the temple area; and when the people started coming to him, he sat down and began to teach them. The scribes and the Pharisees led a woman forward who had been caught in adultery. They made her stand there in front of everyone. "Teacher," they said to him, "this woman has been caught in the act of adultery. In the law, Moses ordered such women to be stoned. What do you have to say about the case?" (They were posing this question to trap him, so that they could have something to accuse him of.) Jesus simply bent down and started tracing on the ground with his finger. When they persisted in their questioning, he straightened up and said to them, "Let the one among you who has no sin be the first to cast a stone at her." A second time he bent down and wrote on the ground. Then the audience drifted away one by one, beginning with the elders. This left him alone with the woman, who continued to stand there before him. Jesus finally straightened up again and said to her, "Woman, where did they all disappear to? Has no one condemned you?" "No one, sir," she answered. Jesus said, "Nor do I condemn you. You may go. But from now on, avoid this sin."

The gospel of the Lord.

INTRODUCTORY PRAYER

What marvels you do for us, Lord!
You place in our hearts the seed of your Word;
you make it grow in the sun of your Spirit.
Help us to harvest with songs of joy
the fruit of eternal life.
And we will be the people of your praise
forever and ever. Amen.

HOMILY

1. Behold, I Am Making a New World

The First Reading is an extract from the second part of the Book of Isaiah (Deutero-Isaiah). It dates from the year 550 and thus prefaces the first return from the Babylonian captivity, in 538. It recalls of the Exodus and the passage through the Red Sea:

God traced a way across the sea
a path in the midst of the deep waters.   Is 43, 16

God will renew these marvels of the Exodus for his people captive in Babylon when he will lead them across the desert of Syria to the Promised Land:

Yes, I am going to make a way across the desert,
and rivers in dry places.   Is 43, 19

This return will be for Israel like the blooming of a new world. Let the people forget their past pain; let them raise their eyes to the future of God:

Do not remember any longer of old;
not think any more of the past.
Behold, I am making a new world.   Is 43, 18-19

What does this prophecy mean for us today?

A New World

The prophecy of the Book of Isaiah is fulfilled in Christ Jesus. In him, God renews his creation. Paul explains:

If someone is in Christ Jesus,
he is a new creation.
The old (world) is gone;
behold, the new (world) has come.   2 Cor 5, 17

The captivity of sin is behind us; it is the past. The deliverance of grace is before us; it is the future. Conversion is not merely regret for the past. Conversion is hope for the future, the certitude of joy on the path of return:

The sowers who sow in tears
will reap while singing.   Ps 126, 5

One sows in tears; one reaps while singing. Do not remember any longer the tears of sowing; listen rather to the songs of joy of the harvest.

Fifth Sunday of Lent

Sow freely in order to reap even more freely. Do not be anxious or tight-fisted, keeping the seed stingily in your hand instead of entrusting it to the dark earth. Listen to the prophet:

> Sow for yourselves righteousness;
> reap a harvest of goodness.
> Break up new lands;
> it is time to seek the Lord. Hos 10, 12

There is only one way to increase the songs of joy of the harvest; it is to sow even more in tears. There is only one way to keep the light of God in our heart; it is to spread it around us. There is only one way to be happy; it is to share in the sufferings of Jesus. There is only one way to rise; it is to accept dying with Christ.[1] Then, on the day of harvest, the Lord will realize in us his word:

> Behold, I am making a new world! Rv 21, 5

This affirmation of the emergence of a new creation in the chaos of our faded and crumpled world, this promise of the springtime of God in the winter of our old age is at the heart of our hope.

Today, before our astonished eyes, Jesus opens a new path across the desert of our life. Today, on the pale horizon of our morning, he makes rise a dawn of light. Today, on the weary road where we are dragging, he displays a path of joy to the Promised Land.

Today, according to the expressed will of God, I must forget the past: "No longer remember of old!" Today, I begin! Today I forget what is behind me; I strain toward the future,[2] toward the joy of return, toward Paradise.

God says this word of grace to me: "No longer worry about the past! It is dead. Let the dead bury the dead. Whatever may be your blunders of yesterday and your sins of old, forget them. I erase everything through my mercy. I no longer remember anything but forgiveness!" Meister Eckhart explains:

> God is a God of the present: as he finds you, he takes you and
> allows you to come to him. He does not ask you what you were,
> but what you are now.[3]

Help us, Lord, to build in our heart the new world filled with your presence. Open our heart to your future. Let your songs of hope rise in the midst of your Church!

198

2. Jesus and the Adulterous Woman

Exegetic Clearing Away

Before analyzing this Gospel, we must clear away some debris from the exegetic terrain.

In the study of a text we can distinguish three levels: the level of canonicity, the level of authenticity, and the level of historicity.

Canonicity

Canonicity asks the following question: Is this text a part of the "Canon" of Scriptures, that is, a part of the texts that the Church, according to the rule (this is the meaning of the Greek *kanon)* of her faith, recognizes as inspired? For example, is the Gospel according to the Hebrews recognized as inspired? The answer is no. Is this account of the Gospel according to John recognized as inspired? The answer is affirmative.

Authenticity

Authenticity asks the following question: Was the text written by the one to whom it is attributed? For example, a particular psalm is attributed to David. It is really David's? Here, this pericope or passage is attributed to John. Is it really from the author whom we call John? The answer is no. In fact, it does not figure in the oldest witnesses of the Gospel of John.

Where does it come from then? The analysis of the vocabulary attributes it with some probability to Luke. It could have been taken out of the Gospel (where it would have come after Lk 21, 27-28) and been introduced into the Gospel of John (between 7, 52 and 8, 12) around the fourth century.

Even though "unauthentic," the text nevertheless belongs to the Gospel. The oldest witness that we have comes to us from Papias, bishop of Hierapolis who wrote about the year 130. This witness is known to us through Eusebius of Caesarie (+339) who writes in his *Ecclesiastic History:*

> He (=Papias) exposes also another story on the subject of a
> woman accused of numerous sins before the Lord, a story that the
> Gospel according to the Hebrews includes.[4]

Historicity

Historicity asks the following question: Does a particular deed related in the Bible really belong to the domain of history? For example, is the story of Jonah and his whale historical? The answer is no; it is a parable. Here, is this story where Jesus forgives the adulterous woman really historical? The answer is yes.

The Law of Moses or the Mercy of Jesus

It is morning. Jesus is teaching in the Temple. The scribes and the Pharisees lead a woman to him. Then they cast the nets of their cunning:

> "Master, this woman was caught in the act of committing adultery. Now, in the Law, Moses commanded us to stone such women. What do you say?"

> They spoke thus to put him to the test in order to be able to accuse him. Jn 8, 4-6

From the beginning, the plotting of the scribes and Pharisees is vicious. How were they able to arrange things so as to catch a woman in the act of adultery as if on command? Where was the masculine partner who, according to the Law, had to undergo the same punishment? The Law commanded stoning? Not exactly; it commanded the punishment of death, but did not specify stoning.[5]

Taking refuge behind their legalism, which in fact was only a cloak of deceit, the scribes and the Pharisees wanted above all to immobilize Jesus in their trap. His teaching indeed seemed insupportable to the theology of the masters of wisdom in Israel. Jesus was proclaiming the universal mercy of God for sinners, publicans, and the "lost sheep of the house of Israel," but he was neglecting and even attacking the scholars who were honoring the Law of Moses by keeping it faithfully in the treasure of their human tradition. Jesus was healing the poor people about whom it could be said: "You were born entirely in sin and now you teach us a lesson,"[6] but he was slighting the specialists in the Law who were still the true nobility of the people of God.

Their dragnet seemed to be working. If Jesus forgave the adulteress, then he was opposing the Law, therefore, the will of God. But if he allowed the execution of the adulteress, then his teaching on mercy fell into their trap. He had to choose: either the Law of Moses without mercy or the mercy of Jesus without the Law of Moses.

Jesus Writes on the Ground

Jesus, bending down,
wrote on the ground with his finger.   Jn 8, 6

This could be translated: "Jesus *wrote* on the ground," or "Jesus *drew (kategraphen)* on the ground." But no translation answers the question: What was he writing? What was he drawing? We can offer many solutions, but with little chance of arriving at the truth. One solution (that Ambrose, Augustine and Jerome contemplated) proposed this text from Jeremiah:

Those who turn away from you are written on the sand for they
forsake the source of living water, the Lord.   Jer 17, 13

The most evident solution is that Jesus refuses to answer. He sees very clearly the net in which the deceit wants to trap him.

Whoever among You is without Sin...

Commenting on this scene, Augustine writes: "They saw the adulteress. They did not look at themselves."[7]

Then Jesus, with a single sentence, tears their duplicity apart. It is a sentence that seems to fall from heaven, laying hearts bare and piercing the mind like an arrow:

Whoever among you who is without sin,
let him be the first to cast a stone on her.   Jn 8, 7

We know what follows. The matter is ended. The woman is saved.

The insupportable scene of the sinful woman in the midst of those who accuse her while being sinners themselves is suddenly illuminated with peace. As the accusers look into their hearts, they beat a retreat, vanquished by their own sins. There remained only the distress of the lone woman and the forgiveness of Jesus, *misera et misericordia,* as Augustine says, misery and mercy.[8]

Jesus and the Sin of Adultery

The stupefying ease with which Jesus granted forgiveness had to shock the Pharisees, who were always more eager to defend the rights of the Law than the duties of mercy.[9] Did this ease not border on laxity, especially in sexual matters? Did it not create a danger for a wholesome and holy morality? Did it not offer women a freedom that the judges—men—would no longer be able to control?

It is probably this fear of laxity which played a role when the early community removed from the evangelic text this pericope in which Jesus grants forgiveness without repentance which criticizes the judges. We know that the early Church, unceasingly threatened by the immorality of surrounding paganism, showed herself severe in penitential matters: She refused to grant forgiveness for the sin of adultery as well as for the sins of homicide and apostasy. To those who had committed such sins she said, "The Church can do nothing for you (she should have said, the Church does not want to do anything for you); entrust yourself to the mercy of God." It was to the credit of Pope Callixtus (217-222) to admit to ecclesial penance all sins without exception. Through the same act, he allowed the episode of the adulterous woman to enter again into the evangelic text. It entered by being placed with much suitability just before this word of Jesus to the Pharisees:

> You judge according to the flesh;
> I do not judge anyone.   Jn 8, 15

Let us come back to our question. What is the position of Jesus towards the sin of adultery? It is extreme. He condemns not only the act of adultery, that to which the Law is limited, but further the look of adultery; therefore, he condemns the sin at the very root where it is born, in the heart of people:

> Whoever looks at a woman to desire her
> has already committed adultery with her.   Mt 5, 28

In our present society where permissiveness in sexual matters is excessive—that is the least that we could say—the Church has sometimes been accused of being too rigid in this domain. It is good to remember that while Jesus, our only Master, knew no compromise with any sin, the Church can only follow her Master in this domain.

Jesus and the Adulteress

If the condemnation of adultery by Jesus is extreme, the forgiveness that he grants the adulteress is also extreme. He totally condemns sin, but totally forgives the sinner. He hates the sin, but saves the sinner. And this forgiveness is granted with marvelous goodness, with incomparable delicacy.

One knew indeed that Jesus forgave; one did not know that he forgave with such indulgence. There is not the least word, not the least allusion to the woman on the subject of her sin. There is no invitation to repent, no imposition of the least penance, no word of condemnation either. Quite the contrary, there is the affirmation that he does not condemn her. He simply frees her. He opens for her a door of hope. He shows her a path of grace: "Go, from now on sin no more!" One can go no further in forgiveness. One cannot imagine a more merciful goodness.

We do not know the mystery of grace that bound the adulteress to Jesus. Did her eyes meet the eyes of Jesus when he stood up after having written in the sand? Those who had accused her finally accused themselves; by refusing to throw the first stone, they acknowledged themselves as sinners. But Jesus had not accused her, he who was without sin—"Who of you will convict me of sin?" he had said[10]—what was he going to say to her? Who can read the heart of the adulteress when heaven has invaded it and forgiveness has erased all vestige of sin? Who, on the other hand, can read the heart of Jesus, who is only tenderness and goodness?

Sometimes the story of the adulterous woman has been compared to the story of Susanna in the Book of Daniel. There is the same accusation of adultery, the same summons before the elders, "elders of the people and judges,"[11] the same appeal to the Law of Moses, the same condemnation to stoning, the same reversal of the situation when the elders recognize themselves as sinners. The Christ of the Gospels appears then as the new Daniel, the judge of messianic times (the meaning of "Dani-El" is "God is judge"). But whereas Daniel saves an innocent woman, a woman who stands like a lily in the midst of the impurity of the elders (the meaning of "Susanna" is "lily"), Jesus forgives and saves a guilty person. Daniel establishes a true tribunal and sets himself up as judge. Jesus affirms expressly: "I have not come to judge the world, but to save the world." Such is the will of his Father.[12] The judgment of God in messianic times is the forgiveness of the sinner. It is enough that our misery meets the mercy of Jesus and forgiveness is granted.

Can one imagine mercy more generous than yours, Lord Jesus?

Jesus Opposite the Scribes and the Pharisees

The scribes and the Pharisees are useful for us simply in the sense that they confirm for us that one cannot with impunity transgress the principle posed by Jesus in the inaugural discourse:

Do not judge
and you will not be judged.
Do not condemn
and you will not be condemned.   Lk 6, 37

They judged the adulterous woman. They condemned her. They were condemned themselves. Or rather—for Jesus did not say one word of condemnation to them—they condemned themselves. By running away one after the other, they avowed that they were sinners.

Did not the justice that they pretended to render in the name of Moses demand that they purify first their own conscience or, as it is commonly said, to "sweep clean before your own door first"?

This Gospel, with extreme audacity, concerns us today on multiple levels. Let us survey two of them.

The Plenitude of Forgiveness

The most obvious meaning of the account is the following: Jesus granted the sinner the plenitude of forgiveness. Following him, the Church—that is, each one of us where Providence has placed us—must offer the sinner mercy similar to the mercy of Jesus.

Perhaps our familiarity with the Gospel has somewhat dulled our faculty of amazement with regard to Jesus. Here is an adulteress who does not manifest any regret for her sin, at least according to the text of the Gospel. Jesus declares that he does not condemn her. She does not give any evidence of conversion; Jesus gives her his mercy. She has no look of thanksgiving, at least according to the text of the Gospel. Jesus frees her.

In the Parable of the Prodigal Son, we found at least a beginning of "confession." The prodigal said:

I shall arise;
I shall go to my father; I shall say to him:
"Father, I have sinned against heaven and against you." Lk 15, 18

Here, we have nothing: not a regret, not an acknowledgement of sin, a firm resolution, not a word of gratitude. Simply this is said: "Jesus remained alone, and the woman stood in the middle."

We have simply the meeting between the misery of man or woman and the mercy of Jesus. That is enough to make forgiveness spring forth. Jesus is more pressed to forgive than the woman seems disposed to regretting.

The forgiveness of the adulteress teaches us this: Only a Church which forgives with the same generosity is the Church of Jesus. And this mystery of the Church, mercy and forgiveness, must be shared by each Christian. Inversely, a Church that does not hasten to forgive with the same generosity is not the Church of Jesus.

Who is Adulterous?

By having us celebrate this Gospel on this Sunday of Lent, the liturgy invites us also to marvel at the forgiveness that Jesus grants today to each one of us. This day is our feast. For the adulteress is also, in a certain way, each one of us, priest or lay, married or celibate.

In fact, the Covenant that binds us to God implies a faithfulness similar to conjugal faithfulness.[13] Now we have tarnished this faithfulness to Christ through our mediocrity; we have sullied it with our personal sins. Who can pretend to make the Church incarnate, this Church "without stain or wrinkle, but holy and blameless,"[14] while bearing the ugliness of sin, while completely "imprisoned" in sin?[15] Who would not blush, while the prophets speak not about one adultery, but about prostitution, that is, incessant repetition of sins? How many times has the Church herself throughout her history, prostituted herself with idols of money, idols of power and idols of pleasure?

The feast that we are celebrating today is forgiveness obtained like that of the adulterous woman, in total gratuitousness. Today, our misery met mercy, and forgiveness inundated our hearts. And the Church, who was a prostitute, received the kiss of Christ and became "pure virgin," the fiancée of the Lord.[16]

Our Thanks to God

The adulteress of the Gospel, unless she had a heart of stone, had to thank Jesus in the silence of her heart (even if that is not said in the text!). Today the whole community thanks the Father for the mercy that he grants in Jesus to the adulterers that we are.

That is what we do in each Eucharist. We thank the Father by offering to him the most jubilant thanksgiving, the only one worthy of his glory: Jesus himself. To the Father who forgives us and loves us in his Son Jesus and in the Holy Spirit, to him our thanks forever and ever.

CONCLUDING PRAYER

Create in our heart a new world!
We are wandering in the barren desert of our life.
Who will be able to lay out before us
a new path to the Promised Land

except you, Lord,
creator of the new world?

We are languishing with thirst in the dry steppe.
Who will be able to make spring up around us
sources of living water

except you, Lord,
creator of the new world?

We are walking, weighed down with sadness,
with the memory of our past sins.
Who will be able to ease our heart with mercy

except you, Lord,
creator of the new world?

We are sowing in tears in a desolate land.
Who will be able to make us reap while singing
in a new land

except you, Lord,
creator of the new world?

We are begging forgiveness for our sins.
Who will be able to take away the weight of our faults
and clothe us with the beauty of heaven

except you, Lord,
creator of the new world?

God of all marvels,
we pray to you, fulfill your promise:
create in our heart a new world
where righteousness will dwell.
And we will bless your love
forever and ever. Amen.

NOTES TO FIFTH SUNDAY OF LENT

1. Cf. Phil 3,10
2. Cf. Phil 3,13
3. Meister Eckhart, German mystic, born around 1260, died in 1327. Text in *Instruction spirituelle* (Paris: Gallimard, 1942), pp. 174-175.
4. Cf. *Histoire Ecclésiastique,* III, 39,17. SC. 31 (1952), p. 152. The apocryphal Gospel according to the Hebrews is anterior to 150 and seems close to pre-canonical Matthew.
5. Cf. Lv 20,10; Dt 22,22.
6. Cf. Jn 9,34.
7. *Homélies sur l'Evangile de Saint Jean,* XXXIII,5. Cf. *Oeuvres de Saint Augustin,* vol. 72 (Paris: Desclée de Brouwer, 1977), p. 704.
8. *Ibid.,* p.702.
9. Cf. Mt. 23,23.
10. Cf. Jn 8,46.
11. Dn 13,41
12. Cf. Jn 3,17 and 12,47.
13. From Hosea (cf. 2,21-22) through the New Testament, the covenant is compared to a marriage between God and his people.
14. Cf. Eph 5,27.
15. Rom 11,23.
16. Cf. 2 Cor 11,2.

PASSION SUNDAY

READING I   Is 50, 4-7

A reading from the book of the prophet Isaiah

The Lord God has given me
  a well-trained tongue,
That I might know how to speak to the weary
  a word that will rouse them.
Morning after morning
  he opens my ear that I may hear;
And I have not rebelled,
  have not turned back.
I gave my back to those who beat me,
  my cheeks to those who plucked my beard;
My face I did not shield
  from buffets and spitting.
The Lord God is my help,
  therefore I am not disgraced;
I have set my face like flint,
  knowing that I shall not be put to shame.
The Word of the Lord.

RESPONSORIAL PSALM   Ps 22, 8-9. 17-18. 19-20. 23-24

R/. (2) My God, my God, why have you abandoned me?

All who see me scoff at me;
  they mock me with parted lips, they wag their heads:
"He relied on the Lord; let him deliver him,
  let him rescue him, if he loves him."

R/. My God, my God, why have you abandoned me?

Indeed, many dogs surround me,
  a pack of evildoers closes in upon me;
They have pierced my hands and my feet;
  I can count all my bones.

R/. My God, my God, why have you abandoned me?

They divide my garments among them,
  and for my vesture they cast lots.

But you, O Lord, be not far from me;
O my help, hasten to aid me.

R/. My God, my God, why have you abandoned me?

I will proclaim your name to my brethren;
in the midst of the assembly I will praise you:
"You who fear the Lord, praise him;
all you descendants of Jacob, give glory to him."

R/. My God, my God, why have you abandoned me?

READING II   PHIL 2, 6-11

A reading from the letter of Paul to the Philippians

Your attitude must be Christ's:
though he was in the form of God
he did not deem equality with God
something to be grasped at.

Rather, he emptied himself
and took the form of a slave,
being born in the likeness of men.

He was known to be of human estate,
and it was thus that he humbled himself,
obediently accepting even death,
death on a cross!

Because of this,
God highly exalted him
and bestowed on him the name
above every other name,

So that at Jesus' name
every knee must bend
in the heavens, on the earth,
and under the earth,
and every tongue proclaim
to the glory of God the Father:
JESUS CHRIST IS LORD!

The Word of the Lord.

Gospel Lk 22, 14-23, 56 or 23, 1-49

The Passion of our Lord Jesus Christ according to Luke

When the hour arrived, Jesus took his place at table, and the apostles with him. He said to them: "I have greatly desired to eat this Passover with you before I suffer. I tell you, I will not eat again until it is fulfilled in the kingdom of God."

Then taking a cup he offered a blessing in thanks and said: "Take this and divide it among you; I tell you, from now on I will not drink of the fruit of the vine until the coming of the reign of God."

Then taking bread and giving thanks, he broke it and gave it to them, saying: "This is my body to be given for you. Do this as a remembrance of me." He did the same with the cup after eating, saying as he did so: "This cup is the new covenant in my blood, which will be shed for you.

"And yet the hand of my betrayer is with me at this table. The Son of Man is following out his appointed course, but woe to that man by whom he is betrayed." Then they began to dispute among themselves as to which of them would do such a deed.

A dispute arose among them about who would be regarded as the greatest. He said: "Earthly kings lord it over their people. Those who exercise authority over them are called their benefactors. Yet it cannot be that way with you. Let the greater among you be as the junior, the leader as the servant. Who, in fact, is the greater—he who reclines at table or he who serves the meal? Is it not the one who reclines at the table? Yet I am in your midst as the one who serves you. You are the ones who have stood loyally by me in my temptations. I for my part assign to you the dominion my Father has assigned to me. In my kingdom, you will eat and drink at my table, and you will sit on thrones judging the twelve tribes of Israel.

"Simon, Simon! Remember that Satan has asked for you to sift you all like wheat. But I have prayed for you that your faith may never fail. You in turn must strengthen your brothers." "Lord," he said to him, "at your side I am prepared to face imprisonment and death itself." Jesus replied, "I tell you, Peter, the rooster will not crow today until you have three times denied that you know me."

He asked them, "When I sent you on a mission without purse or traveling bag or sandals, were you in need of anything?" "Not a thing," they replied. He said to them: "Now, however, the man who has a purse must carry it; the same with the traveling bag. And the man without a sword must sell his coat and buy one. It is written in Scripture,

'He was counted among the wicked,'

and this, I tell you, must come to be fulfilled in me. All that has to do with me approaches its climax." They said, "Lord, here are two swords!" He answered, "Enough."

Then he went out and made his way, as was his custom, to the Mount of Olives; his disciples accompanied him. On reaching the place he said to them, "Pray that you may not be put to the test." He withdrew from them about a stone's throw, then went down on his knees and prayed in these words: "Father, if it is your will, take this cup from me; yet not my will but yours be done." An angel then appeared to him from heaven to strengthen him. In his anguish he prayed with all the greater intensity, and his sweat became like drops of blood falling to the ground. Then he rose from prayer and came to his disciples, only to find them asleep, exhausted with grief. He said to them, "Why are you sleeping? Wake up, and pray that you may not be subjected to the trial."

While he was still speaking a crowd came, led by the man named Judas, one of the Twelve. He approached Jesus to embrace him. Jesus said to him, "Judas, would you betray the Son of Man with a kiss?" When the companions of Jesus saw what was going to happen, they said, "Lord, shall we use the sword?" One of them went so far as to strike the high priest's servant and cut off his right ear. Jesus said in answer to their question "Enough!" Then he touched the ear and healed the man. But to those who had come out against him—the chief priests, the chiefs of the temple guard, and the ancients—Jesus said, "Am I a criminal that you come out after me armed with swords and clubs? When I was with you day after day in the temple you never raised a hand against me. But this is your hour—the triumph of darkness!"

They led him away under arrest and brought him to the house of the high priest, while Peter followed at a distance. Later they lighted a fire in the middle of the courtyard and were sitting beside it, and Peter sat among them. A servant girl saw him sitting in the light of the fire. She gazed at him intently, then said, "This man was with him." He denied the fact, saying, "Woman, I do not know him." A little while later someone else saw him and said, "You are one of them too." But Peter said, "No, sir, not I!" About an hour after that another spoke more insistently: "This man was certainly with him, for he is a Galilean." Peter responded, "My friend, I do not know what you are talking about." At the very moment he was saying this, a rooster crowed. The Lord turned around and looked at Peter, and Peter remembered the word that the Lord had spoken to him, "Before the rooster crows today you will deny me three times." He went out and wept bitterly.

Meanwhile the men guarding Jesus amused themselves at his expense. They blindfolded him first, slapped him, and then taunted him: "Play the prophet; which one struck you?" And they directed many other insulting words at him.

At daybreak the council, which was made up of the elders of the people, the chief priests, and the scribes, assembled again. Once they had brought him before their council, they said, "Tell us, are you the Messiah?" He replied, "If I tell you, you will not believe me, and if I question you, you will not answer. This much only I will say: 'From now on, the Son of Man will have his seat at the right hand of the Power of God.'" "So you are the Son of God?" they asked in chorus. He answered, "It is you who say I am." They said, "What need have we of witnesses? We have heard it from his own mouth."

Then the entire assembly rose up and led him before Pilate. They started his prosecution by saying, "We found this man subverting our nation, opposing the payment of taxes to Caesar, and calling himself the Messiah, a king." Pilate asked him, "Are you the king of the Jews?" He answered, "That is your term." Pilate reported to the chief priests and the crowds, "I do not find a case against this man." But they insisted, "He stirs up the people by his teaching through the whole of Judea, from Galilee, where he began, to this very place." On hearing this Pilate asked if the man was a Galilean; and when he learned that he was under Herod's jurisdiction, he sent him to Herod, who also happened to be in Jerusalem at the time.

Herod was extremely pleased to see Jesus. From the reports about him he had wanted for a long time to see him, and he was hoping to see him work some miracle. He questioned Jesus at considerable length, but Jesus made no answer. The chief priests and scribes were at hand to accuse him vehemently. Herod and his guards then treated him with contempt and insult, after which they put a magnificent robe on him and sent him back to Pilate. Herod and Pilate, who had previously been set against each other, became friends from that day.

Pilate then called together the chief priests, the ruling class, and the people, and said to them: "You have brought this man before me as one who subverts the people. I have examined him in your presence and have no charge against him arising from your allegations. Neither has Herod, who therefore has sent him back to us; obviously this man has done nothing to deserve death. Therefore I mean to release him, once I have taught him a lesson." The whole crowd cried out, "Away with this man; release Barabbas for us!" This Barabbas had been thrown in prison for causing an uprising in the city, and for murder. Pilate addressed them again, for he wanted Jesus to the the one he released.

But they shouted back, "Crucify him, crucify him!" He said to them for the third time, "What wrong is this man guilty of? I have not discovered anything about him deserving the death penalty. I will therefore chastise him and release him." But they demanded with loud cries that he be crucified, and their shouts increased in violence. Pilate then decreed that what they demanded should be done. He released the one they asked for, who had been thrown in prison for insurrection and murder, and delivered Jesus up to their wishes.

As they led him away, they laid hold of one Simon the Cyrenean who was coming in from the fields. They put a crossbeam on Simon's shoulder for him to carry along behind Jesus. A great crowd of people followed him, including women who beat their breasts and lamented over him. Jesus turned to them and said: "Daughters of Jerusalem, do not weep for me. Weep for yourselves and for your children. The days are coming when they will say, 'Happy are the sterile, the wombs that never bore and the breasts that never nursed.' Then they will begin saying to the mountains, 'Fall on us,' and to the hills, 'Cover us.' If they do these things in the green wood, what will happen in the dry?"

Two others who were criminals were led along with him to be crucified. When they came to Skull Place, as it was called, they crucified him there and the criminals as well, one on his right and the other on his left. [Jesus said, "Father, forgive them; they do not know what they are doing."] They divided his garments, rolling dice for them.

The people stood there watching, and the leaders kept jeering at him, saying, "He saved others; let him save himself if he is the Messiah of

God, the chosen one." The soldiers also made fun of him, coming forward to offer him their sour wine and saying, "If you are the king of the Jews, save yourself." There was an inscription over his head:

"THIS IS THE KING OF THE JEWS."

One of the criminals hanging in crucifixion blasphemed him, "Aren't you the Messiah? Then save yourself and us." But the other one rebuked him: "Have you no fear of God, seeing you are under the same sentence? We deserve it, after all. We are only paying the price for what we've done, but this man has done nothing wrong." He then said, "Jesus, remember me when you enter upon your reign." And Jesus replied, "I assure you: this day you will be with me in paradise."

It was now around midday, and darkness came over the whole land until midafternoon with an eclipse of the sun. The curtain in the sanctuary was torn in two. Jesus uttered a loud cry and said,

"Father, into your hands I commend my spirit."

After he said this, he expired. The centurion, upon seeing what had happened, gave glory to God by saying, "Surely this was an innocent man." After the crowd assembled for this spectacle witnessed what had happened, they returned beating their breasts. All his friends and the women who had accompanied him from Galilee were standing at a distance watching everything.

There was a man named Joseph, an upright and holy member of the Sanhedrin, who had not been associated with their plan or their action. He was from Arimathea, a Jewish town, and he looked expectantly for the reign of God. This man approached Pilate with a request for Jesus' body. He took it down, wrapped it in fine linen, and laid it in a tomb hewn out of the rock, in which no one had yet been buried.

That was the day of Preparation, and the sabbath was about to begin. The women who had come with him from Galilee followed along behind. They saw the tomb and how his body was buried. Then they went back home to prepare spices and perfumes. They observed the sabbath as a day of rest, in accordance with the law.

The gospel of the Lord.

INTRODUCTORY PRAYER

May the Lord help us to live in a holy way
during this Holy Week
in the remembrance of his holy Passion.

We bless you, Lord Jesus;
you loved us and offered yourself for us.
Give us the grace to take part in your Passion
by taking our part in the pain and suffering of the world.

And on the Day of your eternal Passover,
when you will come again in glory,
awaken us for the feast of your love.

We ask you this humbly, Lord,
you who suffered with us
and who reign with the Father and the Holy Spirit
in joy forever and ever. Amen.

HOMILY

The Passion According to Luke

Today the holy liturgy offers us the Passion according to Luke. It invites us to meditate in our heart and to keep in our mind the special message of Luke.

This message is unique and marvelous. It reflects the very splendor of the Gospel of Christ. Let us say right away that the same must be said about Mark, Matthew, and John; each Gospel is clothed in the light of Jesus. It is not a matter of giving preference to one Gospel over another, but simply of celebrating the particular beauty of the Passion according to Saint Luke. We will do it by comparing Luke with the other synoptic gospels, Mark and Matthew.

The Lord Jesus

The account of the Passion according to Luke does not have the quality of intense humiliation and extreme meanness that we find in the other evangelists, which the speaker in Psalm 22 expresses well:

I am a worm, no longer a man
disgrace of the human race, outcast of the people. Ps 22, 7

215

Passion Sunday

The speaker is Christ himself. This Psalm begins with this invocation of distress:

My God, my God, why have you forsaken me?   Ps 22, 1

According to Mark and Matthew, this is the prayer of Christ on the cross. But Luke omits this prayer. On the contrary, throughout his account he invites the Christian community to contemplate in Christ Jesus the Lord of glory and majesty, Son of man and Son of God, the Righteous One par excellence.[1] Here are a few examples:

Luke softens considerably the desolation of Jesus' prayer in Gethsemane. Instead of falling on the ground (according to Mark and Matthew), Jesus, more nobly, kneels, and his prayer of distress: "Deeply sad is my soul unto death" is quite simply passed over in silence.[2]

Luke avoids writing that Judas betrayed Jesus with a kiss. He simply notes:

Judas approached Jesus to give him a kiss   Lk 22, 47

The reader will know nothing more about the ignoble kiss of the traitor. But he will learn that Jesus was not surprised by the perfidy of his disciple. He knew it in advance, and he tried one last time to take him away from his treachery:

Judas, is it with a kiss
that you betray the Son of man?   Lk 22, 48

Luke mentions the arrest of Judas in passing, in a past participle: "and having arrested him, they led him away."

Luke could not bring himself to write that Jesus was spat upon and slapped by the crowd.[4] He likewise passes silently over the scourging that humiliates human dignity even more than it rips open the body, as well as the crowning with thorns.[5]

Luke partially ignores the scene in which Jesus is placed in parallel with Barabbas. We are not at all aware of Pilate's questioning as given to us by Matthew:

Whom do you want me to release to you?
Barabbas or Jesus, the Christ?

He likewise omits—but in this, Mark and Matthew do the same—the complete name of Barabbas which, according to ancient traditions,[6] is Jesus-Barabbas. That the famous thief could be called Jesus and that Jesus-Barabbas had been preferred to Jesus-Christ shocked the early community.

This account of the Passion corresponds to the portrait of Jesus that Luke draws in his gospel. Thus, to his death, Jesus remains the Lord of glory who seduces gold by his beauty, the Son of God who dominates events by his power, the Righteous One who deserves all our love.

This portrait of Jesus was a preaching of hope for the Christian community. Through the incessant persecutions that the community underwent in its flesh and in its soul, (as we read in the book of Acts) they continued to live the Passion of Jesus. Let Christians, therefore not lose courage. Jesus risen, lives in the midst of their sufferings. Persecuted by the Judaizers who, at the time that Luke was writing his Gospel, were the heirs of the "elders of the people, chief priests and scribes," the Christians formed the people of the Beatitudes who Jesus had said were "children of God."[7] Accused falsely before the world, they remain righteous and innocent before God. Stained by hatred, they shine in their heart with the beauty of Jesus. Hated by the world, they are loved by God.

Today Luke still invites all Christians, even if their life is broken through suffering, even if they live in the midst of a world splattered with the ugliness of sin, to reflect the beauty of Jesus.

The Death of the Righteous

The death of Jesus presents the ideal of the death of the Righteous. Far from being a defeat, this death that is crowned by resurrection is an example.

The word agony means struggle. Agony is the last battle against all the powers hostile to the love, peace, and joy of God on earth. It is not lived in solitude, like a single balance, for it is a prayer, a dialogue with God, a face to face of love with the Father. It is surrounded by the presence of angels:

An angel appeared to him, coming from heaven, strengthening him.
Entering into agony, he prayed more earnestly.　　　LK 22, 43

The angels who had surrounded his cradle and sang his birth likewise surround his death, which is his "birth into heaven." They do not suppress the suffering anymore than they eased the poverty in Bethlehem, but they surround it with the peace of heaven, that peace which is the first sign of the presence of God in the heart of our pain.

The death of Jesus is a surrender of love into the hands of the Father. Luke cannot resign himself to transcribing Jesus' cry of distress on the cross, that cry that Mark preserved for us in Aramaic:

Elöi, Elöi, lama sabachtani?   Ps 22, 2
My God, my God, why have you forsaken me?   Mk 15, 34

Instead of this word of desolation, he prefers the prayer of Psalm 31:

Jesus says: Father,
into your hands I commend my spirit."   Lk 3, 46

Psalm 31 expresses well this ideal of the death of the Righteous. Perhaps Luke hopes that the faithful will have examined the text and completed the prayer of the Psalm:

I said: "You are my God.
My times are in your hand...
Blessed be the Lord who does for me
wonders of love!"   Ps 31, 15-16, 22

Luke takes up again this ideal of the death of the Righteous in the account of the death of the deacon Stephen. He is the first martyr (that is, *witness*: the meaning of the Greek *martus)* of the Christian community. His exemplary death is illuminated by the prayer of the Crucified. Like Jesus in Gethsemane, Stephen kneels and prays in this way:

Acts 7, 59-60	Luke 23, 46, 34
Lord Jesus,	Father, into your hands
receive my spirit.	I commit your spirit.
Lord,	Father,
do not hold against them	forgive them,
this sin.	for they know
	not what they do.

And just as Jesus was comforted by an angel from heaven, Stephen sees the heavens open and Jesus appears to him in his glory.

Christians never die alone: We die—and rise—with Christ. Happy are those who die in this way, even if it is on a cross of suffering and desolation, while delivering themselves up, as Jesus did, to the love of the Father! Happy are those who die while saying with Jesus: "Father, into your hands I commend my spirit!" Happy are those who die while praying with the Psalm: "Blessed be the Lord who does wonders of love for me!"

The Disciple of Jesus

In the Passion according to Mark and Matthew, Jesus remains alone to face his adversaries. On the other hand, Luke's account of the Passion of Jesus is filled with the presence of "all his friends." The Passion of the Master thus becomes the compassion of the disciples.

First there is *Simon of Cyrene*. Mark relates that the soldiers commandeered him by force to carry the cross. Luke does not even mention the commandeering by the soldiers. He allows us to think that Simon willingly accepted the cross of Jesus and carried it behind him.[8] He is thus the first example of the true disciple of Jesus:

> If someone wants to be my disciple, let him deny himself
> and take his cross each day and follow me   Lk 9, 23

Here is likewise Joseph of Arimathea who buries Jesus in his own newly-hewn tomb, and thus surrounds him with compassion. Luke notes explicitly that he was a "good and righteous" man and that he had refused to associate himself with the decisions and the members of the Council.[9]

We know that women are particularly numerous and active in the Gospel of Luke.[10] In the Passion, those whom Christian tradition will call forever the "holy women" are present everywhere where their love and compassion can be expressed. We meet them when they follow Jesus to Calvary in the first "way of the cross."[11] We find them at the foot of the cross, with all the friends of Jesus:

> Now all his friends stood at a distance,
> as well as the women who followed him from Galilee,
> who were seeing these things.   Lk 23, 48

We find them again when they bury Jesus. They prepare spices and perfumes to anoint the body of the Lord. Finally we know that they will be the first to meet the angels of the Resurrection on Easter morning.[12]

Let us note lastly the very Lukan theme of the presence of crowds throughout the Passion, the messianic crowd of the lowly and the humble, that crowd which was always at the side of Jesus, which drank his words of goodness and forgiveness and which acclaimed his miracles. It is the crowd about which Luke says with enthusiasm:

> The whole crowd rejoiced
> over all the marvels that he was doing.   Lk 13, 17

Passion Sunday

There is a difference in perspective—to say the least!—between the flight of all the Apostles in the garden of Gethsemane, a flight that Mark and Matthew crudely relate, and the presence, according to Luke, of all the friends of Jesus at the foot of the cross. According to the word of Mark:

> And having abandoned him,
> all the disciples fled,   Mk 14, 50

Luke opposes:

> Now all his friends stood there
> (at the foot of the cross).   LK 22, 49

In that ocean of hate which engulfed Jesus, he is assured of the presence of all his friends.

Luke especially notes that intense look that his friends cast upon Jesus; a look that seeks to ease his suffering. It is the look of the Christian community contemplating the suffering Righteous One. When the holy women meet his gaze, Jesus says to them: "Do not weep!" When the good thief meets his gaze, Jesus promises him Paradise. When Peter the renegade meets his gaze, Jesus forgives him and Peter breaks into sobs. Without doubt, it is the centurion who is the most complete model of his contemplation. In him the words of the psalm are fulfilled: "Whoever looks to God will be resplendent."[13] He sees a crucified man and proclaims the Righteous One. He sees a dying man and proclaims the Son of God:

> The centurion, seeing what had happened, gave glory to God, saying:

> "Truly, this man was righteous!"   Lk 23, 47

> "Truly, this man was the Son of God!"   Mk 15, 39

Thus in Luke, the account of the Passion becomes a contemplation of the suffering Christ. Through the tears of Jesus, beyond his gaping wounds of pain, even beyond his death, the Christian community arrives at the risen Lord, the Righteous One par excellence.

Can we today still contemplate Christ in his Passion?

Yes, for the Passion of Jesus continues in the life of our brothers and sisters. It is impossible for us to pass by a cross without recognizing on it the Crucified.

Like Simon of Cyrene we can come to the aid of those who succumb under the weight of sufferings by helping them carry their cross; it is the cross of Jesus. Like the holy women, we can accompany with our compassion those whom sadness is dragging to a Calvary of distress; it is the Calvary of Jesus. Like the centurion, we can stand next to those who are dying while giving glory to God for the marvels that God has accomplished in their death; it is the death of Jesus. Each time that we take our part in the suffering of the world, we meet the Lord Jesus.

The Celebration of Forgiveness

Luke is the evangelist of great pardons.[14] The Passion itself is the celebration of the goodness of Jesus. In spite of the torments that cover the account with a cloak of infinite sadness, the forgiveness of Jesus makes the heart of the account beat and allows us to catch a glimpse of a dawn of peace and hope beyond the treachery, the denials, and the vile actions. Luke excuses almost everyone. But through Luke, it is really the forgiveness of Jesus which shines on the world.

Pilate is almost innocent (undoubtedly through loyalty to Rome, Luke preferred not to charge Roman authority). Three times he notes that Pilate finds in Jesus "no basis for condemnation."[15] He does not condemn Jesus but is content to deliver him "to their will."[16]

The executioners are forgiven because "they do know what they are doing."[17]

Peter, who knew what he was doing, is forgiven by a simple glance which pierces his heart and causes him to break into sobs. Throughout the account, let us note that Peter receives privileged treatment. The reproach of Jesus to Peter, according to Mark:

> Simon, are you asleep?
> Could you not wait one hour?   Mk 14, 37

becomes in Luke a general question addressed to all the Apostles:

> Why are you sleeping?   Lk 22, 46

The triple denial is treated with discretion. Peter's conduct is nevertheless especially painful. Who, since then, has denied Jesus on the day of his first communion? Luke erases all the imprecations and oaths. Only the look of Jesus and the tears of Peter remain:

> The Lord turning looked at Peter...And going out,
> Peter wept bitterly.   Lk 22, 61-62

The group of the Twelve is seen treated with benevolence. Luke refrains from citing the prophecy of Zechariah (13,7):

> I shall strike the Shepherd
> and the sheep will be scattered   Mk 14, 27

a prophecy which unfortunately expressed well the desertion of the Apostles. Luke simply notes that it was the hour of the power of darkness.[18]

Even the servant of the High Priest whose right ear was cut by one of the Twelve benefits from the goodness of Jesus: "Jesus touched his ear and healed it."[19]

The king of the robbers of Paradise remains incontestably the good thief. He is indeed a true thief who, with a single prayer, forces open the doors of the Kingdom and whitens a life of plunder. He recognizes his faults perfectly:

> For us, it is justice.
> We are receiving worthy punishment
> for what we have done.

He proclaims the innocence of Jesus:

> But he has done nothing wrong.   Lk 23, 41

And he implores:

> Jesus, remember me
> when you come into your kingdom.   Lk 23, 42

What sinner, even with a heart burdened with all the despair of the world, would not dare to repeat the prayer of the good thief? What sinner would not have the certitude of hearing, from the very mouth of his Savior, this judgment of mercy:

> Amen, I say to you:
> Today, with me,
> you shall be in paradise!   Lk 25, 43

Conclusion

Like Jesus, we all will pass by the path of death. We all, like Jesus, hope that our death will empty onto resurrection.

We prepare ourselves for this life of light and peace by following the same path of Jesus. What was that path? Luke writes:

> He went around doing good.   Acts 10, 38

May the road of our life be that road of goodness and love that was the road of Christ.

CONCLUDING PRAYER

Look, Lord, at the suffering of the world.
May your cross of light illumine our crosses
and become for us a path to heaven.

Remember us, O Lord,
remember us.

You humbled yourself unto death,
death on the cross,
you, the Lord of glory.
The weak who are crushed by the powerful of this world,

Remember them, O Lord,
Remember them.

You were overwhelmed by sadness in Gethsemani,
you, the joy of the world.
Those who are overcome by sadness
and imprisoned in solitude,

Remember them, O Lord,
Remember them.

You were betrayed by the kiss of Judas,
you, the faithful friend.
The poor who are sold by their brothers and sisters,

Remember them, O Lord,
Remember them.

You were abandoned by all your Apostles,
you, the beloved Master.
The innocent who are unjustly imprisoned,

Remember them, O Lord,
Remember them.

You were denied by your apostle Peter,
you, the blessed Son of God.
Those who are betrayed in his love,

Remember them, O Lord,
Remember them.

You were condemned to death on the cross,
you, the life of the world.
Those who are unjustly accused and condemned,

Remember them, O Lord,
Remember them.

You were helped by Simon of Cyrene,
you, the strength of the faithful.
The friend who helps us to carry our cross,

Remember them, O Lord,
Remember them.

You were crucified in the midst of thieves,
you, the Sun of Justice.
Those who are persecuted for the sake of the Gospel,

Remember them, O Lord,
Remember them.

You died on the cross, abandoned by all,
you, the Savior of the world.
The innocent who are tortured to death,

Remember them, O Lord,
Remember them.

You were buried by Joseph of Arimathea,
you, the Resurrection of the world.
The friend who never forsakes his brother or sister,

Remember them, O Lord,
Remember them.

We want to bless you eternally,
Lord Jesus, who died for our sins
and rose for our life.
Give us the grace to take part in your Passion
by taking part in the suffering of our brothers and sisters.
To you be glory forever and ever. Amen.

NOTES TO PASSION SUNDAY

1. CF. Lk 22, 49; 22, 69-70; 23, 47. In the framework of a homily, one can only give the essential lines of Luke's message. On the characteristics native to Luke, see my *Synapse* (Paris: Desclée du Brouwer, 1975), pp. 266-271.
2. Compare Lk 22, 40-41 with Mk 14, 34-35.
3. Cf Lk 22, 54. Compare Lk, 1 with Mk 15, 1.
4. Cf. Lk 22, 63-65.
5. Compare Lk 23, 24-25 with Mk 15, 15-20.
6. Cf. M. Carrez, *Lesn langues de la Bible* (Paris: Le Centurion, 1983), p. 62.
7. Cf. Mt, 5, 9.
8. Compare Lk 23, 26 with Mk 15, 21.
9. Cf. Lk 23, 50-51
10. Cf. L. Deiss, *Synopse*, p. 349-350
11. Cf. Lk 23, 27-31.
12. Cf. Lk 23, 55-56 and 24, 1-8.
13. Ps 34, 6.
14. Cf. L. Deiss, *Synopse*, p. 346.
15. Cf. Lk 23, 4, 14 and 22.
16. Cf. Lk 23, 25. Pilate, however, in spite of the goodness of Luke in his regard, keeps his part of responsibility in the trial of Jesus.
17. Cf. Lk 23, 34.
18. Cf. Lk 22, 53.
19. Cf. Lk 22,51. It is Jn 18, 10-11 that specifies that the blow came from Peter and that the servant was called Malchus.

EASTER SUNDAY

READING I   ACTS 10, 34. 37-43

A reading from the Acts of the Apostles

Peter addressed the people in these words: "I take it you know what has been reported all over Judea about Jesus of Nazareth, beginning in Galilee with the baptism John preached; of the way God anointed him with the Holy Spirit and power. He went about doing good works and healing all who were in the grip of the devil, and God was with him. We are witnesses to all that he did in the land of the Jews and in Jerusalem. They killed him finally, 'hanging him on a tree,' only to have God raise him up on the third day and grant that he be seen, not by all, but only by such witnesses as had been chosen beforehand by God—by us who ate and drank with him after he rose from the dead. He commissioned us to preach to the people and to bear witness that he is the one set apart by God as judge of the living and the dead. To him all the prophets testify, saying that everyone who believes in him has forgiveness of sins through his name."

The Word of the Lord.

RESPONSORIAL PSALM   PS 118, 1-2. 16-17. 22-23

R/. (24) This is the day the Lord has made;
   let us rejoice and be glad.

Give thanks to the Lord, for he is good,
   for his mercy endures forever.
Let the house of Israel say,
   "His mercy endures forever."

R/. This is the day the Lord has made;
   let us rejoice and be glad.

"The right hand of the Lord has struck with power;
   the right hand of the Lord is exalted.
I shall not die, but live,
   and declare the works of the Lord.

R/. This is the day the Lord has made;
   let us rejoice and be glad.

The stone which the builders rejected
  has become the cornerstone.
By the Lord has this been done;
  it is wonderful in our eyes.

R/. This is the day the Lord has made;
  let us rejoice and be glad.

R/. Or: Alleluia.

READING II   COL 3, 1-4

A reading from the letter of Paul to the Colossians

Since you have been raised up in company with Christ, set your heart
on what pertains to higher realms where Christ is seated at God's right
hand. Be intent on things above rather than on things of earth. After all,
you have died! Your life is hidden now with Christ in God. When
Christ our life appears, then you shall appear with him in glory.

The Word of the Lord.

OR

READING II   I COR 5, 6-8

A reading from the first letter of Paul to the Corinthians

Do you not know that a little yeast has its effect all through the dough?
Get rid of the old yeast to make of yourselves fresh dough, unleavened
loaves, as it were; Christ our Passover has been sacrificed. Let us
celebrate the feast not with the old yeast, that of corruption and
wickedness, but with the unleavened bread of sincerity and truth.

The Word of the Lord.

GOSPEL   JN 20, 1-9

A reading from the holy gospel according to John

Early in the morning on the first day of the week, while it was still
dark, Mary Magdalene came to the tomb. She saw that the stone had
been moved away, so she ran off to Simon Peter and the other disciple
(the one Jesus loved) and told them, "The Lord has been taken from the
tomb! We don't know where they have put him!" At that, Peter and the
other disciple started out on their way toward the tomb. They were
running side by side, but then the other disciple outran Peter and
reached the tomb first. He did not enter but bent down to peer in, and

saw the wrappings lying on the ground. Presently, Simon Peter came along behind him and entered the tomb. He observed the wrappings on the ground and saw the piece of cloth which had covered the head not lying with the wrappings, but rolled up in a place by itself. Then the disciple who had arrived first at the tomb went in. He saw and believed. (Remember, as yet they did not understand the Scripture that Jesus had to rise from the dead.)

The gospel of the Lord.

INTRODUCTORY PRAYER

Alleluia! Christ is risen, the firstborn from the dead!
The springtime of God has come upon our earth;
the dawn of the Resurrection has risen upon our darkness,
the Paschal Lamb is leading us to the springs of life.
We give you thanks God our Father,
through your risen Son, Jesus Christ,
in the joy of the Holy Spirit.

We pray to you:
Renew our heart through your Holy Spirit;
help us to rise with your Son Jesus.
Lead us to the celebration of the eternal Passover
in your Kingdom, forever and ever. Amen.

HOMILY

1. Christ Is Risen!

"Christ is risen!" This song of joy of the angels at the tomb of the Resurrection[1] resounds today in all the Christian communities throughout the world. It proclaims the essential mystery of the Christian messasge: the Resurrection of Jesus.

However, the early biblical evidence is minimal. The most ancient Creed that was recited as a profession of baptismal faith around the years 35-40 was limited to these affirmations:

Christ died for our sins
according to the Scriptures.
He was placed in a tomb,
rose the third day
according to the scriptures
appeared to Peter, then to the Twelve.   1 Cor 15, 3-5

Mark's Gospel, in the most ancient ending,[2] devotes only nine verses to the Resurrection, and the evangelic text stops like a story that would not end:

The women went out and fled from the tomb, for they were all trembling and bewildered. They said nothing to anyone, for they were afraid.   Mk 16,8

The news of the Resurrection of Jesus burst forth in radiance in the heaven of sadness of the early community, and its dazzling brightness burned away all doubts.

At the Heart of the Christian Message

By raising Jesus of Nazareth, God in fact authenticates the whole of Jesus' message: His teaching and his miracles come from heaven. Furthermore, it is this resurrection which becomes the heart of the Good News.

Without Easter, Christianity would never have left the Jewish synagogues, and Christians would have nothing more to do than weep at the Wailing Wall while sighing with the pilgrims of Emmaus: "We were hoping that it was he who would deliver Israel. "[3] But today, faith in the Resurrection of Jesus has opened a road to eternity for all people.

Without Easter, the pithy statements of the Gospel regarding eternity would be hazy at best. For who would dare to affirm that the poor are happy if there were not a future resurrection? But today the poor know that they will obtain the Kingdom on the day of resurrection.

Easter, The Feast of Creation

Each year, the Church begins the feast of the Resurrection of Jesus with the reading of the account of creation; it is the first reading of the Paschal Vigil.

This bond between Easter and creation is very old. In Palestine, in the liturgies of the synagogue, the cycle of the readings was triennial (a little like today when we have the readings of cycles A, B, and C). The first year began in the paschal month of Nisan with the account of creation, the one that we read at the present time. It effectively tied together Passover or Easter and creation. Easter became the feast of creation. A very old homily explains:

> (Easter) is the time when God, artisan and creator of all things, created the universe. This then was the first flowering of creation, the beauty of the world.[5]

Easter, The Spring Feast

It is fitting to remember also that Passover in its origins, that is, before the feast was attached to the memory of the coming out of Egypt, was a spring feast. At the time when Israel was still nomadic, the flocks left their winter enclosures in the spring and went to seek new pastures. The departure was marked by the sacrifice of a lamb. Its blood was sprinkled over the spikes of the tents to drive away the "Destroyer,"[6] that is, the forces hostile to the flocks and the shepherds. The paschal lamb was eaten in a sacrificial meal that sealed the unity of the clan with God.

Later, in the era when Israel became sedentary, Passover became the feast of Unleavened Bread, bread without yeast. It was an agrarian feast which, in Cana, marked the beginning of the harvest. It was called "the feast of the Unleavened Bread for Yahweh."[7] Every piece of old bread was thrown away in order not to be mixed with the bread of the new harvest. The new bread, without yeast, was thought to be purer than the old bread whose dough had fermented.

These ancient feasts may appear like simple archeological curiosities. In reality, they are situated at the heart of our Christian life.

Christ and the New Creation

The old Passover was the feast of creation. The new Passover, Easter, is the feast of the risen Christ who carries the new creation in his body. In him, a little of our earthly dust has entered today into the light of God. In him, a little of the original clay from which we are formed has become "Son of God" for eternity.

And because he is "firstborn of all creation,"[8] and because the firstborn cannot be separated from his brothers and sisters, it is in him that our own body, formed from the same clay, today touches the stars. My own body is shown its sublime destiny, its eternal dwelling; not the dust in the endless night of a tomb, but life without end in the dazzling brightness of God.

How can I not also understand that I must, as Paul says, abandon "the old self"[9] with his decrepitude and his sin in order to rise a "new self" in the youth of Christ? Thus my body, since it came from the womb of my mother, is in genesis of eternity. This resurrection is realized progressively in the effort of each day toward the new life of Christ.

Christ, The Paschal Lamb

The old Passover was the spring feast when the nomadic shepherds offered the paschal lamb to the Lord. The new Passover, Easter, is the feast of the springtime of God when Christ offers himself to God as the Paschal Lamb of the new times. "Christ, our Passover, has been sacrificed,"[10] writes Paul quite plainly as if it were obvious for all Christians that Christ is the Paschal Lamb. Sacrificed as the Paschal Lamb, his blood drives away from our enclosure the "Destroyer" and all forces hostile to God and our happiness. Risen as the Shepherd, he leads his sheep to the pastures of an eternal spring:

The Lamb will be their Shepherd.
He will lead them to the springs of living water.
And God will wipe every tear from their eyes.   Rv 7, 17

How can we not understand each one of us is invited to leave the mired paths of the winter of our sins and to join the springlike pastures of God? To celebrate Easter is to offer oneself (as a lamb) like Christ by bearing our part of the sin of the world and walking with him like a shepherd by guiding our brothers and sisters through this world toward the sheepfold of God.

Christ, The Bread of God

The old Passover was the spring feast of Unleavened Bread, the bread without yeast, made with firstfruits of the harvest. The new Passover, Easter, is the risen Christ, the unleavened bread of the springtime of God, the true bread from heaven, the firstfruits of the harvest of humanity.

How can we not also understand that is no longer possible for us to mix in our life the old bread of sin with the bread of God; the old leaven and its moldiness with the bread of the new harvest? Paul explains:

Purify yourselves from the old yeast
and you will be a new dough
since you are without yeast.   1 Cor 5, 7

3. The Biblical Account of Creation

From the Babylonian tradition we have the poem *Enuma Elish* dating from the eleventh century which tells the story of the creation of the world. The gods are born from the union of Apsou, the male source, with Tiamat, the female source who bears wickedness in her womb. They fight among themselves in the Babylonian pantheon like street gangs. Then Marduk intervenes. He confronts the terrible Tiamat and her mob of monsters, the forces of evil and chaos. He conquers them, as he should. From the monstrous Tiamat he then creates heaven and earth. Each year, on the feast of the Babylonian New Year, the high priest of Esagil would recite this poem of creation, and this liturgical recitation was thought to open the door to springlike renewal.[11]

This Babylonian poem of astonishing length (seven tablets of about one hundred fifty verses each) does not lack poetic grandeur. But what an abyss there is between this account of combat among the gods, of battles and monsters, and the biblical poem, calm as a dawn of spring, where God creates the universe in the peace of his word! Like a litany of praise to the glory of God and his Word, the story of creation is told to us in six stanzas. Each stanza ends with a refrain:

There was evening:
there was morning.
And God saw that it was good.

There is no trace of dualism, as if matter were evil and the spirit good. Creation is not the corpse of the goddess Tiamat; creation is the daughter of the living God. It bears witness in its way to the goodness of God:

God created all beings so that they might exist.
The creatures of the world are wholesome;
there is no deadly poison in them.   Ws 1, 14

From the beginning, therefore, we are warned that a Christian, under the pretext of spiritualism should never despise or ignore the world and its beauty. That would be directly opposed to the plan of God.

The Feast of Light

The first stanza of the poem of creation sings about light:

God said: "Let there be light!"
And there was light.
God saw that the light was good.   Gn 1, 3-4

The old Passover was the feast of light. It was said that it was the "eternal Day." The sun shone twelve hours during the day, and the full moon, twelve hours during the night.

The new Passover, Easter, is the feast of Christ, the Light of God in the new creation. Through his Resurrection on the vernal equinox, Jesus becomes the sun and "life and immortality shine brightly."[12] An old hymn sings about this night clearer than day:

> O night brighter than day,
> O night more dazzling than the sun,
> O night more sparkling than the snow,
> O night more brilliant than our lamps!
> O night sweeter than paradise...
> O night that makes us keep watch with the angels...
> O night in which the Heir
> brings the heirs into their heritage![13]

In the Paschal Vigil, the blessing of the new fire and the paschal candle celebrates Christ, the light. By entering into the church following the paschal candle, we signify that Christ guides us in the darkness of our path to God. By lighting our candles from the flame of the paschal candle, we affirm that our life, extinguished for a moment at the hours of our death, will be relighted at its resurrection. By celebrating the paschal Eucharist, we bear witness that we are walking to that eternal Passover in the heavenly Jerusalem about which it is said:

> It can do without the glare of the sun
> and that of the moon,
> for the glory of God illuminates it
> and the Lamb is its lamp.   Rv 21, 23

The Feast of Humanity

The crowning of the poem of Genesis is the creation of humanity:

> Let us make humankind in our image
> and in our likeness.   Gn 1, 26

We are looking upon a divine deliberation. God speaks out before his heavenly court; he is profoundly engaged in the creative act.

Man is the translation of the Hebrew *Adam*. It is a collective name that designates all of humanity. Adam is never used in the plural.

Easter Sunday

In the Babylonian poem *Enuma Elish*, the creation of humanity is related in this way:

Marduk decided to create a beautiful work.
He speaks out loud to the god Ea
and advises him about what he had said to himself:
"I want to make a network of blood, to form a skeleton,
and to construct a human being and that his name be Man!
I want to create (this) human being, (this) Man,
so that, charged with the service of the gods,
they may be in peace.[14]

Humanity, then, is created to free the gods from the drudgery of service. What a difference from the poem from the Bible where Adam appears not as a flunkey of the gods and a groom of the pantheon, but as the image of the only God and reflection of his splendor:

God created people in his image,
in the image of God, he created them.   Gn 1, 27

When reflecting on this image of God in people, we must neither spiritualize it excessively, or clericalize it, reducing it to the spiritual nature of people. Nothing in biblical anthropology allows the separation of the body from the soul, the carnal from the spiritual. According to the Bible, we do not have a body on one hand a soul on the other; we are body-and-soul. Therefore it is in the unity of his person that he is the image of God.

Biblical tradition affirmed that "in the paradise of God, (Adam) was full of wisdom and marvelous with beauty."[15] Jewish tradition believed that he had been created in full youth, in the splendor of his twenties. The beauty of his hair reflected that of the trees of the forest; the brilliance of his tears, that of the rivers, and the charm of his mouth recalled the infinity of the ocean...[16]

Just as Nebudchadnezzar set up his statue of gold in the plain of Dura to symbolize his presence there and to receive the hommage of his subjects,[17] thus God placed humanity, in the divine image, on earth, and that image reflects God's reign and the splendor of his majesty. Of course, the Creator remains the Master of the universe, but he delegates his "command" to people, his image:

Let them be the master
of the fish of the sea, of the birds of heaven,
of the livestock and of all the wild animals.   Gn 1, 26

Speaking in this way about Adam, are we not forgetting Christ Jesus? How could we since he is the perfect Adam? He stands before Adam as the model before the image, as the Firstborn before his brothers, even more as eternity before time, as the Son of God before the son of man.

> He is the image of the invisible God,
> firstborn of all creatures
> Col 1, 15

sings the hymn of the Letter to the Colossians.

The old Passover was the feast of the first Adam, created in the image of God. The new Passover, Easter, is the feast of the new Adam, the Image of God. Risen, "firstborn from the dead,"[18] he leads all his brothers and sisters into the glory of heaven.

Who can understand this marvel? Our future resurrection is not the simple revivification of a cadaver as was the resurrection of Lazarus or that of the twelve-year-old daughter of Jairus. By calling them back to life, Jesus in fact calls them not to a better life, but to the same life of anguish that they had just left. But in the Resurrection of Easter, Jesus leads humanity into the world of God. We is not freed from our corporeality as Plato wished. He thought that the body was a carnal rag, a prison for the immortal soul. Easter is not the feast of the immortality of the soul, but the resurrection of the whole human person. Nothing of humanity is lost. Everything is glorified. No smile is lost; no joy or love is lost. Neither is any tear lost, those precious tears that God collects in his wineskin, as the psalm says,[19] and that his love transforms into pearls of joy and eternity.

Thus, at the heart of the world is this body of the risen Christ; greater than the world. At the heart of matter is this Christ, indwelt by the Spirit. At the heart of time, there is the Christ of eternity. From earthly dust is born the Son of God. From weakness surges glory. From death rises eternal life.[20]

How can we thank you, Lord Jesus, for so many marvels!

The Feast of Man and Woman

God is the author of sexual differentiation. It is said:

> Male and female he created them.

The individual is truly "human" only in the unity of this sexual diversity. This is affirmed here with majestic simplicity. There is no trace of sexual anguish in the sacred text, even less no divinization of sex as in the Babylonian religions, nor any requirement of particular asceticism in regard to sex.

Easter Sunday

There is also in Genesis the affirmation of beauty, even of a certain splendor of sexuality. Actually, after each work, God stops, turns around so to speak, and contemplates it:

God saw that it was good.

After the creation of man and women, it is said:

God saw all that he had made.
It was very good. Gn 1, 31

The Hebrew *tob*, "good," is rendered in the Greek translation of the Septuagint by the word *kalos* which signifies more precisely beautiful. We know that Greek likes to unite the two concepts of good and beauty. There is even a word, *kalokagathia*, which signifies *beauty-goodness* at the same time.

One day when I was speaking about *kalokagathia* in a homily, a man—perhaps in his seventies—came to me after Mass and asked me: "Do you know what I call have called my wife since we were married? My kalokagathia, my beautiful-and-my-good."

According to God's Word, sexuality is good. It is even very good. One can also add that it is beautiful. That, more than any other creation, it bears the reflection of the splendor of God. A man who does not know how to respect, admire, and love a woman is not worthy of God. And the one who respects, admires, and loves a woman is in the plan of God. This is also true for women in regard to men.[21]

Of course, the author is not naïve to the point of believing that the male-female union is always a source of paradisical happiness. The Bible presents a whole litany of wicked women—and also perverse men—with whom it is preferable not to live under the same roof. But the wickedness of the creature cannot defile creation: it only defiles the one who is wicked and forgets to love.

On this feast of the Resurrection where love was stronger than death, let us pray the each gesture of human love, the most humble as well as the most sublime, may become a path of resurrection, a road to eternity.

Creation and the Eternal Easter

The look of God upon his creation is one of astonishing optimism. For him, the earth is really a path to heaven. This long story that passes through the whole Bible, a story which is holier than one could imagine since it empties onto the eternal shores and upon the Son of God, begins with the creation of the earth, the sea, light, plants, animals, man, and woman. According to God, it is the earth that prepares heaven, creation that prepares redemption, nature that prepares grace.

The attitude of a Christian can therefore only be one of wonder, joy, and praise before creation. Whoever does not admire creation is not worthy to contemplate the beauty of God on the day of eternity. Whoever does not know how to admire spring and its roses cannot celebrate the eternal Easter and its flowers of heaven.

May the glory of the Lord be forever!
The Lord rejoices in his works.   Ps 104, 31

May we imitate our creator. May we give him glory! May we rejoice in his works! And on the days of suffering, may we remember that death itself is a path to the eternal Easter.

Toward the New Heavens and the New Earth

The refrain "God said" is repeated ten times in the poem of Genesis. These ten creative words prefigure the ten words of Sinai where God creates the people of the Covenant. The Word is the bond that unites God to his creation and his people.

In Jesus this bond became a bond of love. Summing up the creative work of God, the Psalm affirms:

The earth is full of the love of the Lord.   Ps 33, 5

If this word of the Psalm is true, if it is certain that the whole earth is full of God's love, then it is also true that God's love dwells in the heart of the jonquils and in the clusters of the foxtails, in the bell flowers of the cowslips which chime in the spring, and in the lace petticoat which adorns the fern, in the laughter of the nightingale rising early to sing matins, and in the leap of the gazelle which leaps in the savannah, in the quivering light of Andromeda which has cried out the glory of God for billions of years...Yes, if this word is true, then the love of God dwells also in our heart.

237

The day will come when the trumpet will sound for the eternal Easter, when the sabbath which concludes the last day of creation will begin for eternity, when the first day of the new heavens and the new earth will be born "where justice will dwell,"[22] when God will be "all in all,"[23] when the whole world and what is most precious in the world, the heart of each man and each woman, will overflow with that love.

Then we will cry out with joy, we will sing, we will dance with creation which has become forever fraternal, fully paschal. How will we dance? I do not know exactly. I simply know that God is infinitely more marvelous that we could ever imagine.

Alleluia! To him glory forever! Amen.

CONCLUDING PRAYER

We praise you, O risen Christ,
the true springtime of God which shines
on the winter of the world.
Make the flowers of eternal joy
bloom in the garden of our heart.

Alleluia! Alleluia!

We praise you, O risen Christ!
the new dawn of the day without end
and sun of joy
Make the light of eternal life
shine on the darkness of our mornings.

Alleluia! Alleluia!

We praise you, O risen Christ!
the Paschal Lamb of the feast of spring
and our royal Shepherd.
Lead us to the springs of living water,
to the pastures of eternal spring.

Alleluia! Alleluia!

We praise you, O risen Christ!
the true bread of God, kneaded from the first fruits
of the new harvest.
Purify us from the old yeast,
and fill us with your eternal youth.

Alleluia! Alleluia!

We praise you, O risen Christ,
the Firstborn from the dead
splendor of eternal glory.
Open the tombs of our death
onto eternal peace.

Alleluia! Alleluia!

We praise you, O risen Christ,
the smile of heaven on our earth
and tenderness of the Father.
Be the bond of love which seals
the union of man and woman
for the eternal feast.

Alleluia! Alleluia!

Your Resurrection, Lord Jesus, created
the new heavens and the new earth.
Open for us the doors of paradise
for the celebration of the eternal Easter
near your Father,
in communion with the Spirit of love,
forever and ever. Amen

NOTES TO EASTER SUNDAY

1. Lk 24,6
2. Exegesis unanimously recognizes today that the second ending of Mark (16,9-20), which recapitulates several apparitions, was not part of the early Gospel. Therefore it is not authentic (that is, it is not from Mark's hand) but nevertheless remains canonical (the Church recognizes it as inspired in the same way as the whole of Mark).
3. Lk 24, 21
4. See L. Deiss, *Springtime of the Liturgy* (Collegeville, Minn.: The Liturgical Press, 1979), pp. 99-100.
5. See *Homélies Pascales*, SC 27 (1950), p. 145.
6. Ex 12, 23
7. Lv 23, 6. The texts of the Priestly source distinguish the two feasts (Lv 23, 5-14; Nm 28, 16-17). Deuteronomy unites them (Dt 16, 1-8).
8. Col 1, 15.
9. See Rom 6, 6
10. 1 Cor 5, 7.

11. See the text in *Les religions du Proche-Orient*, (Paris: Ed. Fayard-Denoel, 1970), pp. 38-70.

In the text of Genesis, two accounts of creation are distinguished:

–The first, (Gn 1, 1-4, 4a—the one we read) comes from the source called Priestly. It dates from the period of the Exile (around the sixth century)

–The second (Gn 2, 4b-25) comes from the source called Yahwist (God is called Yahweh) and dates from about 950.

These two accounts undoubtedly convey the oldest doucments. They reflect the accounts that were told of old under the tents of Abraham, in the Judean countryside, and in the Babylonian exile. They in no way present the scientific origin of humanity, an origin that God entrusts to our research. But they give a religious teaching of permanent value on God and on our destiny.

12. 2 Tm 1, 10.
13. See L. Deiss, *Springtime of the Liturgy*, pp. 259-260.
14. *Les religions du Proche-Orient* p. 59.
15. See Ez 28, 12.
16. See L. Ginzberg, *The Legends of the Jews*, vol. 1 (Philadelphia: The Jewish Publication Society of America, 1937), pp. 54-62.
17. See Dn 3, 1.
18. Col 1, 18.
19. See Ps 56, 9.
20. See 1 Cor 15, 42-43.
21. The sexual plan can be passed over but only for a superior reason "in view of the Kingdom of heaven" (Mt 19, 12). It can never be ignored, even less disparaged.
22. 2 Pt 3, 13.
23. 1 Cor 15, 28.

SECOND SUNDAY OF EASTER

READING I   ACTS 5, 12-16

A reading from the Acts of the Apostles

Through the hands of the apostles, many signs and wonders occurred
among the people. By mutual agreement they used to meet in
Solomon's Portico. No one else dared to join them, despite the fact that
the people held them in great esteem Nevertheless more and more
believers, men and women in great numbers, were continually added to
the Lord. The people carried the sick into the streets and laid them on
cots and mattresses, so that when Peter passed by at least his shadow
might fall on one or another of them. Crowds from the towns around
Jerusalem would gather, too, bringing their sick and those who were
troubled by unclean spirits, all of whom were cured.

The Word of the Lord.

RESPONSORIAL PSALM   Ps 118, 2-4. 13-15. 22-24

R/. (1) Give thanks to the Lord for he is good,
  his love is everlasting.

Let the house of Israel say,
  "His mercy endures forever."
Let the house of Aaron say,
  "His mercy endures forever."
Let those who fear the Lord say,
  "His mercy endures forever."

R/. Give thanks to the Lord for he is good,
  his love is everlasting.

I was hard pressed and was falling,
  but the Lord helped me.
My strength and my courage is the Lord,
  and he has been my savior.
The joyful shout of victory
  in the tents of the just:

R/. Give thanks to the Lord for he is good,
  his love is everlasting.

The stone which the builders rejected
  has become the cornerstone.

241

By the Lord has this been done;
　it is wonderful in our eyes.
This is the day the Lord has made;
　let us be glad and rejoice in it.

R/. Give thanks to the Lord for he is good,
　his love is everlasting.

R/. Alleluia.

READING II   Rv 1, 9-11. 12-13. 17-19

A reading from the book of Revelation

I, John, your brother, who share with you the distress and the kingly
reign and the endurance we have in Jesus, found myself on the island
called Patmos because I proclaimed God's word and bore witness to
Jesus. On the Lord's day I was cought up in ecstasy, and I heard behind
me a piercing voice like the sound of a trumpet, which said, "Write on
a scroll what you now see." I turned around to see whose voice it was
that spoke to me. When I did so I saw seven lampstands of gold, and
among the lampstands One like a Son of Man wearing an ankle-length
robe, with a sash of gold about his breast.

When I caught sight of him I fell down at his feet as though dead. He
touched me with his right hand and said: "There is nothing to fear. I am
the First and the Last and the One who lives. Once I was dead but now
I live—forever and ever. I hold the keys of death and the nether world.
Write down, therefore, whatever you see in visions—what you see now
and will see in time to come."

The Word of the Lord.

GOSPEL   JN 20, 19-31

A reading from the holy gospel according to John

On the evening of that first day of the week, even though the disciples
had locked the doors of the place where they were for fear of the Jews,
Jesus came and stood before them. "Peace be with you," he said. When
he had said this, he showed them his hands and his side. At the sight of
the Lord the disciples rejoiced. "Peace be with you," he said again.

　"As the Father has sent me,
　so I send you."
　Then he breathed on them and said:

"Receive the Holy Spirit.
If you forgive men's sins,
they are forgiven them;
if you hold them bound,
they are held bound."

It happened that one of the Twelve, Thomas (the name means "Twin"), was absent when Jesus came. The other disciples kept telling him: "We have seen the Lord!" His answer was, "I'll never believe it without probing the nail-prints in his hands, without putting my finger in the nail-marks and my hand into his side."

A week later, the disciples were once more in the room, and this time Thomas was with them. Despite the locked doors, Jesus came and stood before them. "Peace be with you," he said; then, to Thomas: "Take your finger and examine my hands. Put your hand into my side. Do not persist in your unbelief, but believe!" Thomas said in response, "My Lord and my God!" Jesus then said to him:
"You became a believer because you saw me."
Blest are they who have not seen and have believed."
Jesus performed many other signs as well—signs not recorded here—in the presence of his disciples. But these have been recorded to help you believe that Jesus is the Messiah, the Son of God, so that through this faith you may have life in his name.

The gospel of the Lord.

INTRODUCTORY PRAYER

We bless, you, Lord Jesus.
Throughout the week
you have kept us in the joy of your Resurrection.
We pray to you:
Come into the midst of our community
again today
and say to us, as you said of old to your disciples:
"Peace be with you!"
Then, with one heart and one soul
we will celebrate the power of your love
forever and ever. Amen.

HOMILY

1. Behold, I Am Alive Forever and Ever

On this octave Sunday of Easter, the liturgy begins the the Book of Revelation. This book, sparkling with images of savage beauty shines the light of the risen Christ on the Christian community. Its message of hope and joy is going to accompany us up to Pentecost and thus prepare us for the coming of the Holy Spirit.

The interpretation of this book is sometimes difficult, because we are not very familiar with the apocalyptic literary style and with the images used. Here are a few introductory remarks.

Revelation

The Greek work *apokalypsis* from which we derive our word apocalypse signifies literally a re-velation, that is, a taking away of the veil *(velum)* which covers hidden mysteries. In the apocalyptic literature which flourished around the time of Christ, these mysteries ordinarily concerned events which called to mind the destiny of the people of God and the irruption of the end times. The very title of the Revelation is presented in this way:

> The revelation (apocalypse) of Jesus Christ:
> God gave it to him
> to show his servants
> what must take place soon.
> He made it known by sending his angel
> to his servant John.   Rv 1, 1

Author

The author is named John and is described as a prophet.[1] But nowhere is he identified with the apostle John from the group of the Twelve. In fact, the tradition of the first three centuries is not unanimous in attributing Revelation to the apostle John; the analysis of the vocabulary and the theological themes common to the Gospel and to the Revelation does not allow definite conclusions to be drawn.

Therefore we find ourselves presented with three questions: Who is John, the author of Revelation? Who is this "beloved disciple," presented as the author of the Gospel? Is John, the author of Revelation, and the beloved disciple identifiable with the apostle John from the group of the Twelve?

The mist of the past has covered these questions with a veil of beauty and has simplified them to the extreme: all the Johanine literature comes from the apostle John. Present biblical criticism (for perfectly valid reasons) has put in doubt these old certitudes; it is humbly seeking the truth.

Concerning the Book of Revelation, present thinking speaks not about a single author, but rather about a tradition or a "Johannine" community gathered around John.[2] That community could have left Palestine after the year 66 or 70, moving to Ephesus. Its literary activity, supported by John, is going to extend for a period of time starting from the year 80. It will end after the death of John at the beginning of the second century.

Date

The Church of the Revelation was under persecution. The first century knew two persecutions: that of Nero and that of Domitian. We can therefore propose as a date for Revelation either the period following the persecution of Nero and the ruin of Jerusalem (65-70), or the years at the end of the reign of Domitian (81-96). If we admit several redactional levels in Revelation—which would explain the presence of numerous doublets—we can place the final edition of the Book of Revelation toward the end of the first century. We know that ancient tradition, recorded by Irenaeus,[3] puts John's death during the reign of Trajan (98-117).

The Problem of Christian Hope

By the year 95, the Christian community had at its disposal all the literature of the New Testament. What then was the new revelation that the Book of Revelation could offer?

After two thousand years of Christian existence, we can hardly imagine the problems of faith and especially of hope posed by the situation in which the Church was struggling after the death of Jesus. An outburst of hatred and violence, as much on the part of the old synogague as on the part of Roman power, was unleashed upon the Christians; it threatened to make them lose heart.

Jesus had been enthroned as King and Lord by his Resurrection from the dead. But the persecutions of Nero and Domitian continued to slaughter the faithful; they burned like torches in the public gardens of Rome.

Jesus had triumphantly gone up to heaven, escorted by the angels; he had opened a door of hope into Paradise. But while waiting, the faithful suffered atrociously on earth, devoured by lions in circus games.

Jesus had sent the Spirit of Pentecost whose effusion was to mark the end times. In his first homily, Peter had said with ardor: "The last days have arrived!" And resting upon the prophecy of Joel, he added that one would see "wonders above in heaven, signs here below on earth, of blood, fire and a column of smoke…" Undoubtedly he also hoped in his innermost heart that the wicked would be punished; that would be good for them! But how long in coming was this "Great and glorious day of the lord!"[4] How far it seemed from the word of Jesus: "Courage! I have overcome the world!"[5] For, while waiting, it was the wicked who seemed to triumph. Rome continued to impose through force and diffused across the empire the idolatrous cult of its defiled emperors.

According to Peter's letter,[6] Christians form "the chosen people, the holy nation, the people that God obtained to proclaim his praises." But according to Tacitus,[7] they were considered as an "execrable superstition," and he adds: "In order to silence the rumors relative to the burning of Rome, Nero blamed the individuals detested for their abominations, whom the common herd calls Christian." Later, they were even accused of incestuous morals, of orgiastic banquets involving the immolation and eating of little children.[8] What a pity!

Jesus was the Lord of history. But in the eyes of the world, history was in the process of triumphing over the Lord of history.

And the question rises in the heart: "Risen Jesus, where are you?"

That was the question being asked around the year 95, at the turn of the first century. It is the question that we are asking today, at the turn of the twentieth century.

We have celebrated Easter; we have sung "Alleluia!" We have bought our spring clothes; we have put on a smile. Our whole being has rejoiced with the song: "This is the day the lord has made, let us rejoice and be glad!" A week has gone by. What remains of our Alleluias? Where is Jesus in our life? Where is his Resurrection?

Of course, we have not been exposed to the lions of the circus, but "our adversary the devil is prowling like a roaring lion seeking someone to devour."[9] Who can say that they have never been bitten? We have not been thrown into dungeons for Christ, but we remain imprisoned in our shabbiness. And how many of our brothers and sisters in the world are awaiting their deliverance? "Remember those who are imprisoned," says the Letter to the Hebrews, "as if you were prisoners with them."[10] We may not have been slandered for orgiastic or incestuous practices, but now how rare are those who believe in the holiness of the institution of the Church! In a word, when we consider the personal history of each one of us or the general history of the Christian community, can we say that this history is progressing in joy towards the definitive victory of God in us?

It is to that question that the Revelation responds.

Do Not Be Afraid (Rv 1, 17)

"Do not be afraid": This is the first answer of the Revelation.

Of course, the coming of the Son of Man who holds seven stars in his hands, whose mouth pronounces judgment cutting as a double-edged sword, whose face shines like the most brilliant sun,[11] is a vision of glory and infinite majesty which makes a creature tremble. And it is true; the wicked who refuse to come back to God will die of fright when the risen Christ comes.

> And on earth will come an agony of nations, tormented by the
> noise of the sea and the surf. Men will faint from fear and anxiety
> over what is coming on the earth. Lk 21, 25-26

But for those who seek the Lord by serving him in the simplicity of their heart, the coming of God is the coming of his joy and his peace in their hearts. Jesus says to us today as he said to John: "Do not be afraid! Do not fear to meet God! Do not be afraid to encounter love! Your life is going toward a feast, toward eternity. It is maturing in affliction; it is preparing a harvest for eternity!"

I Was Dead, but Behold, I Am Alive (Rv 1, 18)

A man who died hanging on a cross, his heart pierced by the lance of the centurion, who was buried in the tomb of Joseph of Arimathea, this man, Jesus, is risen. We all come back to the dust of the tomb. That is our last dwelling. It is said in the psalm:

(Lord), you make mortals return to dust
by saying: "Return, sons of Adam!"   Ps 90, 3

But Jesus came back to life. And he proclaims: "Behold, I am alive forever, for the eternity of God. I hold the keys to the sojurn of the dead. And because I am 'firstborn from the dead' and Son of man, because you are my brothers and sisters, I am leading all of you into the eternity of God!"

To the Christians at the time of the persecutions of Nero and Domitian, as to the Christians of our time martyred by incessant human wickedness or by their own weaknesses, the Revelation brings the judgment of God. Death is no longer the last word on human destiny; it is a passage toward life. The dust on the tomb is no longer our ultimate dwelling; it is the expectation of the new heavens and the new earth. Sufferings, persecutions, and martyrdom are paths toward the Kingdom. The intensity of present trials indicates entrance into the Kingdom:

We must pass through many trials
to enter into the Kingdom of God.   Acts 14, 22

I Am the Alpha and the Omega: I Am the First and the Last

Jesus says, "I am the Master of the history of the world, the Master also of the history of your life. I am the Alpha, that is, the First, the beginning. It is in me that everything was created. Therefore your own life was also created in me; it is in me that life takes its source. I am also the Omega, the end, the Last. It is in me that everything finds its completion for life eternal. I am the eternity of your own life. No matter what Neros and Domitians are persecuting you, you are going toward the meeting with your Father. This world sometimes writhes in pain. But this is not the pain of death but the pain of the birth of new heavens and the new earth."

"As I am the triumph of poor Achilles." Now, this Achilles was a little "retarded." He had forgotten to grow intellectually. We welcomed him through charity into our major seminary. Nevertheless Achilles knew how to wash the dishes.

One evening, while he was watching television and smoking a cigarette after dinner, he put his hand over his heart. He breathed a sigh: "Ah!" Then he closed his eyes. Or rather he opened them to the splendor of God. And the Father of heaven said to him: "Come now, Achilles, dishwashing is over! Come into my arms. I am your Father! I did not give you many joys in your life, but you are now in the midst of eternal joy! I did not fill you with much intelligence, but now you understand as much as the professors with swelled heads who sleep next to you in the cemetery. Nor did I give you many friends; now you have entered into the family of heaven; you are my child." And innocent Achilles was quite surprised, I imagine, to find himself singing these words from the Book of Revelation:

I saw the new Jerusalem
come down from heaven from God,
beautiful as a bride adorned for her husband...
No more death, no more tears,
no more crying nor pain,
for the old world has passed away! Rv 21, 2, 4

Endurance with Jesus

In the last combats which put the faithful in opposition to the powers of Evil, the key to victory is perseverance, endurance with Jesus. John is called our brother and our companion "in endurance with Jesus."

The Greek term that we translate as "endurance" or "perseverance" is *hypomone*. The word is delightful. It means literally "to remain" *(menein)* "under" *(hypo),* whence the meaning of perseverance or endurance. We find ourselves placed under persecutions, under trials, under wickedness; we receive them on the head. It is as though we were under the gutter of a roof that is pouring out the torments of persecutors. But we hold out. It is an obstinate endurance which surmounts the test of duration because it is rooted in hope and confidence in God.[12] In the family of Christian virtues, perseverance and hope are sister virtues. Paul speaks about the "perseverance of hope."[13] It is in this perseverance that the secret of Christian fruitfulness is found. Perseverance is the last word in the explanation of the parable of the sower:

That which is sown in good soil are those who, having heard the Word in a beautiful and good heart, keep it and bear fruit with perseverance. Lk 8, 15

That was precisely the endurance of Jesus: "He endured *(hypemeinen)* the cross unto death, then bore his fruit in the Resurrection." That is also the condition of the believer crucified by persecutions. John says to us with fascinating candor:

Whoever must perish chained,
let him be chained!
Whoever must perish by the sword,
let him perish by the sword!
Here is the endurance and faith of the saints.   Rv 13, 10

We call to mind that chapters two and three of the Book of Revelation present the seven letters that John addresses to the seven Churches. In the numerology of the time the number seven indicated plentitude or totality. Beyond the seven Churches, the universal Church is designated. Now, in Revelation, perseverance *(hypomone)* is mentioned exactly seven times. The plentitude of the victory of the Church takes place in the plentitude of her perseverance!

And what then is the root that bears this marvelous hope as a flower? What then is this foundation upon which we can place the rock of our hope? Paul explains:

It is love
that endures *(hypomeinei)* everything.   1 Cor 13, 7

It is love that makes us hold out when we find ourselves under gutters that pour upon us torrential rains of persecutions, and love that makes us persevere until the sun of Christ returns.

It is love that makes us hope beyond death that the smile of the Risen will shine upon us and illuminate our night.

It is love that makes us cry: "Lord Jesus, radiant Morning Star, shine at last in our heart! Yes, come, Lord Jesus!"[14]

2. The Community of The Risen

"With one heart" is the refrain that comes back in the song that describes the life of the early community. In the first description of the community, Luke writes:

With one heart *(homothymadon)* they returned each day to the temple.
They broke bread in their homes, eating in joy and
simplicity of heart.   Acts 2, 46

In the second description, he notes likewise:

> The multitude of the believers had only one heart and
> one soul.
>   Acts 4, 32

Finally, in today's text he says:

> They all stood with one heart *(homothymadon)* under Solomon's
> Portico.
>   Acts 5, 12

Undoubtedly Luke idealizes somewhat. We know that the early community experienced tensions. Luke does not hide the conflicts. But here he is setting forth the idyllic image of the community of the Risen. It is a union of hearts, a communion of souls.

Of course, we are not talking here about dissolving one's personality in the community for the sake of a certain loving mimicry that would like us Christians to be sheep bearing the same wool and being shorn the same day. Rather it is a matter of each one bringing his or her personal riches to enrich the whole of the ecclesial community.

A Radiant Community

Luke insists on the radiance of the community in the service of the people. It is a radiance of beauty, grace, and goodness.

> They found a favorable welcome with all the people. Acts 2, 47
> They all enjoyed great favor.   Acts 4, 33
> All the people eulogized them.   Acts 5, 13

This Sunday's Reading adds further this extraordinary scene:

> They went so far as to bring the sick into the streets by placing
> them on beds and pallets: thus, when Peter passed, he would
> touch one or the other with his shadow.   Acts 5, 16

The most astonished person in this story had to be Peter himself: To have a shadow that healed the sick, a healing shadow!

Perhaps you heard about an incident which took place in India: An untouchable, a pariah, was killed because he had the audacity to allow his shadow to fall on a man of high class. When hate or contempt reigns, everything becomes crazy. When love triumphs, everything becomes grace.

I think that we will never have a healing shadow like Peter. However, we must have a healing presence; I mean a presence that alleviates pain, that eases agony, and that drives away sadness.

Conclusion

This is "the Day of the Lord" when John saw the heavens open and heard the words of the Revelation.[15]

It is also the Day of the Lord, Sunday, when we contemplate in our Sunday assembly the Risen Christ and hear his word of life.

But, if we wish, all days can be "Days of the Lord" for us. For it is at each moment that Jesus says to us: "Do not be afraid! I am the Living One. And I remain with you!"

Can we answer any better than with these words from the Book of Revelation?

To the one who loves us,
who delivered us from our sins by his blood,
who made of us a kingdom
of priests for is God and Father,
to him glory and power
for ever and ever! Amen.

CONCLUDING PRAYER

With one heart and one soul
let us implore the risen Christ.

My Lord and my God!

O risen Christ,
in the word that is proclaimed to us.
May it resound in our hearts
like a song of spring.
Then, with Thomas, we will be able to acclaim you:

My Lord and my God!

Reveal to us your presence,
O risen Christ,
you are the Alpha and the Omega,
the love of our life and its eternity
the first to love us
the last smile at our death.
With Thomas, we acclaim you:

My Lord and my God!

O risen Christ,
you are the Living One; you awaken
those who sleep in the land of dust.
Take us away from the grasp of death.
Save us in the eternity of your life.
With Thomas, we acclaim you:

My Lord and my God!

O risen Christ,
you hold the keys to the sojurn of death.
Bolt the dungeons of wickedness;
open for us the door of happiness.
Save us in the eternity of your joy.
With Thomas, we acclaim you:

My Lord and my God!

O risen Christ,
you are our Peace;
you destroy hate
and you reconcile earth and heaven.
Save us in the eternity of your peace.
With Thomas, we acclaim you:

My Lord and my God!

Your hand, Lord Jesus, imprisons the stars,
and your face is more radiant than a springtime sun.
Save us in the eternity
of the new heavens and the new earth.
With Thomas, we will then acclaim you eternally:

My Lord and my God!

Amen.

NOTES TO SECOND SUNDAY OF EASTER

1. See Rv 1, 13, 4 and 22, 8.
2. One leaves open the question of knowing if the disciple "that Jesus loved" is really the apostle John from the group of the Twelve.
3. See *Against Heresies*, II, 22, 5.
4. See Acts, 2, 17-20.
5. Jn 16, 33.
6. 1 Pt 2, 9.
7. See *Annales* XV, 44.
8. These are the accusations that are told to us by Minucius Felix in *Octavius* IX, 6; XXXI,1-2. On this subject see J. Daniélou and H. Marrou, *Nouvelle Histoire de L'Eglise*, vol. I, (Paris: Ed. du Seuil, 1963), pp. 112-127.
9. 1 Pt 5. 8.
10. Heb 13, 3.
11. See Rv 1, 16.
12. In the Septuagint, *hyupomone* is the regular translation of the Hebrew *gâwah* (or one of its derivatives), which expressed the idea of waiting, of intense desire, whence the idea of hope and of trust. In the New Testament, *hypomone* is found sixteen times in Paul, twice in Luke, and never in Matthew, Mark or John.
13. See 1 Thes 1, 3 and 2 Thes 1, 4.
14. Cf. Rv 22, 16, 20.
15. See Rv 1, 10.

THIRD SUNDAY OF EASTER

READING I ACTS 5, 27-32, 40-41

A reading from the Acts of the Apostles

The high priest began the interrogation of the apostles in this way: "We gave you strict orders not to teach about that name, yet you have filled Jerusalem with your teaching and are determined to make us responsible for that man's blood." To this, Peter and the apostles replied: "Better for us to obey God than men! The God of our fathers has raised up Jesus whom you put to death, 'hanging him on a tree.' He whom God has exalted at his right hand as ruler and savior is to bring repentance to Israel and forgiveness of sins. We testify to this. So too does the Holy Spirit, whom God has given to those that obey him." The Sandhedrin ordered the apostles not to speak again about the name of Jesus, and afterward dismissed them. The apostles for their part left the Sanhedrin full of joy that they had been judged worthy of ill-treatment for the sake of the Name.

The Word of the Lord.

RESPONSORIAL PSALM Ps 30, 2. 4. 5-6. 11-12. 13

R/. (2) I will praise you, Lord,
   for you have rescued me.

I will extol you, O Lord, for you drew me clear
   and did not let my enemies rejoice over me.
O Lord, you brought me up from the nether world;
   you preserved me from among those going down into the pit.

R/. I will praise you Lord,
   for you have rescued me.

Sing praise to the Lord, you his faithful ones,
   and give thanks to his holy name.
For his anger lasts but a moment;
   a lifetime, his good will.
At nightfall, weeping enters in,
   but with the dawn, rejoicing.

R/. I will praise you, Lord
   for you have rescued me.

Hear, O Lord, and have pity on me;
  O Lord, be my helper.
You changed my mourning into dancing;
  O Lord, my God, forever will I give you thanks.

R/. I will praise you, Lord,
  for you have rescued me.

R/. Or: Alleluia.

READING II   Rv 5, 11-14

A reading from the book of Revelation.

I, John, had a vision, and I heard the voices of many angels who
surrounded the throne and the living creatures and the elders. They
were countless in number, thousands and tens of thousands, and they all
cried out:

  "Worthy is the Lamb that was slain
  to receive power and riches, wisdom and strength,
  honor and glory and praise!"
  Then I heard the voices of every creature in heaven and on earth
  and under the earth and in the sea; everything in the universe
  cried aloud:
  "To the One seated on the throne, and to the Lamb,
  be praise and honor, glory and might,
  forever and ever!"
  The four living creatures answered, "Amen," and the elders fell
  down and worshiped.

The Word of the Lord.

GOSPEL   Jn 1, 1-19

A reading from the holy gospel according to John

At the Sea of Tiberias Jesus showed himself to the disciples [once
again]. This is how the appearance took place. Assembled were Simon
Peter, Thomas ("the Twin"), Nathanael (from Cana in Galilee),
Zebedee's sons, and two other disciples. Simon Peter said to them,
"I'm going out to fish." "We'll join you," they replied, and went off to
get into their boat. All through the night they caught nothing. Just after
daybreak Jesus was standing on the shore, though none of the disciples
knew it was Jesus. He said to them, "Children, have you caught

anything to eat?" "Not a thing," they answered. "Cast your net off to
the starboard side," he suggested, "and you will find something." So
they made a cast, and took so many fish they could not haul the net in.
Then the disciple Jesus loved cried out to Peter, "It is the Lord!" On
hearing it was the Lord, Simon Peter threw on some clothes—he was
stripped—and jumped into the water.

Meanwhile the other disciples came in with the boat, towing the net full of
fish. Actually they were not far from land—no more than a hundred yards.

When they landed, they saw a charcoal fire there with a fish laid on it
and some bread.

"Bring some of the fish you just caught," Jesus told them. Simon Peter
went aboard and hauled ashore the net loaded with sizble fish—one
hundred fifty-three of them! In spite of the great number, the net was
not torn.

"Come and eat your meal," Jesus told them. Not one of the disciples
presumed to inquire "Who are you?" for they knew it was the Lord.
Jesus came over, took the bread and gave it to them, and did the same
with the fish. This marked the third time that Jesus appeared to the
disciples after being raised from the dead.

When they had eaten their meal, Jesus said to Simon Peter, "Simon, son
of John, do you love me more than these?" "Yes, Lord," Peter said,
"you know that I love you." At which Jesus said, "Feed my lambs."

A second time he put his question, "Simon, son of John, do you love
me?" "Yes, Lord," Peter said, "you know that I love you." Jesus
replied, "Tend my sheep."

A third time Jesus asked him, "Simon, son of John, do you love me?"
Peter was hurt because he had asked a third time, "Do you love me?"
So he said to him: "Lord, you know everything. You know well that I
love you." Jesus told him, "Feed my sheep.

"I tell you solemnly:
as a young man
you fastened your belt
and went about as you pleased;
but when you are older
you will stretch out your hands,
and another will tie you fast
and carry you off against your will."

(What he said indicated the sort of death by which Peter was to glorify God.) When Jesus had finished speaking he said to him, "Follow me."

The gospel of the Lord.

INTRODUCTORY PRAYER

We bless you, God our Father,
through your risen Son, Jesus Christ.
in the Spirit of love and peace.

At each celebration, you invite our community,
in spite of the poverty of our heart,
to participate in the liturgy of heaven.
Our prayer you unite to the prayer of the angels,
our thanksgiving, to the thanksgiving of the saints,
our worship, to the worship of all your creatures.
With the myriads of angels that surround your throne,
we acclaim you:

You are worthy, Lord our God,
to receive power and worship,
wisdom and strength, honor, glory, and blessing
forever and ever. Amen.

HOMILY

1. Peter's Discourse before the Sanhedrin

The First Reading, taken from the Book of Acts, presents the third discourse of the Apostles after their appearance in court before the Sanhedrin. The essential part of this discourse is presented in three affirmations:

The God of our fathers has raised Jesus.	Acts 5, 30
He exalted him through his power and established him as Savior.	
He brought to Israel conversion and the forgiveness of sins.	Acts 5, 31

One recognizes in this diagram the customary structure of missionary discourses: the proclamation of the Resurrection of Jesus, the affirmation of his lordship, the invitation to conversion.

To Obey God

To the interdiction placed by the Sanhedrin on announcing the mystery of Jesus, the Apostles reply:

It is necessary to obey God
rather than men.   Acts 5, 29

Yes, that is better! Obedience to God is actually the very result of salvation.

It was the result of salvation for all the martyrs who died because they refused to kneel before the idolatrous pretentions of the states or before the lies of the sanhedrins. Today it is still the result of salvation for those who refuse to kneel before the tyrannies of money, power, and pleasure.

We continue the announcement of the Resurrection of Jesus. How are we proclaiming it? By preferring to obey God rather than men. Still today, that is better for us.

We and the Holy Spirit

In order to be judically valid according to the law of Deuteronomy,[1] all testimony had to rest on the attestation of at least two witnesses.

We are witnesses of all that,
we and the Holy Spirit
whom God gave to those who obey him.   Acts 5, 32

"We and the Holy Spirit" the reckoning is good. But what a reckoning! On the one hand there is the Spirit of glory and absolute holiness, and on the other hand there is a man inhabited by fragility and sin. And yet, it is in this union of the Spirit of God and the human spirit that the witness to the Resurrection of Jesus is rooted.[2]

Even today, every word about Jesus should first be nourished in a dialogue with the Spirit. No one should dare speak about the Resurrection if he has not spoken first with the Spirit who lives in him.

2. The Liturgy of Heaven

In the Second Reading taken from the Book of Revelation, John contemplates the heavenly liturgy as it is celebrated in the eternity of God. He hears the acclamation of the innumerable multitudes of angels, of the four Living Creatures and the Elders:[3]

Third Sunday of Easter

They cried out:

> *"Worthy is the Lamb who was slain*
> *to receive power and wealth,*
> *wisdom and power,*
> *honor, glory, and blessing!"*　　　　　　Rv 5, 12

The doxology utilizes seven adjectives, which signify the plenitude of the acclamation.

The choir of angels is innumerable: "thousands of thousands, myriads of myriads," writes John. But here the numbers no longer mean anything except the impossibility for us to grasp the infinity of those spiritual creatures. Our God is not a solitary God. An immense, festive family surrounds him and joyfully celebrates the splendor of the Father and the victory of Christ risen, the slain lamb.

Cosmic Praise

Heaven leads the entire cosmos in his praise. To the multitudes of angels are joined

> *all the creatures*
> *in heaven, on earth, under the earth and on the sea,*
> *and all the beings which are found in them.*　　　Rv 5, 13

"All the creatures…" The angels around the throne lead the universe in a roundelay of joy. Praise and worship become cosmic. Choir of the stars, canticle of the sun, ballad of the moon, serenade of the galaxies that gambol in the infinity of heaven, psalmody of the flowers, pas-de-deux of the forest creatures, glissade of the birds of the air, jig of the sea creatures, song of the evening wind, all the myriads of unknown creatures, join the angelic hosts to sing to the slain Lamb, to bless the Lord who created all of you, even you smallest of atoms, through love!

The cosmos finds its unity when it sings to its creator. Heaven is not closed upon his splendor; it opens the earth to his beauty. It is this unity with the angelic world that the liturgies of the first centuries sang:

> You are attended by thousands upon thousands
> and myriads upon myriads of Angels and Archangels,
> of Thrones and Lordships,
> of Principalities and Powers.

Beside you stand the Seraphim…
They sing your holiness.
With theirs, receive also
our acclamations of your holiness:
Holy, holy, holy is the Lord Sabaoth![4]

Receive Also Our Acclamations

Each time that we sing the Sanctus, our community joins hands with angelic hosts. It unites its praise to the praise of the cosmos; it opens itself to the acclamation of the liturgy of heaven.

Heaven is also our heart, to the extent that God lives in our heart. In this cosmic liturgy, there is a constant back and forth between earth and heaven. The humble stammering of our heart is united with the eternal song of angelic myriads.

I think that it is good to make friends with the angels, especially with our guardian angel, an intimacy with that crowd of friends in the celebration around the throne of God. Sometimes it is necessary to know how to stop the bustle of life, to bless God with the angels and to speak and pray with our guardian angel. With this "lost" time we buy a supplement of peace and joy. In this way we are fulfilling the prayer of the psalm:

I sing to you in the presence of angels.
Lord, eternal is your love!   Ps 138, 1, 8

3. Today's Gospel

This Sunday's Gospel is divided into three parts:
• The miraculous catch of the fish.
• The meal in the presence of the Risen.
• The institution of Peter as pastor of the Church.

The Miraculous Catch of Fish

This miraculous catch is very close to the one that Luke (5, 1-11) places at the beginning of the public life. The two accounts insist on the vocation of Peter and underline his primacy in the Church. But by situating this account after the Resurrection, John affirms that the ministry of Peter and, consequently, the very structure of the Church are founded on the Resurrection of Jesus. The authority in the Church thus appears in the world like the radiance of the glory of the Risen.

The Return to Capernaum

We imagine with difficulty the immense disappointment that gripped the hearts of the Apostles after the death of the Lord. They had abandoned everything to follow him for three years. And now it was he, the Master, who had abandoned them to go up to heaven. They remained there, like star-gazers in sorrow, their noses pointed toward the clouds. And to console them an angel asked them:

> Men of Galilee,
> why do you stay there looking at the sky?   Acts 1, 11

Peter returned afterwards to Capernaum. He found his nets rotting; for three years they had not been used, and his boat was leaking!

He also found the criticisms of those who had not followed Jesus. They were exulting. "They" had told him so. "They" knew it in advance: that business with Jesus the Nazorean could not work. Even in Nazareth, the family of Jesus had said, "He is out of his mind." They had added: a drinker of wine who surrounded himself with women of little virtue.[5] Peter had followed him; therefore, did he think that he was better than the others? All he had to do was stay with his wife and mother-in-law, next to his lake, next to his buddies.

That evening, Peter is obviously not in a good mood. He used to make great declarations:

> Though all may have their faith in you shaken,
> my faith will never be shaken!   Mt 26, 33

Today, he is brief: "I am going fishing." The others also are brief: "We are going with you." The apocryphal Gospel of Peter portrays well the atmosphere of this taking up of the nets:

> We, the twelve disciples of the Lord, were weeping and grieving,
> and each one, saddened by the event, returned home. As for me,
> Simon Peter, and Andrew, my brother, we took up our nets and
> went to the sea.[7]

That night they do not catch anything. They return early in the morning. Jesus is standing on the shore. They notice him 100 yards away without recognizing him. And then the marvelous adventure of the miraculous catch of fish begins.

One Hundred Fifty-Three Large fish

Simon Peter climbed back in the boat;
he pulled the net to land:
it was filled with one hundred fifty-three large fish.   Jn 21, 11

Did they really count them? How did they arrive at 153 "large fish?" Did they calibrate them in order to recognize those that were classified large and those that were counted among the small, therefore, negligible? And what about the shellfish? Jesus knew well that a net thrown into the sea brings back all sorts of things…

In the early Church, when one told that story and mentioned the number 153, the whole community uttered a sigh of admiration: "Ah!"

It is necessary to know, and all the elders knew it, that 153 is a triangular number: it is the sum of the first seventeen numbers: 1 + 2 + 3 + 4, etc. + 17 = 153. The number 17, on the other hand, is the sum of 7, the number which signifies perfection, and 10, the number which indicates plentitude. Now, if one makes an equilateral triangle by placing one point at the summit then two points below, three, four, etc., up to seventeen, one obtains an equilateral triangle of 17 points all around and of a total of 153 points.

The number 153 then represents perfection and the totality from which nothing can be taken away and to which nothing can be added without destroying the harmony of the whole. It is the very image of the Church.

We remember the parable of Jesus:

The Kingdom of heaven is like a net that is thrown into the sea
and collects all sorts of things.   Mt 13, 47

Peter's net collects the totality of the perfection of all the fish. According to the natural sciences of the epoch, one also counted 153 large fish. Therefore, all people are called to allow themselves to be caught in the net of love of the risen Lord.

And this Church will be perfect only if she is complete. She will be happy only if the catch is successful and brings in 153 fish. Clearly, the happiness of the Church will be complete only when the last chosen one enters into the joy of the Kingdom. We will be happy only if we work for the happiness of all our brothers by leading them to Christ Jesus.

The Seven Disciples

Who is going to fish for Jesus and his Church? Let us survey the names and count them. John says that those present were Simon Peter (1) with Thomas (2), Nathaniel of Cana in Galilee (3), the sons of Zebedee, that is, James and John (5), and two other disciples whose names have not been kept; in total seven. Let us note that the word disciple *(mathetes)* occurs exactly seven times in this account. In the symbolism of numbers, as it was understood in the time of Christ, the number 7 was supposed to express perfection.[8] The catch of fish is made by the whole of the disciples of Jesus. All are sent to bring in the 153 large fish, as all are sent to proclaim the Gospel.

Jesus is on the shore. The boat of the Church is still on the sea of time and testing. Therefore, let us cast our net on the right side. On the left side, when one fishes without Jesus, one catches nothing, and it is night. But on the right side, the side of blessing, there where the blessed of the Father will be gathered, one catches the totality of the fish, and it is the day of the Risen One.

A Net without "Schism"

Here is a final remark. John writes:

> Although the fish were very numerous,
> the net was not torn.   Jn 21, 11

John's text is very evocative: The net did not have any "schism" *(eschisthe)*, that is, any tear. Clearly, schism is introduced into the Church when the fish are not all in the net. When they are in it, there is no schism.

The Meal in the Presence of the Risen

Between the miraculous catch of fish and the institution of Peter as Shepherd of the sheep, John places the meal of the disciples in the presence of the Risen. It is one of the most extraordinary pages of the Gospel. It is also one of the most moving.

Upon disembarking onto the shore,
the disciples saw a fire of burning coals
with some fish on it, and some bread...
Jesus said to them:
"Come eat."
None of the disciples dared to ask him:
"Who are you?"
for they knew it was the Lord.
Jesus approached;
he took the bread and gave it to them,
as well as some fish.   Jn 21, 9, 12-13

Jesus was going to invest Peter with the highest ministry on earth: Shepherd of his Church. In the morning sun which was playing on the waves of the lake, in the patches of mist which were still touching the water, Christ Jesus, radiant with the light of the Resurrection, was going to celebrate for his Apostles and for the angels, in the presence of the sea gulls who were dancing on the waves and the fish who were still wriggling, a liturgy of enthronement. Now, what does Jesus do? He knows well, as the popular saying goes, that "a hungry man will not listen to reason." The Apostles returned very tired from their night of fishing. They were hungry. Jesus, the Lord of infinite majesty, had lit a fire on the shore; he had broiled some fish on the coals. He had prepared bread. Jesus the Risen cooks for his Apostles! Then he offers each one a piece of bread with this fish cooked by the Creator of the universe!

The Humanity of the Risen Christ

John underlines first the reality of the body of the Risen. We remember that on the evening of Passover, according to Luke[9], Jesus had eaten fish grilled in front of the Apostles to show them the reality of his risen body.

Here, however, the gesture of Jesus goes further. It signifies the permanence, beyond the Reusurrection, of his "humanity;" of his goodness, his benevolence for his own. The glory of the Resurrection did not harden his heart in indifference toward his disciples. The eternity of God did not take him away from the humble cares of the present time. He even remembers, although he comes from heaven, that fishing during the night creates hunger. Although he lives with the angels, he still knows how to light a fire of coals and broil fish. Moreover, he knows how to love as one loves on earth while loving as one loves in heaven. The heart of the Risen remains a heart fully "human."

That truth touches us also in the most intimate part of our heart. It embraces us with happiness. What Jesus did of old for his own, he still continues to do today for us. If of old he cooked for his Apostles, do you not think that he would do even more for us; that is, that this glory of the Risen lives in the heart of our joys and our pains?

The Humanity of the Church

What Jesus did of old for his disciples, we must continue to do today for our brothers and sisters when they are hungry. It is useless to speak about God to someone whose stomach is crying, to someone whose heart is suffering, to someone whose soul is in agony, if one has not sought first to come to his aid. The Church will have to cook fish on coals for a long time yet before being able to speak about the Resurrection and to offer that bread of heaven which is Christ Jesus.

Blessed be the bishops who know how to light the fire and to grill fish for their faithful! Blessed be the professors who, before teaching "great truths" to their brothers and sisters, begin by serving them with hands of love! Blessed be Marie-Therese, the little sister who knows how to hunt gazelles with the pygmies of the equatorial forest, and my confrere, Father Stephen who, like Peter, knows how to catch fish in a balancing boat on the African coast before revealing to the poorest of the poor the riches of God! Blessed be above all the Lord Jesus! He alone knows how to speak about heaven and intermix it with earth.

The Institution of Peter as Pastor of the Church

Three times Jesus asks Peter:

"Simon, son of John,
do you love me more than these?"

Peter answers three times: "Yes, Lord, you know that I love you." Jesus says to him then:

Feed my lambs! Jn 21, 15

Feed my sheep! Jn 21, 17

The vocabulary varies somewhat from one question to another and from one answer to another. Undoubtedly it is a question there of stylistic variations.[10] They do not seem to have theological points.

The Triple Repetition

In a civilization based on the written word, it is enough to signal once for a commitment to be considered final. In a civilization founded on the spoken word, one used the triple repetition as a confirmation.[11]

Without doubt, there is also a discreet allusion to the triple denial: Peter must cancel out his denials.

However, we would be wrong to see in this repetition a type of reparation demanded by Jesus. That would absolutely not be the "way" of Jesus. He is infinitely above these human "ways." He forgave the adulterous woman without making the least allusion to her sin, without demanding anything from her. How could he not forgive his Apostle in the same way? There is rather in this triple question the affirmation that the measure of Peter's love is the measure of Jesus' forgiveness.

Like Peter, we are sinners as we come before the Risen. More than three times Jesus has forgiven us. More than three times he has asked us: "Do you love me?"

May we all, before answering, look into our heart...

The "Pastorate" in the Church

Peter receives the ministry that is considered the most important in the Church, and sometimes, as the most honorary in the eyes of the world. According to Jesus, the greatest love must respond to the greatest ministry. The primacy of Peter must be a primacy of love. This is really the meaning of Jesus' question: "Simon, son of John, do you love me more than these?"

Even today, every ministry, even the most humble, is first a vocation to love the Lord. Every pastorate is a call to love. The most eminent this pastorate is, the more intense must this love be. "Primacy" in service can only be a primacy in love.

Perhaps you will think: "How tremendous is the vocation of the priest, but I, as a lay person, have no ministry in the Church." You do not have a ministry in the Church? But you have a vocation. You do not have the ministry of priest, bishop, or pope? But you have the vocation of husband, wife, parent, celibate, brother, sister, or friend. The way that God created you is the way that he calls you to love him.

It is in this way that you serve the Risen. To him the primacy of our love forever and ever!

PRAYER

Risen Christ, we pray to you:
Make the morning of your love,
shine on us, O Lord.

Make the morning of your Resurrection shine on us.

Like the disciples, may we be able
to discover the splendor of your face
on the shores of eternity.

Make the morning of your Resurrection shine on us.

Like the disciples, may we be able
to catch in the nets of your love
those who seek your face.

Make the morning of your Resurrection shine on us.

Like the disciples, may we be able
to satisfy ourselves at the feast that you prepare
on the shores of your Resurrection.

Make the morning of your Resurrection shine on us.

Like the disciples, may we be able
to shepherd the sheep of your flock
and lead them to the sheepfold of eternal life.

Make the morning of your Resurrection shine on us.

Like the disciples, may we be able then to say to you:
"Lord, you know everything.
you know well that I love you
eternally!"
Amen.

NOTES TO THIRD SUNDAY OF EASTER

1. See Dt 19, 15.
2. Paul affirms likewise that his testimony is accompanied by the action of the Holy Spirit 1 Thes 1,4; 1 Cor 2,4.
3. The "Living" represent the universe signified by four cardinal points. The "Elders" can be the chosen of the Old Testament.
4. The Eucharistic Prayer of the Euchology of Serapion (+ after 362). See L. Deiss, *Springtime of the Liturgy* (Collegeville, Minn.; The Liturgical Press, 1979), p. 194.
5. See Mk 3,21, Lk 7,34 and 8, 2-3
6. Luke speaks about the "high fever" of Peter's mother-in-law.
7. See L. Vagany, *L'Evangile de Pierre*, Coll. "Etudes Bibliques" (1930), pp. 337-339.
8. Revelation the number 7 appears explicitly 54 times. There are 7 churches, 7 Spirits, 7 candelabras of gold, 7 stars, 7 seals, 7 trumpets, 7 thunders, 7 plagues, 7 bowls.
   Note well that one does not say the number 7 indeed expressed perfection, but simply that it was intended to express it. John used the signification of the numbers without taking otherwise a position on this symbolism (quite as Jesus used the Aramaic vocabulary without canonizing that vocabulary).
9. See Lk 24, 42-43
10. Thus John uses two words for "to love" *(agapan* and *philein),* two words for "to shepherd" *(boskein* and *poimainen),* two words for "to know" *(eidenai* and *ginôskein)* and speaks sometimes about "lambs" and sometimes about "sheep."
11. Thus, when Abraham wants to buy the grotto of Machpelah at Hebron to bury Sarah in the "Holy Land," the "Promised Land," according to the Covenant, he asks the question three times: "Grant me a burial site so that I might bury my dead." And three times, the sons of Seth answer him: "My lord, listen to us rather...Bury your dead" (Gn 23,5,11,15).

FOURTH SUNDAY OF EASTER

READING I   ACTS 13, 14, 43-52

A reading from the Acts of the Apostles

Paul and Barnabas travelled on from Perga and came to Antioch in
Pisidia. On the sabbath day they entered the synogague and sat down.
Many Jews and devout Jewish converts became their followers and
they spoke to them and urged them to hold fast to the grace of God.

The following sabbath, almost the entire city gathered to hear the word
of God. When the Jews saw the crowds, they became very jealous and
countered with violent abuse whatever Paul said. Paul and Barnabas
spoke out fearlessly, nonetheless: "The word of God has to be declared
to you first of all; but since you reject it and thus convict yourselves as
unworthy of everlasting life, we now turn to the Gentiles. For thus were
we instructed by the Lord: 'I have made you a light to the nations, a
means of salvation to the ends of the earth." The Gentiles were delighted when they heard this and responded to the word of the Lord
with praise. All who were destined for life everlasting believed in it.
Thus the word of the Lord was carried throughout the area.

But some of the Jews stirred up their influential women sympathizers
and the leading men of the town, and in that way got a persecution
started against Paul and Barnabas. The Jews finally expelled them from
their territory. So the two shook the dust from their feet in protest and
went on to Iconium. Their disciples knew only how to be filled with joy
and the Holy Spirit.

The Word of the Lord.

RESPONSORIAL PSALM   Ps 100, 1-2. 3. 5

R/. (3) We are his people:
   the sheep of his flock.

Sing joyfully to the Lord, all you lands:
   serve the Lord with gladness;
   come before him with joyful song.

R/. We are his people:
   the sheep of his flock.

Know that the Lord is God;
  he made us, his we are;
  his people, the flock he tends.

R/. We are his people:
  the sheep of his flock.

The Lord is good:
  his kindness endures forever,
  and his faithfulness, to all generations.

R/. We are his people:
  the sheep of his flock.

R/. Or: Alleluia.

READING II   Rv 7, 9. 14-17

A reading from the book of Revelation

I, John, saw before me a huge crowd which no one could count from every nation and race, people and tongue. They stood before the throne and the Lamb, dressed in long white robes and holding palm branches in their hands.

Then one of the elders said to me:

  "These are the ones who have survived the great period of trial;
  they have washed their robes and made them white in the blood
  of the Lamb.

  "It was this that brought them before God's throne:
  day and night they minister to him in his temple;
  he who sits on the throne will give them shelter.
  Never again shall they know hunger or thirst,
  nor shall the sun or its heat beat down on them,
  for the Lamb on the throne will shepherd them.
  He will lead them to springs of life-giving water,
  and God will wipe every tear from their eyes."

The Word of the Lord.

GOSPEL   JN 10, 27-30

A reading from the holy Gospel according to John
Jesus said:

"My sheep hear my voice.
I know them,
and they follow me.
I give them eternal life,
and they shall never perish.
No one shall snatch them out of my hand.
My Father is greater than all, in what he has given me,
and there is no snatching out of his hand.
The Father and I are one."

The gospel of the Lord.

INTRODUCTORY PRAYER

We bless you, God our Father,
source of peace and fountain of joy.
You yourself invite us
to come to you with songs of joy.

We pray to you:
Let each day spent in your presence
be for us a day of feasting.
Let each liturgical celebration
bring us nearer to the throne of our glory.
And let each step in our life,
in spite of the long path of the great trial,
be for us a doorway of hope
into the new heavens and the new earth
where we will sing your eternal praise. Amen.

HOMILY

1. The Announcement of the Gospel to the Gentiles

The First Reading, taken from the Book of Acts, relates to us the foundation of the Church in Antioch of Pisidia[1] by Paul and Barnabas at the time of the first missionary journey. It is there that one of the most important turning points of the mission of the Church takes place at the dawn of Christianity around the years 45-49.

It can be presented this way:

- Paul, in his preaching, always begins by addressing himself to the Jewish community.
- The Jewish community on the whole ordinarily refuses the message of Jesus.
- Paul then addresses himself to the Gentiles.

This pattern is found again, with some close variants, at Iconium, at Thessalonica, at Corinth, at Ephesus, and finally at Rome. Now it is at Iconium that Paul makes for the first time, in a decisive manner and with magnificence, this step toward the Gentiles.

Luke's account presents, like a type of résumé, not the speech that Paul and Barnabas made under the circumstances, but what they should have been able to do:

Paul and Barnabas declared to the Jews boldly:
It is to you first that it was necessary
to address the Word of God.
Since you reject it
and do not consider yourselves worthy of eternal life,
we are turning to the Gentiles.   Acts 13, 46

Obviously, the text presents a controversial point: No one will believe that the Jews do not consider themselves "worthy of eternal life..." In order to support the new orientation of their mission, Paul and Barnabas, through the hand of Luke, then invoke "the commandment of Jesus and the prophecy of the Servant of Yahweh" according to Isaiah 49.6:

This is the commandment that the Lord gave to us:
"I have made you the light of the Gentiles
so that, thanks to you, salvation may come
to the ends of the earth."   Acts13, 47

Jews and Gentiles

There is a simplistic and superficial way to consider mission. One may think that it is the failure of the preaching to the Jews which entails as a consequence the mission to the Gentiles. At the messianic banquet organized by Jesus, the Gentiles become the guests filling the places of those who neglect to come. The refusal of Israel causes the acceptance of the Gentiles. Failure with one is compensated by success with the others.

But this reasoning does not stand up before the biblical facts. It seems that God would need fo fill the room of the messianic banquet at any cost. This reasoning seems to rest on a liturgical interpretation of the parable of the Discourteous Guests, where it is said:

> The (first) guests were not worthy.
> Make other guests enter
> so that my house may be full.   Lk 14, 23

We should not confuse a parable with a theology of mission to the Gentiles, which will take the place of Israel. Quite the contrary, it is written:

> Many will come from the east and the west
> and will take their places at the table
> with Abraham, Issac, and Jacob
> (and not in place of Abraham...)
> in the Kingdom of heaven.   Mt 8, 11

God's Plan

How can we, within the measure of our limited intelligence, understand God's plan of light?

God invites us, Jews and Gentile, to enter into his love. He does not need the refusal of the Jews to fulfill his plan with regard to the Gentiles. In God's heart, no one replaces anyone. For we are all loved with the same and total love; first the people of the promise, then the people of the Gentiles. Jesus appears truly as the "light to enlighten the Gentiles" and the "glory of the people of Israel."[2]

But among the Gentiles, as among the Jews, some refuse the love offered; others accept it. What Luke says about the community at Rome applies to all:

> Some allowed themselves to be persuaded by the words of Paul;
> others refused.   Acts 28.14

Today

These questions can seem obsolete today. In reality, they are of burning interest. We know who Israel is. We know the love with which God surrounds Israel. Paul melts with tenderness when he reminds us:

Theirs is the adoption as sons, the glory, the covenants, the
legislation, the worship, the promises, and also the patriarchs
from whom Christ is born…
God, eternally blessed. Amen.   Rom 9, 4-5

We also know who we are. Wild olive shoots grafted through
grace into the holy root that is Israel,[3] we know our original
poverty. Before the call of God and the gift of faith, we can only
take up the role of the Gentiles of Antioch:
The Gentiles were glad.
They gave glory to the word of the Lord.   Acts 13, 48

There is a fascinating word in Revelation. You cannot forget it once you
have heard it, for it digs into the heart. I think that it will also be engraved
forever in our hearts. God affirms that he never extinguishes the torch, but
he sometimes changes its place.[4] How many times in the history of the
Church has this word been confirmed!

Formerly Northern Africa—what we call today Morocco, Algeria, and
Tunisia—was Christian. We know the names of the church Fathers who
lived there: Tertullien, Cyprien, and Augustine, who was one of the great
geniuses of the Church, without forgetting the early, moving passion of the
martyrs Felicitas and Perpetua. Today, does a single Christian exist who
is of North-African origin? God did not extinguish the torch, but he
changed its place.

Formerly Syria and Asia Minor were Christian and gave to the Church:
Ignatius of Antioch, Polycarp,Theophile, Method of Olympia, Epiphane,
and great among the greats, Basil, Gregory Nazianzen, and Gregory of
Nyssa. Even today, we live by their holiness and we are filled with their
knowledge. Without them, the Church would not be what she is today.
Neither do we forget that it was there that the Gospel according to Matthew
(perhaps in Antioch of Syria), as well as the Johannine literature (maybe
at Ephesus) were born, and also those writings in which our liturgy is
rooted: the Didache, the Didascalia of the Apostles, and the Apostolic
Consitutions.Today, religious distress reigns in those countries, and a tiny
Christian minority survives there. God did not extinguish the torch, but he
changed its place.

Where are the Christian communities of Antioch of Syria today? There, in
Antioch, the disciples of Jesus were called "Christian" for the first time[5]
and from there the whole missionary movement departed and evangelized
the Middle East and Europe. At the time of the New Testament, Antioch

was the third largest city in the world, after Rome and Alexandria, with a population of more than half a million inhabitants. In the sixth century, the patriarchate of Antioch included eleven metropolitans and one hundred twenty-six bishops.[6] Today, the only thing remaining of Antioch is a pile of ruins where goats come to graze during the day and owls hunt at night. God did not extinguish the torch, but he changed its place.

The light of Christ shines in our hands today; no one is certain of being able to keep it. We live in the midst of Christian communities; no community is certain of remaining one forever.

> Whoever takes pride in standing firm,
> let him take care not to fall! 1 Cor 10, 12

Whoever takes pride in being the light of the world as Jesus asked us to be—"You are the light of the world"[7]—must take care not to become darkness. Whoever bears the torch of Christ must take care not to lose it.

What should we do? There is only one way not to extinguish the light of Christ in our hands: Light the torches around us. There is only one way to keep the faith: communicate it to our brothers and sisters. There is only one way to keep Christ, "the hope of the glory,"[8] in our midst: proclaim him to our brothers and sisters. True Christianity, like that of Paul and Barnabas, is missionary or it does not exist.

Such is our vocation. Such is also the joy of our life.

2. The Eternal Joy of the Redeemed

Last Sunday, John opened a door of light for us upon the heavenly liturgy. We contemplated the angelic multitudes celebrating the Lamb and the God of eternity. Today, he invites us to admire the triumph of the chosen:

> I saw an immense crowd
> that no one could count,
> from every nation, race, people and language.
> They stood before the throne and before the Lamb,
> clothed in white robes
> and with palm branches in their hands. Rv 7, 9

The question which immediately rises in the heart is the following:

> Those who are clothed in white robes,
> who are they, and where do they come from? Rv 7, 13

John's vision is a prophecy of our destiny. This "immense crowd" grows as we, who are saved by Christ, gather together before the throne of God to unite ourselves to the choir of the redeemed. It is there, at the heart of that immensity, in that song of eternity, with all our brothers and sisters, that we find our place for praising forever in a youth endlessly renewed. Where do they come from?

They come from the trial, from the great trial
(les thlipseos tes mégales).

The word *thlipsis* literally means 'pressure,' whence 'trial,' 'tribulation' or even 'affliction' (the word affliction has the same root as *thlipsis).*

Affliction or trial is the daily bread of Christian life. The path to heaven is the path of great trial. For some this supreme trial is martyrdom. For others, it is simply the trial of faith as it is lived in daily life. In the farewell of Paul and Barnabas to the Christians of Antioch of Pisidia, Luke explains:

They strengthened the hearts of the disciples,
encouraging them to persevere in the faith,
for "we must go through many trials
to enter into the Kingdom of God."   Acts 14, 22

Here we are clothed in white robes, palm branches in our hands, singing to exhaustion the heavenly canticle. How powerless are the words of earth to describe the splendor of heaven! How difficult heavenly joy is to imagine, whereas the pains of earth which gnaw at us each day are so easy to feel! How are we to understand:

They washed their robes
and whitened them in the blood of the Lamb.   Rv 7, 14

In biblical vocabulary, blood signifies life. To be whitened in the blood of the Lamb, therefore, is to be purified in the life of Jesus, to be implicated in his Resurrection, to mix one's life with the Risen's, to immerse one's sadness into his joy, to dissolve one's immortality in his eternity. Creation which surrounds so fraternally is like the smile of God who creates everything for our joy. At the dawn of the first day, while God built the universe, the angels who were present cried out with pleasure. This is described nicely in the book of Job:

God placed the cornerstone of the world
among the joyous concerts of the morning stars
and the unanimous acclamations
of the sons of God (that is, the angels)   Job 38, 6-7

Then God created our own life, and we get involved in that long walk "through many trials."

Finally the new heavens and the new earth will come. The angels will continue their festive roundelays, for God will wipe every tear from our eyes and together with the angelic multitudes we will eternally acclaim his love.

3. The Good Shepherd

This Sunday's Gospel echoes the parable of the Good Shepherd:

> My sheep listen to my voice;
> I know them
> and they know me. Jn 10, 27

Mutual Understanding

This mutual understanding of the Shepherd and the sheep assures the unity of the flock. The more we know the voice of Christ, the more we enter into his love, the more we enter also into his unity with the Father.

Even today this mutual understanding should be the rule in the Church as much for the pastors as for the sheep. The pastors have to learn from the sheep at least as much as the sheep learn from the pastors. The holiness of one sustains the holiness of the others and glorifies the holiness of Jesus. Augustine explains:

> Indeed, if the sheep are good, the shepherds
> also are good. For it is good sheep that make
> good shepherds.

> But all the shepherds form only one single Shepherd.
> They are only one. They lead to pasture, but it
> is Christ who tends (the flock).[9]

With Songs of Joy

The Responsorial Psalm likewise touches upon the theme of the Good Shepherd:

> The Lord made us; we are his;
> we are his people
> and the flock he leads. Ps 100, 3

The Psalm adds a precious reflection. We are walking toward that eternal celebration about which Revelation speaks. We are going there through a long path of many trials, but we must go there joyfully:

Go to the Lord
with songs of joy.   Ps 100, 2

How then can we recognize the true flock of Jesus? It is the one that sings songs of joy on its way; it is the one that goes straight toward eternity with cries of joy.

Happy are those who, day after day, draw near to the Lord in the joy of loving him or serving him, and of singing to him forever and ever. Amen.

CONCLUDING PRAYER

Let us pray to the Lord, our Good Shepherd.
May he keep us in his love.

You, Lord, are our Good Shepherd.
You call us each by name.
Help us to recognize your voice
and to follow the calls of your love.

Lord, keep us in your love

You, Lord, are our Good Shepherd.
You give your life for your sheep.
Stay near to us in the great trial
and keep us in your hand.

Lord, keep us in your love.

You, Lord, are our Good Shepherd.
You lead us to the springs of living water.
Ease our thirst for eternity.
Wipe every tear from our eyes.

Lord, keep us in your love.

You, Lord, are our Good Shepherd.
You gather us into a single flock.
Take away from your Church the scandal of divisions.
Make of us one heart and one soul.

Lord, keep us in your love.

Fourth Sunday of Easter

We also commend to you, Lord,
the sheep who are still outside the fold.

Gather us, Lord Jesus, around the throne of your Father.
With the immense crowd of the redeemed,
with the multitudes of angels,
we will bless you then
forever and ever. Amen.

NOTES TO FOURTH SUNDAY OF EASTER

1. The city of Antioch of Pisidia was situated almost at the center of Asia Minor, at 1,100 meters altitude. Presently only some ruins remain.
2. Lee Lk 2, 23.
3. See Rom 11, 16-18.
4. See Rv 2, 5.
5. See Acts 11, 26.
6. See F. Van der Meer, Ch. Mohrmann. *Atlas de l'Antiquité chrétienne* (Paris, Brussels: Ed. Swquoia, 1960), P. 186.
7. Mt 5, 14.
8. Col 1, 27.
9. *Sermo XLVI, 30.* Cf. *Corpus christianorum, Series Latina, 41.* pp. 555-556.

FIFTH SUNDAY OF EASTER

READING I ACTS 14, 21-27

A reading from the Acts of the Apostles

After Paul and Barnabas had proclaimed the good news in Derbe and made numerous disciples, they retraced their steps to Lystra and Iconium first, then to Antioch. They gave their disciples reassurances, and encouraged them to persevere in the faith with this instruction: "We must undergo many trials if we are to enter into the reign of God." In each church they installed elders and, with prayer and fasting, commended them to the Lord in whom they had put their faith.

Then they passed through Pisidia and came to Pamphylia. After preaching the message in Perga, they went down to Attalia. From there they sailed back to Antioch, where they had first been commended to the favor of God for the task they had now completed. On their arrival, they called the congregation together and related all that God helped them accomplish, and how he had opened the door of faith to the Gentiles.

The Word of the Lord.

RESPONSORIAL PSALM Ps 145, 8-9. 10-11. 12-13

R/. (1) I will praise your name forever, my king and my God.

The Lord is gracious and merciful,
    slow to anger and of great kindness.
The Lord is good to all
    and compassionate toward all his works.

R/. I will praise your name forever, my king and my God.

Let all your works give you thanks, O Lord,
    and let your faithful ones bless you.
Let them discourse of the glory of your kingdom
    and speak of your might.

R/. I will praise your name forever, my king and my God.

Let them make known to men your might
    and the glorious splendor of your kingdom.
Your kingdom is a kingdom for all ages,
    and your dominion endures through all generations.

Fifth Sunday of Easter

R/. I will praise your name forever, my king and my God.

R/. Or: Alleluia.

READING II   Rv 21, 1-5

A reading from the book of Revelation

I, John, saw the heavens and a new earth. The former heavens and the former earth had passed away, and the sea was no longer. I also saw a new Jerusalem, the holy city, coming down out of heaven from God, beautiful as a bride prepared to meet her husband. I heard a loud voice from the throne cry out: "This is God's dwelling among men. He shall dwell with them and they shall be his people, and he shall be their God who is always with them. He shall wipe every tear from their eyes, and there shall be no more death or mourning, crying out or pain, for the former world has passed away."

The One who sat on the throne said to me, "See, I make all things new!"

The Word of the Lord.

GOSPEL   JN 13, 31-33. 34-35

A reading from the holy gospel according to John

Once Judas had left [the cenacle], Jesus said:

"Now is the Son of Man glorified
and God is glorified in him.
[If God has been glorified in him,]
God will, in turn, glorify him in himself,
and will glorify him soon.
My children, I am not to be with you much longer.
I give you a new commandment:
Love one another.
Such as my love has been for you,
so must your love be for each other.
This is how all will know you for my disciples:
your love for one another."

The gospel of the Lord.

INTRODUCTORY PRAYER

We bless you, God our Father.
Through the Resurrection of your Son Jesus,
you create the new heavens and the new earth.

We pray to you:
Come to establish your dwelling
in the midst of our community.

Help us, day after day, to live
according to the new commandment of love,
and lead us to the new Jerusalem
where we will sing the marvels of your salvation,
through your Son Jesus Christ,
in the joy of the Holy Spirit,
forever and ever. Amen.

HOMILY

1. The First Missionary Journey of Paul and Barnabas

In the First Reading from the Book of the Acts of the Apostles, Luke tells about the end of the first missionary journey of Paul and Barnabas (around the years 46-48). Before returning to Antioch of Syria, Paul and Barnabas decide to visit the communities that they had founded at Lystra, at Iconium, and at Antioch of Pisidia.

We might ask what they were hoping to find in those places of the first combats. At Antioch of Pisidia, they had been persecuted and driven away; at Iconium they had avoided stoning just in time. At Lystra, Paul had actually been stoned and left for dead.[1] Why would they return to those hornets' nests?

Luke explains:

Paul and Barnabas...strengthened the courage of the disciples.
They encouraged them to persevere in the faith.   Acts 14, 22

Paul and Barnabas want to exhort the neophytes to have courage and perseverance. They give them the golden rule of Christian combat:

We must pass through many trials
to enter into the Kingdom of God.   Acts 14, 22

This Christian necessity of trial is not invented just for the needs of pious exhortation. In reality, in the First Letter to the Thessalonians, written round the year 51, two or three years after the first journey of evangelization, Paul explains clearly:

> Let no one be troubled by these trials. You know that it is for them that we are made. Also, when we were with you, we told you that we would have to undergo trials. And that is what has happened; you know it. 1 Thes 3, 3-4

We do not have any explanation to comment in a valid way on the necessity for the disciples to undergo persecutions. We can simply assert this: The message of Jesus, demanding even the forgiveness of enemies, is of such loftiness that it necessarily gives rise to the bad temper of the world. It is the holiness of Jesus that is at the root of the trials of the Church.

Organization of the Communities

The courage of the disciples and the exhortation of the Apostles is not enough to organize the early communities. Luke relates:

> They appointed presbyters *(presbyterous)*
> for each one of their churches. Acts 14, 23

The organization of the community rests on a college of *presbyters*. This organization is directly inspired by the college of elders in the Jewish communities. It is wise to understand that the churches were not all necessarily organized on the same model, that differences certainly could have existed between the Judeo Christian churches and the churches coming from paganism. But all of them had at their head, in each city, a college of presbyters. Writing to Titus, Paul reminds him:

> If I left you in Crete, it was to accomplish the organization and to establish presbyters in each city. Ti 1, 5

These presbyters receive the name *episcopos*, overseer, guardian, when one considers their pastoral office in the Christian community.

In the terms *presbyteros* and *episcopos* there is a grave problem—at the same time a grave hope—for the present Church. We can only mention it in passing in the body of a homily. But we must mention it intensively in the body of our prayer. Here it is.

The term *presbyteros, "presbyter"* is rendered in our vocabulary by the term "priest." The term *episcopos* gave us the term "bishop." But we know that no part of the New Testament speaks about priest in the sense of *hiereus,* one who would have been at the head of the Christian community.[2] When the New Testament speaks about priest *(hiereus)* it is always to apply this term either to Christ (in the Letter to the Hebrews)[3] or to each baptized person. Christ made all Christians—men, women, and children—"priests *(hiereis)* for his God and Father."[4]

The Church which at the beginning was presided over by a college of presbyters[5] adopted a monarchial structure (bishop, priest, and deacon) around the end of the second century in Asia.[6] Strictly sacerdotal or priestly vocabulary appeared with Cyprien (+ about 258) and was imposed at the same time as the monarchical organization of the Church definitively grew stronger. This organization triumphed in 1870 at Vatican I in the definition of pontificial infallibility. Ecclesiology then became, in the words of Father Congar, a hierarchy, and the history of the Church came to be not so much the history of the people of God as the history of the papacy.

A Lesson for Today

It is useless to want to go back in time in order to return to the Church of the first centuries and her native purity. History does not advance backwards. But history can inspire the solutions of the future. Speaking about the Church, Vatican II presented her first as the people of God and only then looked at her hierarchical structure.[7] This vision and the mystery of the Church as the People of God more than as a pyramidal structure, was wanted, defended, and explicitly taught by the Council.

It is always permissible to dream, even to dream that the Church might appear in the eyes of the world what she is in the presence of God: the people of God. Will I have the joy before dying of seeing such a manifestation of my beloved Church, for example, a Council composed half of men, half of women, with the participation of all–lay, priests, bishops, and the pope?

This reality of the Church, the people of God, is of capital importance for the present evangelization of the world. When Paul announced the old Gospel, he founded local churches. When we announce the Gospel today, we found "missions." The communities founded by Paul had to serve them, all the ministers–the presbyters–that they needed, including those who would assure the presidency of the Eucharist or grant forgiveness in the name of Christ Jesus.

In any case, I am sure that the holiness of the Church, which is her charity, rests in the hands of all Christians, therefore, in our hands. It is not the monopoly of the hierarchy or of the priesthood.

I am very conscious that by saying this I am short-circuiting the problem of the very structure of the Church. I also know the issue is not a simple problem of theology but the very face of the Church; therefore, the very splendor of the face of Christ.

Facing this problem, we labor with bare hands. We have as a recourse only the love of our heart. But perhaps the weight of love is heavier than the weight of the priesthood and the hierarchy. Who had the most influence on the history of the Church: Pope Pius IX (+1873)–who remembers him today?– or Pope Leo XIII (+1896) who reigned gloriously (as they say) at the end of the nineteenth century, or that little Carmelite who died in obscurity on September 30, 1897, and who was called Therese of the Infant Jesus?

The evolution of mentalities is made slowly, silently, under the action of the Holy Spirit. A Chinese proverb says that a forest that is growing makes less noise than a tree that is being knocked down. Immense trees, that were thought to be eternal, have been knocked down these past twenty years, or rather have fallen by themselves. The forest, touched by the breath of the Spirit, is silently growing.

2. The New Heavens and The New Earth

A new day will come…The Day will come when God will wipe every tear to make of it a pearl of love, when he will stifle every sob to transform it into a cry of joy, when he will destroy death to change it into eternity:

The Lord will wipe every tear from their eyes.
There will no longer be any death,
nor grief, nor crying, nor pain,
for the old world has passed away.

Death, along with our birth, is the only absolute of our life, the only date imposed by God. All other dates we can choose, except those two.

Death is also the most personal event of our existence. We avoid thinking about it too much because it wounds our sensibility. We speak about it sometimes as an abstraction, as one speaks, for example, about history (but not our own history) or even about life (but not our own life). And yet, in our solitary walk, it is toward death that we are walking unceasingly and ineluctably. In the almost imperceptible decline of our physical strength, in the progressive loss of a certain intellectual agility or flexibility of the mind, in the unavowed erosion of middle age which opens onto old age, it is toward death that we are irremediably hastening. Enveloped in a cloak of solitude, we make an appointment with our end.

And here today in this time of Easter the Word of God attests to us: What you are affirming there is false. Absolutely.

Behold, I Am Making Everything New

You speak about being imprisoned in the solitude of a tomb. But God says to you: "Here is the dwelling (literally: the tent) for God among people. He will dwell with them."

You speak about tears. Here is what God says to you: "I shall wipe every tear from their eyes."

You speak about death. God shows you a betrothal.

You speak about sadness, about crying, about pain. God speaks to you about a joy similar to that of a bride adorned for her husband. He is going to create Jerusalem, "Joy," and his people, "Delight."[8]

You are afraid of dying of thirst in a valley of despair. God is going to make springs of living water[9] gush forth for you in the desert of your life.

You speak about stumbling in darkness. Indeed, one day there will be neither the glare of the sun nor the brightness of the moon. But that is because the Lamb itself will illuminate your heaven.[10]

You are afraid of dying in a dungeon of solitude. God says to you: , Emmanuel, God-with-us, will be your God forever.

Finally you speak about old things. You depend on the witness of Qoheleth, the prince of boredom, who sighed his bitterness in this refrain: "Everything is boring...There is nothing new under the sun."[11] But God reverses Qoheleth and affirms,: "Behold, I am making everything new!" When?

We ask avidly: When then, Lord, will you create the new heavens and the new earth? When will the eternity of your joy devour the time of our pain? When will the song of angelic multitudes swallow in its harmony the dissonances of the cries of the earth?

God answers us: Your heaven is to be with Christ. Your heaven, if you want, can begin today!

> If someone is in Christ,
> he is a new creation.

2 Cor 5, 17

3. The New Commandment

This Sunday's Gospel presents an extract from the discourse of Jesus at the Last Supper, after the washing of the feet.

All the words of Jesus are precious and have the value of a testament. These words are especially precious, for they are spoken near to his death.

> I give you a new commandment;
> it is to love one another.
> As I have loved you,
> you also love one another.
>
> Jn 13, 34

The Commandment of Love

Throughout the entire Word of God, the Lord gives us the commandment of love. Throughout its history, Israel, in its daily prayer, remembered the law of love:

> Hear, O Israel, the Lord our God
> is the only Lord.
> You shall love the Lord your God
> with all your heart, with all your soul,
> and with all your strength.
>
> Dt 6, 4-5

Why then does Jesus say that this commandment is new?

What is new in the history of Israel is Jesus. What is new in our way of loving is that we must love *as* Jesus loved. He loved us unto death. Then he rose. What is new is that all our joys, all our pains, all our loves, and the best of our heart he saved by placing them in his Resurrection.

This new commandment does not cease to pose questions for us. We love. Are our loves indwelt by his Resurrection? Do we love as Christ loves?

We love our wives, our husbands, our children. Do we love them, day after day, as Christ loves us? Are our loves illuminated by the Resurrection of the Lord?

There are also those whom we hardly love. Do we, day after day, seek to conquer our indifference with regard to them and love them as Christ loves us? He gave his life for us. Are we ready to give our life for our brothers and sisters?

Are these questions foolish? In a sense, yes. Only those who allow the love of Christ to invade their heart will be able to love with this new love.

Love, The Sign of Christians

Love is the distinctive sign of Christians. In some way it is the "institutuion"[12] upon which the mystery of the Church is built. Augustine says, magnificiently:

> Only love distinguishes the children of God from the children of the devil.

> All may well make the sign of the cross of Christ. All respond: "Amen." All sing: "Alleluia." All be baptized, enter into churches, build the walls of basilicas. But the children of God are distinguished from the children of the devil only by love. Those who love are born of God. Those who do not have it are not born of God. There is the great sign, the great distinction.

> You can have all that you want; if you lack only love, the rest is of no use to you. But if you lack all the rest and you have love, you have fulfilled the law.[13]

May the Lord help us to fulfill the Law in this way by living in love. To him glory forever and ever. Amen.

PRAYER

Let the new heavens and the new earth
come upon us, Lord,
and save us through your love.

Risen Christ,
see the tears of distress in our eyes.
Change them into pearls of love.

Save us through your love.

Risen Christ,
hear the groanings of our agony.
Transifgure them into cries of joy.

Save us through your love.

Risen Christ,
see the barren land of our hearts.
Build there the dwelling of your glory.

Save us through your love.

Fifth Sunday of Easter

Risen Christ,
see the wrinkles of our aging world.
Transform them into the smile of the new heavens.

Save us through your love.

Risen Christ,
look at your Church disfigured by sin.
Make her resplendant as a young bride
adorned for her bridegroom.

Save us through your love.

Risen Christ,
look at the sadness of our earthly loves.
Rejuvenate us through your new love.

Save us through your love.

God our Father,
you make all things new
in the Resurrection of your Son Jesus;
fulfill now your promise:
Change our hardened hearts
into a new heaven and a new earth. Amen.

NOTES TO THE FIFTH SUNDAY OF EASTER

1. See Acts 13,50-52; 14,5 and 14,19-20.
2. Of course, these communities celebrated the Eucharist, but Luke, who is so sensitive to the questions of communities and their needs, nowhere mentions the presidency of a *priest-hiereus.*
3. Priest: Heb 5,6. High Priest: 5,5. Great High Priest: 4,14. Etc.
4. See Rv 1,6; 5,10; 20,6.
5. We know through Clement of Rome that toward the end of the first century, the Church of Corinth was still directed by a college of presbyters. See A. Jaubert, Sc 167 (Paris: Ed. du Cerf, 1971) pp. 83-84. We know through Hermas that toward the middle of the second century the Church of Rome still had the same organization. R. Joly *(Hermas, Le Pasteur,* SC 53, 1958, p.41) writes: One discovers in *Le Pasteur* no allusion to the monarchical episcopate."
6. According to the witness of the letters of Ignatius of Antioch whose date is debated (around 165?). See R. Joly, *Le dossier d'Ignace d'Antioche,* Ed. de l'Universite de Bruxelles, 1979.
7. In the Dogmatic Constitution on the Church, *Lumen Gentium.*
8. Is 65, 18.
9. Rv 21. 6.
10. Rv 21, 13.
11. Eccl 1, 8-9.
12. The word is from C. Spicq, *Agapé,* vol. 3 (Coll. "Etudes bibliques," 1959), p. 172.
13. *Commentaire de la Premiere Epître de saint Jean,* V.7, Cf. SC 75 (1961), p. 260.

SIXTH SUNDAY OF EASTER

READING I   ACTS 15, 1-2. 22-29

A reading from the Acts of the Apostles

Some men came down to Antioch from Judea and began to teach the brothers: "Unless you are circumcised according to Mosaic practice, you cannot be saved." This created dissention and much controversy between them and Paul and Barnabas. Finally it was decided that Paul, Barnabas, and some others should go up to see the apostles and elders in Jerusalem about this question.

It was resolved by the apostles and the elders, in agreement with the whole Jerusalem church, that representatives be chosen from among their number and sent to Antioch along with Paul and Barnabas. Those chosen were leading men of the community, Judas, known as Barsabbas, and Silas. They were to deliver this letter:

"The apostles and the elders, your brothers, send greetings to the brothers of Gentile origin in Antioch, Syria and Cilicia. We have heard that some of our number without any instructions from us have upset you with their discussions and disturbed your peace of mind. Therefore we have unanimously resolved to choose representatives and send them to you, along with our beloved Barnabas and Paul, who have dedicated themselves to the cause of our Lord Jesus Christ. Those whom we are sending you are Judas and Silas, who will convey this message by word of mouth: 'It is the decision of the Holy Spirit, and ours too, not to lay on you any burden beyond that which is strictly necessary, namely, to abstain from meat sacrificed to idols, from blood, from the meat of strangled animals, and from illicit sexual union. You will be well advised to avoid these things. Farewell.'"

The Word of the Lord.

RESPONSORIAL PSALM   Ps 67, 2-3. 5. 6. 8

R/. (4) O God, let all the nations praise you!

May God have pity on us and bless us;
    may he let his face shine upon us.
So may your way be known upon earth;
    among all nations, your salvation.

R/. O God, let all the nations praise you!

Sixth Sunday of Easter

May the nations be glad and exult
  because you rule the peoples in equity;
  the nations on the earth you guide.

R/. O God, let the nations praise you!

May the peoples praise you, O God;
  may all the peoples praise you!
May God bless us,
  and may all the ends of the earth fear him!

R/. O God, let all the nations praise you!

R/. Or: Alleluia.

READING II   RV 21, 10-14. 22-23

A reading from the book of Revelation

The angel carried me away in spirit to the top of a very high mountain
and showed me the holy city Jerusalem coming down out of heaven
from God. It gleamed with the splendor of God. The city had the
radiance of a precious jewel that sparkled like a diamond. Its wall,
massive and high, had twelve gates at which twelve angels were
stationed. Twelve names were written on the gates, the names of the
twelve tribes of Israel. There were three gates facing east, three north,
three south, and three west. The wall of the city had twelve courses of
stones as its foundation, on which were written the names of the twelve
apostles of the Lamb.

I saw no temple in the city. The Lord, God the Almighty, is its temple –
he and the Lamb. The city had no need of sun or moon, for the glory of
God gave it light, and its lamp was the Lamb.

The Word of the Lord.

GOSPEL   JN 14, 23-29

A reading from the holy gospel according to John

Jesus said to his disciples:

"Anyone who loves me
will be true to my word,
and my Father will love him;
we will come to him
and make our dwelling place with him always.

He who does not love me does not keep my words.
Yet the word you hear is not mine;
it comes from the Father who sent me.
This much have I told you while I was
still with you;
The Paraclete, the Holy Spirit
whom the Father will send in my name,
will instruct you in everything,
and remind you of all that I told you.
'Peace' is my farewell to you,
my peace is my gift to you;
I do not give it to you as the world gives
peace.
Do not be distressed or fearful.
You have heard me say,
'I go away for a while, and I come back
to you.'
If you truly loved me
you would rejoice to have me go to the Father,
for the Father is greater than I.
I tell you this now, before it takes place,
so that when it takes place you may believe."

The gospel of the Lord.

INTRODUCTORY PRAYER

We bless you, God our Father, at this time of Easter,
because the Resurrection of your Son Jesus
opens for us a door to eternal freedom.
You deliver us from the slavery of sin;
you break for us the bonds of death;
you enrich us with the freedom of children of God.

We pray to you:
Fill our life with the joy of your love,
and help us to arrive one day
in that land of eternal freedom
where you reign with your Son Jesus and the Holy Spirit
forever and ever. Amen.

HOMILY

1. The Assembly of Jerusalem

The First Reading speaks to us about what was sometimes called the Council of Jerusalem. This assembly was the great feast which opened to the Gentiles the door of entry into the Gospel, the celebration of the joy of salvation, and access to the freedom of the children of God.

Let us state some dates precisely[1]. Jesus dies on the 14th day of Nisan of the year 30. Paul's conversion takes place in the spring of the year 35. The first mission of evangelization is situated about ten years later, around 46-48. The council of Jerusalem takes place around Easter 48.

Let us also state some events precisely. It is generally admitted that Luke, in chapter 15 of the Book of Acts (from where our reading is taken) blocked out two controversies as well as the solutions that were given for them:

- A controversy on the obligation of the Gentiles converted to the Gospel to submit themselves to the Jewish Law. This controversy took place in the presence of Peter and Paul.

- A controversy on the relations between the Christians coming from paganism and Judeo-Christians. This controversy was dominated by the authority of the apostle James.

This mixture of events and decisions should not detract from an understanding of the text that the Lectionary proposes to us today.

The Law of Moses or the Law of Christ?

The question that was asked at Antioch was the following: Was it necessary to oblige the Gentiles converted to faith in Christ to submit themselves to the Jewish Law, or was faith in Jesus Christ sufficient for salvation?

What did the Law represent? It was the most precious treasure in the world to the faith of Israel. It was the Word with which God had fed his people throughout history and through which the people dialogued with their God. Were they to sacrifice this ancient treasure, whose value was certain, to the newness of the Gospel?

That was the burning question debated at Antioch. Paul was rather radical and not always easy-going in disposition, nor were his adversaries, the traditionalist Pharisees. He speaks about them by treating them as "intruders and false brothers." He is so nervous when he speaks about them that he forgets to finish his sentence:

Because of these intruders, these false brothers who stole in to
spy on the freedom that we have in Jesus Christ, in order for us to
reduce to slaves, men to whom we refuse to yield, not for a
moment, in subjection, in order to safeguard for you the truth of
the Gospel...   Gal 2, 4-6

The conflict of the traditionalists with Paul and Barnabas must have been
particularly lively since Luke, who ordinarily smooths the rough edges,
speaks about a controversy as a "not little" discussion. Finally it was
decided that

Paul and Barnabas, with some brothers, would go up to Jerusalem
to the Apostles and the presbyters to discuss this question. Acts 15, 2

The final decision was served by a letter to the community of Antioch. It
was carried by Paul and Barnabas, accompanied by Jude and Silas.

Christian Freedom

That decision is essentially a proclamation of Christian freedom: The
Gentiles do not have to pass under the yoke of the Mosaic Law. They
possess the freedom of the Gospel.

It is simply asked of them not to offend the sensibility of the Judeo-
Christian brothers, especially in the domain of ritual purity. Three regulations are mentioned. They must abstain from meat offered to idols.[3] They
must also avoid the meat of strangled animals and blood, for such would
scandalize Jewish piety a great deal. Finally, they must also avoid
illegitimate unions, for example incest.

But the most important rule of the apostolic letter, the one that dominates
those three prohibitions, is the following:

We have decided not to burden you with other obligations than
these which are indispensable.   Acts 12, 28

Therefore, the golden rule of the early community is that of minimal
obligation. In negative terms, no more regulation than necessary. In
position terms, the least regulation possible. Should not this apostolic rule,
which is also a rule of good sense, be the ideal of all legislation for our
present communities?

Sixth Sunday of Easter

Freedom in the Service of the Gospel

We are indebted to Paul's pugnacity and to his spiritual audacity in having lead us to a land of the freedom of Christ. When we see traditionalist Jews on television with their black frock coats and phylacteries, wearing large hats on their curls, in their prayer shawls, swaying while praying the sacred texts and facing the Wailing Wall, we say to ourselves, "There are some of the traditions which we would have had to submit and from which we have been freed."

Of course, we respect those traditions. We venerate them even more than those of any other religious community, for they are the traditions of the children of the Promise. They are the chosen people; we are the wild shoots grafted onto the true branch. This having been said, the problem of freedom exists today for us as in the time of Paul.

We are free, but free to do what? A freedom is precious only if it serves. If you tell someone who is dying of hunger that he is free, will that give him something to eat? The real problem is the following: What are we doing with this freedom that Christ earned for us? A freedom that is not used for the service of the Kingdom is a wounded, sometimes mutilated, freedom.

We are no longer subject to the observances of the Sabbath. Very well. But do we use our Sunday freedom to do nothing or to do good deeds?

We are free from the fasts of the Law. But do we use this freedom to feast or to share our bread with one who is hungry, to share our love with one who is alone?

We are free from formulas of prayer used in the Jewish tradition. But do we use the time gained in this way for futilite activities or to make our life one which is intimate with the Lord?

The assembly in Jerusalem was the council of freedom, the council for trust in the Holy Spirit. It was then that Christians became the freest people on earth. I only hope that our Church may always appear in the eyes of the world as a place of freedom and not as the symbol of distrust towards everything new!

At a Church gathering, some young Protestants appeared with large placards on which was written: "We are the napthaline of the world."[4] Christ had said: "You are the light of the world."[5] Unfortunately, there is still a great deal of napthaline in the regulations of our churches, whether they are Catholic, Protestant, or Orthodox. Nepthaline is effacious against moths, but it creates no new life. We have neither the kippa nor the thalit of the Jewish tradition, but we have invented a thousand "traditions" which have taken the mask of regulations, or even of rules, and which are only weaknesses of the past.

Let us pray that our Church may truly be the people of freedom, the community of the future.

Collegiality and the Holy Spirit

The decision to send the apostolic letter was made colegially by "the Apostles and the presbyters with the entire Church." It was made "unanimously," *homothymadon*, literally with one breath, one soul. Finally in the letter itself, the Apostles present themselves as brothers writing to brothers.[6] One would not know how to realize better the ideal that Jesus had proposed to his Church: "You are all brothers and sisters."[7]

But the most essential point is still the introduction of the letter itself. It is said there:

> The Holy Spirit and we
> have decided...
>   Acts 15, 28

One is tempted to ask: Is it really true or is it simply a writing error? It cannot be a slip of the pen since Luke had Peter make a similar statement in the disclosure before the Sanhedrin:

> We and the Holy Spirit
> are witnesses of these things.
>   Acts 5, 32

The relations of the community with the Spirit of Jesus had to be very familiar and consistent. What lesson is there in this for our communities and for ourselves? If only every decision that we made would always be the result of an understanding and of a dialogue with the Spirit of Jesus!

The minimum effort that one might suggest is that we pray that the Spirit may guide us when we have to make important decisions. Sometimes our spirit is so gloomy that, as the Scripture says,[8] we no longer know how to distinguish our right from our left. Now the Spirit is light.

The ideal to which we must desire is to make each moment of our life a dialogue with the Spirit of Jesus.

Is that very difficult? No, for the Spirit is not far from us. He dwells in our heart.

2. The New Jerusalem

In the Second Reading, John describes the new Jerusalem to us. He is really describing the heavenly Church, built in the eternity of God. But that heavenly Church is partially foreshadowed by the messianic Church on earth.

City of God

The City of God is built by the love of God, beautiful as a bride, descended from heaven, clothed with divine glory. No human power, even the most holy, would know how to construct her and raise her from earth to heaven. If the Lord does not build that city, the masons labor in vain.[9]

The twelve doors in its walls bear the names of the twelve tribes of Israel. Its walls rest on twelve foundations bearing the twelve names of the Apostles of the Lamb. The messianic and celestial Church, therefore, rests at the same time on the twelve tribes and the twelve Apostles, on Israel and the new people of God, and on the Old Testament and the Gospel. That also means that whoever would like to enter into that City and understand the Gospel without understanding the Old Testament would be like one who wishes to enter into a city without passing through its doors.

The heart of that city is its Temple. But it is precisely a city without a temple. For God is its Temple; God is its heart. John explains:

> In the city, I did not see a Temple,
> for its Temple is the Lord, God Almighty,
> and the Lamb.   Rv 21, 22

It is said further:

> The city does not need
> the light of the sun or the moon,
> for the glory of God enlightens it,
> and the source of its light is the Lamb.   Rv 21, 23

No one will any longer be light for his brother, for all will shine in the light of God.

A Church to Love

Who could not love that heavenly Church, clothed in splendor, described by John? But how can one love the earthly Church, clothed in the rags of her humanity, the Church whose wrinkles and ugliness we know only too well?

It is precious, in theory, to distinguish between the Church as an institution on earth and the Church as a community in heaven. But it is fruitless to make this distinction determine the practice of our love. For both these Churches form one Church of Jesus: one in the humility of her humanity and the other in her heavenly beauty. We may readily admit, however, that it is difficult to go from the image of the Church as the young bride of Christ[10] to the image of the Church as an institution represented by some old cardinals. Only faith can illuminate our view.

It is also worthwhile to remember that when we discover wrinkles on the face of the Church, those are our own mistakes that we are noticing. The best prayer for the Church is the prayer for the holiness of her children. It is our own holiness.

The Church that God Built

Tradition often meditated on the mystery of the Church. Ambrose (339-397) did it with tenderness and magnificence:

> The mother of the living is the Church that God built.
> For a cornerstone she has Christ Jesus himself.
> It is in him that all the construction
> is adjusted and rises to form a temple.
>
> Let him come then, God! Let him build the Woman,
> the first woman (Eve) as a helper for Adam,
> but the latter (the Church) as a helper for Christ!
> It is not that Christ needs a helper,
> but it is we who seek and desire
> to come to the grace of Christ through the Church.
>
> Even now she is being built:
> even now she is being formed;
> even now the Woman is fashioned;
> even now she is created.
>
> Even now the spiritual House
> is rising for a holy priesthood.
> Come, Lord God, build this Woman:
> build this City!

Here is the Woman, the Mother of all;
here is the spiritual dwelling; here is the city,
the one which lives eternally,
for it knows not how to die.
This is really it, the city of Jerusalem
which now has appeared on earth.
Such is the hope of the Church:
she will be carried, raised, taken away to heaven.

To build her, many were sent.
Sent, the partiarchs! Sent, the prophets!
Sent also, the archangel Gabriel!
Innumerable angels were directed to her,
and the multitude of the heavenly army begin to praise God
when the construction of the city nears.
Many are sent to her,
but it is Christ alone who builds her.

Let us also contemplate the Father.
Listen to him: He is present, the benevolent God.
He will not forsake his Temple.
He also wants to build every soul;
he wants to imprint his image in them;
he wants all the living stones
of the earth to go up to heaven.[11]

3. Peace and the Holy Spirit

This Sunday's Gospel presents the end of the first discourse of Jesus' farewell at the Last Supper. Jesus leaves his disciples by wishing them peace according to the Jewish custom. But at the same time he insists on the special character of messianic peace:

It is peace that I leave you;
it is my peace that I give to you.
It is not in the way of the world
that I give it to you.   Jn 14, 27

People wish each other peace *(Shalom)* then leave. Jesus wishes peace, but he remains with his own.

Peace in our heart is the most obvious sign of the presence of God in our life. It is not the peace of immobility or even of death (which is the peace of cemeteries). On the contrary, it is the peace of Jesus in the plentitude of joy–"May your joy be complete,"[12] he said–in the effervescence of a life which is unceasingly renewed.

The Holy Spirit, the Reminder of the Church

Jesus affirms further:

> The Holy Spirit will teach you everything;
> he will remind you
> of everything I have said to you.   Jn 14, 26

In the expression "He will remind you," John uses a very descriptive verb, *hypo-mimnesko*. The verb is somewhat redundant. It is composed of *mimnesko*, to "recall", to "remind," and of *hypo,* "above", whence to "remind-above," to make "sou-venir." Thus there is an insistance on the anamnestic function of the Spirit. He is in some ways the memory of the Church. He does not teach new truths, but he gives new understanding of old truths. Jesus gave the plentitude of revelation; the Spirit gives us the plentitude of its understanding.

We sometimes allow the marvels of God in our life to be lost in the sands of our memory. Or further, we act as though these benefits were due, which is another way of forgetting. Do you want an example? Upon awakening this morning, did we thank God for this new day that his love created for us, or did we consider it something owed to us? It is the Spirit who reminds us of the kindness of God and makes thanksgiving spring up in our heart:

> Give thanks to the Lord, shout his name...
> Remember the marvels that he has done!   Ps 105,1,5

Vicar of Christ

What Jesus was for the Apostles at the time of the Gospel, the Holy Spirit is then for us today at the time of this long Pentecost which is the life of the Church.

Tradition also liked to contemplate in the Spirit the "vicar" (*vicarius)* of Christ, that is, the one who holds the place of Christ.[13]

I would like to end this homily briefly by citing this word from John Chrysostom: "What use would a homily be, if it were not accompanied by prayer?"[14]

May the Spririt of Jesus transfigure our prayer into eternal praise! Amen.

CONCLUDING PRAYER

For every grace, let us bless you, God.
For every fault, let us implore your forgiveness.

For the dawn of peace and joy that your Spirit
made rise in your Church in apostolic times,
blessed be you!
For the trouble and confusion that false nostalgia
for the past
provokes in our communities today,
pardon us, Lord!

Kyrie eleison.

For the paths of light and truth
on which your Spirit leads us,
blessed be you!
For the twisted roads of our lies
on which we stumble,
pardon us, Lord!

Kyrie eleison.

For the freedom of children of God
that blooms in your Gospel,
blessed be you!
For the chains that we create
to restrain the liberty of our brothers and sisters,
pardon us, Lord!

Kyrie eleison.

For confidence in the future
that you bring forth in us through your Spirit,
blessed be you!
For the fear and agony
with which our distrust tears our heart,
pardon us, Lord!

Kyrie eleison.

For the beauty of our life
which builds a Jerusalem of light,
blessed be you!
For the ugliness of our sinful faces
which tarnishes the splendor of your Church,
pardon us, Lord!

Kyrie eleison.

May God have mercy on us and bless us;
may he make shine on us the light of his face,
his Son Jesus, our Lord. Amen.

NOTES TO SIXTH SUNDAY OF EASTER

1. We are adopting the positions of S. Ducokz, *Chronologies néotestamentaires* (Paris-Gembloux: Ed. Duculot, 1976), pp. 84-87.
2. See Acts 15, 2.
3. See 1 Cor 8.
4. Cited by Y. Congar, *la Parole et le Souffle* (Paris: Ed. Desiclée, 1984), p. 123.
5. Mt 5, 14.
6. See Acts 15, 22, 23 and 25.
7. See Mt. 23, 8.
8. See Jonah 4, 11.
9. See Ps 127, 1.
10. See 2 Cor 11, 2.
11. *Traité sur L'Evangile de S.Luc*, II, 86-87, 94. See Sc 45 (1956), pp.113-114, 117.
12. Jn 16, 24.
13. See for example Tertullien, *Traité sur la Pescription contre les Heretiques*, XIII, 5: SC 46 (1957), P. 106. Origen, *Homélies sur S. Luc*, XXII, 1; SC 87 (1962), p. 300.
14. *Sur l'incompréhensibilité de Dieu*, III. SC 28 (1951), p. 196.

ASCENSION

READING I ACTS 1, 1-11

The beginning of the Acts of the Apostles

In my first account, Theophilus, I dealt with all that Jesus did and taught until the day he was taken up to heaven, having first instructed the apostles he had chosen through the Holy Spirit. In the time after his suffering he showed them in many convincing ways that he was alive, appearing to them over the course of forty days and speaking to them about the reign of God. On one occasion when he met with them, he told them not to leave Jerusalem: "Wait, rather, for the fulfillment of my Father's promise, of which you have heard me speak. John baptized with water, but within a few days you will be baptized with the Holy Spirit."

While they were with him they asked, "Lord, are you going to restore the rule to Israel now?" His answer was: "The exact time it is not yours to know. The Father has reserved that to himself. You will receive power when the Holy Spirit comes down on you; then you are to be my witnesses in Jerusalem, throughout Judea and Samaria, yes, even to the ends of the earth." No sooner had he said this than he was lifted up before their eyes in a cloud which took him from their sight.

They were still gazing up into the heavens when two men dressed in white stood beside them. "Men of Galilee," they said, "why do you stand here looking up at the skies? This Jesus who has been taken from you will return, just as you saw him go up into the heavens."

The Word of the Lord.

RESPONSORIAL PSALM PS 47, 2-3. 6-7. 8-9

R/. (6) God mounts his throne to shouts of joy;
   a blare of trumpets for the Lord.

All you peoples, clap your hands,
   shout to God with cries of gladness,
For the Lord, the Most High, the awesome,
   is the great king over all the earth.

R/. God mounts his throne to shouts of joy;
   a blare of trumpets for the Lord.

God mounts his throne amid shouts of joy;
   the Lord, amid trumpet blasts.

Sing praise to God, sing praise;
  sing praise to our king, sing praise.

R/. God mounts his throne to shouts of joy;
  a blare of trumpets for the Lord.

For king of all the earth is God;
  sing hymns of praise.
God reigns over the nations,
  God sits upon his holy throne.

R/. God mounts his throne to shouts of joy;
  a blare of trumpets for the Lord.

R/. Or: Alleluia.

READING II   EPH 1, 17-23

A reading from the letter of Paul to the Ephesians

May the God of our Lord Jesus Christ, the Father of glory, grant you a spirit of wisdom and insight to know him clearly. May he enlighten your innermost vision that you may know the great hope to which he has called you, the wealth of his glorious heritage to be distributed among the members of the church, and the immeasurable scope of his power in us who believe. It is like the strength he showed in raising Christ from the dead and seating him at his right hand in heaven, high above every principality, power, virtue and domination, and every name that can be given in this age or the age to come.

He has put all things under Christ's feet and has made him thus exalted, head of the church, which is his body. The fullness of him who fills the universe in all its parts.

The Word of the Lord.

GOSPEL   LK 24, 46-53

The conclusion of the holy gospel according to Luke

Jesus said to the Eleven: "Thus it is written that the Messiah must suffer and rise from the dead on the third day. In his name, penance for the remission of sins is to be preached to the nations, beginning at Jerusalem. You are witnesses of all this. See, I send down upon you the promise of my Father. Remain here in the city until you are clothed with power from on high."

He then led them out near Bethany, and with hands upraised, blessed them. As he blessed, he left them, and was taken up to heaven. They fell down to do him reverence, then returned to Jerusalem filled with joy. There they were to be found in the temple constantly, speaking the praises of God.

The gospel of the Lord.

INTRODUCTORY PRAYER

We bless you, Lord Jesus,
on this day of your Ascension.
You are the Lord of infinite glory
and you remain our brother for eternity.
You reign next to your Father in the heavens
and you remain in our midst until the end of time.

We pray to you:
You gave us this earth
to make your glory dwell in it.
May the love of the beauty of this world
be for us a path to the splendor of heaven.
May the desire for the good things of the earth
teach us to prefer celestial realities.
And may the humble work of each day
in the service of your Kingdom
reveal your presence and your love
to all our brothers and sisters.
To you be glory
forever and ever. Amen.

HOMILY

1. Exegetic Explanations

Luke presents to us two accounts of the Lord's Ascension. Each account has scriptural and theological profundity.

The first account is found at the end of his gospel.[1] The Ascension appears like the immediate crowning of the Passion and Resurrection. It seems to take place on the very day of Easter, for no temporal distance separates the mystery of the Resurrection from the mystery of the Ascension. Here Luke reflects the theology of John. In John's gospel, the crucifixion and glorification are deeply united: The crucifixion of Jesus is an elevation, an exaltation.[2] For us, this theology signifies that cross and resurrection are intimately bound in our lives. Each cross accepted with love is an entrance into the Resurrection of Christ.

The second account of the Ascension is found at the beginning of the Book of the Acts of the Apostles.[3] There the Ascension marks the beginning of the mission of the Church.[4] Therefore the Ascension is a beginning more than a departure. Luke signifies in this way that each ascension of our soul, each elevation to God, is also a mission to our brothers and sisters. Our death itself is not a departure but a beginning of eternity.

One might say that the Ascension is really the most spectacular mystery in the life of Jesus. In order to describe this mystery, Luke utilizes the vocabulary and images common to his day, the only ones that his readers could understand. But, as elsewhere in the Bible, it is always advisable to distinguish between the conceptual material that is used (the vocabulary and the images) and the spiritual message that is signified.

Forty Days

Forty days: That is the length of time that Christ lived with his own people after his Resurrection:

> Forty days he appeared to them and spoke to them about the
> Kingdom of God.   Acts 1, 3

It is, therefore, the time that the apostles used to "wean themselves" from Christ according to the flesh and to accustom themselves to the risen Christ according to the Spirit. Those forty days are to be considered a number having theological value. They bring to mind the forty days of Christ's fasting, which prepared him for public life. One can also think about the forty years of Exodus. Just as God accompanied the people of the Exodus for forty years to prepare them to enter into the Promised Land, Jesus walked with his disciples for forty days to speak to them about the Kingdom of God.

The Ascent into Heaven

The ascent into heaven is clearly a symbolic image. We could say that Jesus did not "ascend" into heaven if by that we mean a local ascent into the interstellar heaven (as we ascend into the clouds when we are in an airplane). The heaven of Jesus is not the starry firmament in which the sun and the moon dance with the stars and billions of galaxies. That heaven is an immense desert. It is interesting only for the Hubble telescope.

We must add that the body of Jesus is a glorified body. We cannot, therefore, recognize him with the eyes of our flesh. We must contemplate him in faith.

Perhaps it is also time to rid ourselves of other ideas of heaven that fill our minds and encumber us like a heavy chain around our neck.

The idea that heaven is a future compensation is one example. This idea is represented in this way: In heaven, we will revel in proportion to all the bitterness of the present life that we will have endured with patience. This compensatory-heaven is built on trivial bookkeeping that seeks to balance the sufferings here below with the pleasures up above. It pleases us because, unfortunately, we have a mercenary mentality. Of course there will be a compensation. But it will be one of love. The love of God surpasses all our poor human calculations; the measure of joy that he will give to us is a joy beyond measure. Paul speaks of this "compensation" when he says:

> I consider that our present sufferings are without comparison
> with the glory that is to be revealed in us.   Rom 8, 18

Yes, God is greater than the hope of humanity. He is infinitely better than what our heart can desire or even imagine.

In our unconscious mind, there is also the idea of a movie-heaven. It is rooted in the idea that we have about the beatific vision. We imagine that we will be in a movie-heaven where we will gaze upon divine immensity in boring immobility, or further, dressed in white robes and holding palms in our hands,[5] we will be out of breath singing canticles to fill eternity while hoping secretly that the eternal movie will sometimes become funnier and our canticle more stirring. What poor limited creatures we are!

But then, you will say, tell us what heaven is! I will not tell you. Not because I do not want to, but because I cannot. I simply know that God is greater than my heart and that his immense joy fills all creation.

Luke writes that Jesus disappeared from the eyes of his apostles "into a cloud."[6] The cloud of the Ascension calls to mind the cloud that led the people of the Exodus across the desert or even the cloud that covered Mount Sinai when God spoke to his people.[7] As at the transfiguration, the entrance of Jesus into the cloud signifies his belonging to the sphere of God. This cloud is the radiance of God. It seizes like light, encompasses like perfume, warms like love.

The Triumph of Humanity in Jesus

The most obvious mystery of the Ascension is the triumph of humanity in the risen Jesus.

What are we? Fragile flesh. Our life is only a puff of wind; we find ourselves threatened at each moment. A tiny artery ruptures in our head, and we are on the edge of death!

What are we? A darkened spirit that has no credible explanation when faced with the least suffering and is thrown into full disarray when faced with death.

What are we? We are each a heart moved by fear, a heart desiring to love and be loved, even before loving heaven. And when we love, we are like prisoners who cannot fully reach each other, who tap against the partition of their cells in order to forget their bars. A prison cell where a thousand riddles run around without finding escape.

Well, that is exactly what Jesus carried to heaven: our humanity. That is what he saved.

Our hands, like his hands, one day will hold in heaven what they have held here on earth.

Our eyes, like his eyes, will be saved, for one day I will see God face to face, in the same way that a man sees the woman he loves and a woman sees the man she loves!

Our heart, as it loves: That is what is saved. The heart of a mother who loves her child: That is the love that is saved, saved and transfigured, not simply saved in the way that an antique dealer keeps and preserves an old thing but transfigured by the Resurrection, rejuvenated with a thousand splendors. Saved like a child who falls into the arms of its father! For God is our Father.

Saint Catherine Labouré tells about the time when the Virgin appeared to her at the chapel of the Rue du Bac in Paris:

> I made only one move toward her (putting myself) on my knees
> on the steps of the altar, my hands leaning on the knees of the
> Holy Virgin.[9]

I dream of that day when I, too, like Catherine, will be able to place my wrinkled brow on Mary's knees and say to her: "It is you, the Mother of Jesus, the woman clothed with the sun and crowned with stars! How I have longed to see your face!"

A day will come, the day of my ascension, when I will meet Joseph, and with eyes full of joy, I will say to him, "It is you, the carpenter of Nazareth who loved little Miriam! What good fortune you had! All men do not have a Miriam to love, a Miriam to marry! It is surely of you that the Holy Spirit said in the Book of Proverbs: 'To find a wife is to find happiness.'"[10]

A day will come, the day of my ascension, when I will be able to say: It is you, my good angel, my guardian angel! How busy you were sometimes trying to protect me! Thank you for having accompanied me on all the paths of my life."

A day will come, the day of my ascension, the day of joy, when my eyes will meet the eyes of my Lord Jesus. I will see him face to face, as I see you, better than I see you. And then I will say to him...What will I say to him? Probably nothing. For I will see everything in his eyes. I will see in them my own joy. I will see the place that his love has prepared for me from all eternity.

And if a single one of these words that I have just said were not true, then the whole Christian faith would fall into ruin. Then there would be nothing more to love, nothing more to believe.[11]

Jesus presents the mystery of his Ascension in this way:

> I leave to prepare a place for you...
> I will come back to take you with me
> so that where I am,
> you will be also.   Jn 14, 2-3

In the prayer after communion, the liturgy prays in this way: "God, put in our hearts a great desire to live with Christ, in whom our human nature is already near to you."

2. The Prayer of the Ascension

On this feast of the Ascension, the liturgy puts on our lips the prayer of the letter to the Ephesians. A wonderful prayer, but in a difficult and labored text. For often, when Paul wants to say everything, when he wants to say too much, he beats the words to bend them to what he wants to say. I am translating this prayer literally:

May the God of our Lord Jesus Christ,
the Father of glory,
give you a spirit of wisdom and revelation,
so that the eyes of your heart being enlightened,
you may know the hope
to which he calls you,
which is the riches of the glory
of his inheritance among the saints.   Eph 1, 17-18

The question that comes to mind immediately is the following: Does our heart have eyes to see? Tradition likes to speak about the *fides oculata*, that is, the faith which is—how can one translate—*oculata?*—provided with eyes. Without those eyes of the heart, which tradition translated so nicely as *lumina cordis*, lights of the heart, we remain in darkness; we cannot see Christ in heaven, who is our love, nor the heaven of Christ, which is our inheritance. Around the year 96 Clement of Rome wrote:

Through Jesus Christ, we cast our eyes on the heights of
heaven...
It is he who opens the eyes of our heart. It is he who revives
our vain
and darkened intelligence in his light.[12]

3. The Farewell Gospel

Beethoven wrote a lovely sonata called *Lebewohl,* "the Farewells." It begins tenderly in E-flat major. But from the second line, it swings into a somber E-flat minor. This music wants to be a language. We part company by smiling: "Good-bye and good luck!" But as soon as we turn our back, we languish in an aching silence, our heart on the verge of tears.

Beethoven's music is perfect for describing earthly good-byes. But it is not at all suitable for describing the heavenly farewell of Jesus to his disciples, a farewell which, it is said, fills them with "great joy."[13]

Luke's text is paradoxical and mysterious, as if Jesus, while remaining with his Apostles, was already living in a marvelous hereafter beyond time and space.

The time is uncertain. It is the very day of Passover. The pilgrims of Emmaus have returned to Jerusalem late in the evening. The sudden apearance of Jesus to his Apostles with the interlude of the broiled fish (24, 36-43), the last instructions (24, 44-49), the departure to go to the place of the Ascension, and the return to Jerusalem all bring us at least to the middle of the night. And if the Apostles go directly to the Temple to "bless God" (24, 53), we find ourselves in the small hours of the morning.

The place is equally uncertain. In the Gospel, the Ascension takes place at Bethany; in Acts it takes place on the Mount of Olives. Now, as the crow flies, Bethany is about one kilometer from Bethphage, which is one kilometer from the Mount of Olives, which is five hundred meters from the golden Door of Jerusalem. Bethphage, Bethany, and the Mount of Olives are mentioned by Luke as the starting point of the messianic entrance of Jesus into Jerusalem before his Passion. Luke writes that this triumphant procession was organized "as Jesus was approaching from Bethphage and Bethany, near the Mount of Olives."[14] It is from these same places that the triumphant entrance of Jesus into the heavenly Jerusalem was organized.

The very description of the Ascension is made with great discretion:

> He separated himself from them
> and was taken away to heaven. Lk 24, 51

We are not absolutely sure that the text of the second phrase, "He was taken away to heaven," is accurate. It lacks excellent witnesses and some editions prefer to place it in parenthesis. It also lacks the angels dressed in white, the "glory" that clothes Jesus with the light of heaven, and the sending of the Apostles into mission.

With Great Joy

But infinitely more precious than everything else is the great joy of the Apostles:

> They returned to Jerusalem with great joy
> (*méta charas mégales*). Lk 24, 52

The expression *chara mégale*, "great joy," is rare in Luke. We read it exactly two times: here, at the departure of Jesus, and another time, at his coming, in the announcement of the angels to the shepherds of Bethlehem:

> Behold I bring you great joy, *charan mégalen*, for all
> the people. Lk 2.10

Just as the coming of Jesus was a source of great joy for all the people, his departure at the ascension, far from drying up the source of this happiness, on the contrary made joy spring forth in the heart of the Church. The great joy of Bethlehem was the presence of Emmanuel in the midst of his people. The great joy of the Ascension is his presence forever in the heart of his Church. Thus the Ascension appears not like a departure, but like the continuation of his presence, in mystery. It is inappropriate, as was done formerly, to extinguish the paschal candle after the proclamation of the Gospel. Rather we must rejoice that the joy of its flame burns among us throughout the whole liturgical cycle.

The Promise of the Father

Joy must be earned. How do we earn the joy of the presence of the Absent One? How do we keep it?

Jesus says to his Apostles:

> I will send the Promise of my Father upon you. Lk 24, 49

This "Promise of the Father" is the Holy Spirit, as the parallel text from the Book of Acts shows:

Lk 24, 49	Acts 1, 4. 8
And I shall send	He commanded them…
	to wait for
the Promise of my Father	the Promise of the Father
upon you	that you have heard from me.
But you, remain in	But you will receive
the city until	
you have been clothed with	
power from on high.	the power of the Holy Spirit
	coming upon you.

Luke liked to associate the idea of Spirit (or *spirit),* with the idea of power *(dynamis).* It is said about John the Baptist that he "will precede the Lord with the spirit and power of Elijah." It is said about Mary that "the Holy Spirit will come upon you and the power of the Most High will overshadow you. Finally about Jesus it is said that "he was anointed with the Spirit and power."[15] The Spirit of God is linked with the power of God. By playing on the words, one could say that the Spirit, the breath of God, gives his breath to the Apostles who otherwise would run out of breath doing the work which Jesus assigns them. So here, the Spirit helps them to go beyond the sadness caused by the departure of Jesus and keeps them in the joy of his presence.

The Church is never orphaned.

And we ourselves, in the worst solitudes, if we know how to open our heart to the "Promise from on high," will receive the strength to go beyond our agonies and to find the face of Christ.

The Presence of the Risen in the Word

Jesus is present to his Church in his Word.

The life of the Lord, especially his undergoing death and the glory of his Resurrection and the fulfillment of Scripture:

> Everything had to be fulfilled
> that was announced through the Scriptures:
> the suffering of the Messiah
> and his resurrection on the third day.   Lk 24,46

We do not really understand why "it was necessary" that Jesus suffer. And who wants to discuss with God his plan of redemption? But we understand very well the necessity of the Resurrection: It alone gives us the key to the understanding of the Old and the New Testament.

Without the Resurrection of Jesus, Abraham and Sarah, Issac and Rebecca, Jacob and Leah would sleep forever in the cave of Machpelah;[16] Job would remain without hope on his dunghill, and all the prayers in the Psalms would have been uttered in vain:

> I believe that I will see the goodness of the Lord
> in the landing of the living.   Ps 27, 14

Without this Resurrection, the path of our own life would stop in an impasse, the impasse of death; without this Resurrection our smiles would fade in agony. Paul sums up well this situation without resurrection when he writes:

> If Christ is not risen…if it is for this life alone that we have
> put our hope in Christ, then we are the most unfortunate
> of people.   1 Cor 15, 19

This understanding of Scripture is directly tied to the gift of the Spirit, the Promise of the Father. It was a clear principle of ancient exegesis that the same grace of the Holy Spirit was needed to understand the Scriptures that had been needed to write them. Speaking about his teacher Origen, Gregory Thaumaturgus affirms that he was "in communion with the divine Spirit" and adds:

The same power is necessary for those who prophesy and for
those who listen to the prophets; no one would be able to listen to
a prophecy if the same Spirit who prophesied in it did not grant
him the understanding of his words.[17]

Without doubt, the observation is overstated because the charism of
uttering the Word of God cannot be identified with the charism of understanding it and explaining it. What is true is that the two charismata
come from the one Spirit.

Upon reading Gregory's text, I tremble. And all of those who have the
ministry of explaining the Word of God, whether they be bishops or lay
catechists, should tremble with me. The question is raised; no one can
escape it.

Are we sufficiently indwelt by the Spirit to transmit not human words, but
the authentic Word of Jesus? Between God and the community, is our word
a screen or is it a reflection of God? If we are screens, it will be to our
sadness. If we are reflections, it will be to our joy.

Perhaps you will say to yourself: "That is your problem." I agree. But really
no one is exempt from the problem. Everyone faces the same question: Are
you sufficiently indwelt by the Spirit to receive the Word of God? Are you
realizing the ideal about which Paul was speaking when he said to his
Thessalonians:

> You have received the Word not as a word of man, but for what it
> really is: the Word of God. 1 Thes 2, 13

Luke has a wonderful passage:

> Jesus opened their mind to the meaning of the Scriptures. Lk 24, 45

May the Lord open for us also a path of understanding of the Scriptures!
May his Resurrection explain his Word to us! May his Spirit, the Promise
of heaven, help us to discover the face of the Risen on each page of
the Bible!

The Blessing of The Risen One

> Lifting up his hands, he blessed them. Lk 24, 50

This blessing of Jesus intrigues the exegesis which seeks points of
comparison in order to understand Scripture better.

Ascension

The blessing of Jesus has sometimes been compared to a priestly blessing, such as the high priests used to give.[18] It is, in fact, the only priestly gesture that one finds in the life of Jesus.But there is at best only small interest in comparing Jesus to a priest of the Levitical priesthood, because he is the very source of all priesthood. It is like comparing the beauty of a moonbeam with the splendor of the sun itself!

We are also reminded of a farewell blessing like the one that Jacob, Moses, and David gave before dying.[19] Those blessings were their last look upon their children and upon their people. They were also a look upon God. The blessing that David gave is in a unique way a rendering of praise to God.

However, we should understand the major difference between all those blessings and the blessing given by Jesus. The former are blessings of dying people descending to the grave; the latter is the blessing of a Living One who is going up to heaven. The former are farewells; the latter, a presence.

This last blessing of Jesus can be understood as the blessing with which Abraham was filled at the dawn of Israel's salvation, the blessing which then passed across the tumultuous waves of history, carrying along holiness and sin, the blessing which filled the Virgin Mary–as it is said in the Magnificat–the blessing which stretches even now to the dimensions of the universe. Citing the promise made to Abraham, Peter says:

> God has raised his servant (Jesus)
> and sent him to bless you.   Acts 2, 36

Here is the last gesture of the earthly life of Jesus. Nevermore will he appear to his Apostles, share broiled fish with them, and walk with them on the road. His earthly life ends with that blessing. The long chain that links Abraham to the Church as recipients of God's promise also ends, in its last link, in the blessing hand of the Risen One.

To this last link and to this blessing is attached the hope of all humanity. Blessing his Apostles, Jesus was looking at each one of us, for, through his grace, we have become "the children of the prophets and the Covenant."[20]

Of course this blessing is also priestly because the risen Jesus is now the heavenly priest beyond all priesthood!

Of course this blessing also includes the blessing of Jacob, of Moses, and of David since the Risen One is Lord of the patriarchs, the prophets, and the kings!

Of course this blessing fulfills the desire of Abraham since Jesus, the son of Abraham, is also the Son of God!

How would the Father recognize us on the last day if we were not marked by the blessing of his Son? "Grace is like a paradise of blessing," says Wisdom.[2] It is this "paradise of blessing" that the grace of the Risen One has opened for us.

The Praise of the Church

What is the response of the faithful to the blessing of Jesus? Luke gives it in this way:

> They were unceasingly in the Temple,
> praising God.

Lk 24, 53

This is the last sentence of Luke's Gospel. Here also ends the chain that links the Old Testament to the new Church. Luke's Gospel had begun with the celebration of Zachariah in the Temple. It ends with the celebration of the Apostles in the Temple. The cycle is finished. But to the last link of the chain is now attached the praise of the Church. The end of the Gospel is the beginning of universal praise.

The Ascension, the feast of the blessing of Jesus, is also the feast of the praise of the Church. This praise, celebrated by the Apostles on the day of ascension, will never end; it will last eternally.

May the Lord will one day allow us to participate in that praise forever and ever. Amen.

CONCLUDING PRAYER

It is you, Lord, who create
the splendor of your billions of stars,
and who make them dance in your palace of light.

> *Grant that while opening our eyes*
> *on the beauty of this world*
> *we may learn to prefer*
> *the splendor of your heaven.*

It is you, Lord, who give
understanding to the creatures of the forest
and wisdom to the flowers of the field.

Ascension

Grant that while walking in the garden of your creation
we may discover the road of the new heavens
and the new earth.

It is you, Lord, who invent
the laughter of the flute, the call of the trumpet,
the fury of the great organ.

Grant that while playing the music of this earth
we may learn to prefer
the songs of heaven.

It is you, Lord, who create
the grace and strength of our youth,
the holiness of those who seek your face.

Grant that while blessing the life on this earth
we may learn to prefer
the eternity of your heaven.

It is you, Lord, who create
the joy of our dances, the laughter of our songs,
the gaity of our festive meals.

Grant that while rejoicing on this earth
we may learn to desire more
the feast of your heaven.

It is you, Lord, who create
the joy of our loves, the smile of our children,
the warmth of our earthly hearths.

Grant that our human loves
may be a path
to the love of heaven.

All your paths, O Lord,
are paths of ascension to heaven.
May each step of our life,
in joy as in pain,
bring us nearer to eternal life
next to your Father, with the Spirit of love,
forever and ever. Amen.

NOTES TO ASCENSION

1. Lk 24, 50-53.
2. Cf. Jn 3, 14.
3. Acts 1, 6-11.
4. Acts 1, 18.
5. Cf. Rv 7, 9-12.
6. Acts 1, 9.
7. Ex 13, 21 and 19, 16.
8. Cf. Lk 9, 34.
9. R. Laurentin, *Vie de Catherine Labouré* (Paris: Desclée de Brouwer, 1980), p. 84.
10. Prv 18, 22.
11. After having made a similar supposition, Paul continued in this way: "But no, Christ is risen from the dead, firstfruits of those who have fallen asleep" (I Cor 15, 20).
12. Clement of Rome, *Letter to the Corinthians* (around 96) 36.2. SC 167 (1971), pp. 158-160.
13. Lk 24.52..
14. See Lk 19.29.
15. See Lk 1.17 and 35. Acts 10.38.
16. See Gn 23 and 49.31.
17. *Remerciement á Origéne*, XV (179). Trans. H. Crouzel, SC 148 (1969), P. 171. This discourse dates from around 238.
18. This is the way the high priest Simeon blessed: "He lifted his hands toward the whole assembly of Israel to give the blessing of the Lord in a loud voice" (Sir 50.20). Heb 7.14 calls to mind that Jesus was not a priest according to the levitical priesthood.
19. See Gn 49.28; Dt 33.1; 1 Chr 29.10.
20. Acts 3.25.
21. Sir 40.27.

SEVENTH SUNDAY OF EASTER

READING I
ACTS 7, 55-60

A reading from the Acts of the Apostles

Stephen, filled with the Holy Spirit, looked to the sky above and saw the glory of God, and Jesus standing at God's right hand. "Look!" he exclaimed, "I see an opening in the sky, and the Son of Man standing at God's right hand." The onlookers were shouting aloud, holding their hands over their ears as they did so. Then they rushed at him as one man, dragged him out of the city, and began to stone him. The witnesses meanwhile were piling their cloaks at the feat of a young man named Saul. As Stephen was being stoned he could be heard praying, "Lord Jesus, receive my spirit." He fell to his knees and cried out in a loud voice, "Lord, do not hold this sin against them." And with that he died.

The Word of the Lord

RESPONSORIAL PSALM
Ps 97, 1-2. 6-7. 9

R/. (1.9) The Lord is king, the most high over all the earth.

The Lord is king; let the earth rejoice;
   let the many isles be glad.
Justice and judgment are the foundation of his throne.

R/. The Lord is king, the most high over all the earth.

The heavens proclaim his justice,
   and all peoples see his glory.
All gods are prostrate before him.

R/. The Lord is king, the most high over all the earth.

You, O Lord, are the Most High over all the earth,
   exalted far above all gods.

R/. The Lord is king, the most high over all the earth.

R/. Or: Alleluia.

READING II
Rv 22, 12-14. 16-17. 20

A reading from the book of Revelation

I, John, heard a voice saying to me: "Remember, I am coming soon! I bring with me the reward that will be given to each man as his conduct deserves. I am the Alpha and the Omega, the First and the Last, the Beginning and the End! Happy are they who wash their robes so as to have free access to the tree of life and enter the city through its gates!

"It is I, Jesus, who have sent my angel to give you this testimony about the churches. I am the Root and Offspring of David, the Morning Star shining bright."

The Spirit and the Bride say, "Come!" Let him who hears answer, "Come!" Let him who is thirsty come forward; let all who desire it accept the gift of life-giving water.

The One who gives this testimony says, "Yes, I am coming soon!" Amen! Come, Lord Jesus!

The Word of the Lord.

GOSPEL   JN 17, 20-26

A reading from the holy gospel according to John

Jesus looked up to heaven and said:
"I do not pray for my disciples alone.
I pray also for those who will believe in me
through their word,
that all may be one as you, Father, are in me, and I in you;
I pray that they may be [one] in us,
that the world may believe that you sent me.
I have given them the glory you gave me
that they may be one, as we are one—
I living in them, you living in me—
that their unity may be complete.
So shall the world know that you sent me,
and that you loved them as you loved me.
Father,
all those you gave me
I would have in my company
where I am,
to see this glory of mine
which is your gift to me,
because of the love you bore me before
the world began.

321

Just Father,
the world has not known you,
but I have known you;
and these men have known that you sent me.
To them I have revealed your name,
and I will continue to reveal it
so that your love for me may live in them,
and I may live in them."

The gospel of the Lord.

INTRODUCTORY PRAYER

We bless you, God our Father,
source of all joy and fountain of mercy,
for all the graces which fill each day of our life.
We thank you especially
for that eternal love you granted to us
even before the creation of the world
and that you give to us today in your Son Jesus.

We pray to you:
Keep us in the joy
of serving you and loving you more each day
in your Son Jesus, in the unity of the Holy Spirit,
forever and ever. Amen.

HOMILY

1. The Martyrdom of Stephen

In the First Reading from the Book of the Acts of the Apostles, Luke presents to us the account of the martyrdom of Stephen. The word martyr signifies witness. Through his martyrdom, Stephen is the first witness of the Risen Christ.

The account of Stephen's death is modeled on the account of Jesus' death. As in Jesus' trial, false witnesses accuse Stephen of having uttered threats against the Temple and against the Law. As with the trial of Jesus,

Stephen's trial takes place before the Sanhedrin.[1] As in the case of Jesus, punishment takes place outside the city.[2] Like Jesus, Stephen implores forgiveness for his prosecutors. Like Jesus, he commits his soul to God.

Reading this account, the early community verifies that the path of the disciple is really the path of the Master. Stephen walks in the steps of Jesus.

The community also learns that this path is a path that radiates the Gospel. On that day, Luke relates,

> A violent persecution broke out against the Church of Jerusalem.
> All except the apostles were scattered into the countries of Judea
> and Samaria.   Acts 8, 1

By scattering the disciples, the persecution "scattered" the Good News. The persecution wanted to kill the Gospel; it made it more radiant:

> Those who have been scattered went from place to place pro-
> claiming the word of the Good News.   Acts 8, 4

Here again, the death of Stephen imitates the death of Jesus. It is a dissemination of the Good News.

The Contemplation of the Risen Christ

At the center of the account, Luke places the revelation of the Risen Christ to Stephen:

> Filled with the Holy Spirit,
> Stephen looked to heaven.
> He saw the glory of God
> and Jesus standing at the right hand of God.
> He said:
> Look, I see the heavens open
> and the Son of Man
> standing at the right hand of God.   Acts 7, 55-56

Luke likes to talk about the Spirit of Jesus to such a degree that he has been called the Evangelist of the Holy Spirit, and the Acts of the Apostles could just as well be called the Acts of the Holy Spirit. We are not surprised then to find the presence of the Spirit throughout the account. Stephen belongs to a group of Christians who are "full of the Spirit and wisdom," and he himself is "full of faith and the Holy Spirit." The Jews who oppose him are presented as "stiff-necked, with uncircumcised ears and hearts who all resist the Holy Spirit;" and when they argue with him, they cannot hold up their heads "against the wisdom and the Spirit who made him speak."[3]

Finally it is in the light of the Spirit that Stephen sees heaven open and Jesus in his glory of heaven. Therefore, the Spirit is wisdom on his lips and light in his eyes.

The Church continues the ministry of Stephen. Like him, she is a martyr in the full sense of the word: On the one hand by bearing witness to the Resurrection of the Lord and on the other hand by suffering for this witness. We cannot give this witness if the Holy Spirit is not on our lips as he was on the lips of Stephen. And we cannot see the Risen Christ if the Spirit is not in our eyes. The Spirit lives in the very heart of this witness.

> When you are brought here before the synagogues, magistrates,
> and authorities, do not worry about how to defend yourselves or
> what to say. For the Holy Spirit will teach you at that very hour
> what you should say. Lk 12, 11-12

The life of the witnessing and persecuted Church is thus a life with the Spirit.

2. Come, Lord Jesus

We have just read the last page of the last book of the Bible. Here is the end of what theology calls the "Revelation." Hereafter God will no longer speak through the book until the Day when we shall see him face to face, when we shall understand without words what his love is.

And this time, the time of our life that remains to be lived, is dominated by the double affirmation of Jesus:

> Look, I am coming soon!
> Yes, I am coming soon! Rv 22, 12.20

Therefore, the last "Good News" that the Lord says to each one of us is the following: The Lord is near to you. He is at the heart of your joy, at the heart of your pain, in the tenderness of a love, and in the birth of a child's smile. He is in your efforts to live his Gospel better. He is in your crosses, in your agonies, and in your despair. And to cast upon him your begging eyes is enough for him to come to you:

> The Lord is near to those who call on him,
> to all those who call on him in truth. Ps 145, 18

He is especially near to those who seek him in suffering:

> The Lord is near to the brokenhearted. Ps 34, 19

For a broken heart is the usual door through which the Lord enters into your life.

Those who call on the Lord, who carry in their broken hearts the desire to see his face, already carry the Lord in their hearts. They experience how sweet is the word of Jesus: "Look, I am coming soon!"

To Enter the Gates of the City

It is said further:

> Happy are those who wash their robes
> to share in the fruits of the tree of life
> and to be able to enter the gates of the city.   Rv 22, 14

There are exactly seven beatitudes in the Revelation. This is the last, the seventh, the one which opens the doors of Eternity. It enables us to go back into the garden from which Adam and Eve were chased away and to cut the fruits from the tree of life: not a fruit of death like the one that Adam and Eve cut in the first paradise, but a fruit of life:

> To the one who overcomes, I will give the right to eat from the
> tree of life in the paradise of God.   Rv 2, 7

It is said further:

> I, Jesus...am the root
> and the Offspring of David,
> the bright Morning Star.   Rv 22, 16

Happy are those who, in the dawning mists of the eternal Day, allow this morning star to shine in their hearts.[4] For then their hearts will already become the heaven of Jesus Christ.

What then is the requirement to be able to "enter the gates of the city" and to enter into eternal joy? One must have washed one's robe, must have whitened it, as it is said, "in the blood of the Lamb."[5] This clearly means that it is necessary to purify oneself by plunging into the very life of Christ.

The prophet Baruch had invited Jerusalem to change and to adorn itself for God:

> Jerusalem, take off your robe of sadness and misery; put on for
> ever the beauty of the glory of God; envelope yourself with the
> cloak of God's justice.   Bar 5, 1

Sadness and misery are the rags of exile. Beauty, glory, and holiness are the clothes of eternity. Undoubtedly, it is difficult to find in the wardrobe of the Church robes of glory and cloaks of justice. Paul seeks to explain these images when he writes:

> Baptized (that is, plunged) in Christ,
> you have been clothed with Christ. Gal 3, 27

Paul likes the image "to be clothed with" or "to put on Christ." He explains: to put on Christ is to shed one's darkness; it is to be dressed in the light of Christ. It is to live in justice, holiness, and truth.[6]

Come, Lord Jesus!

To the affirmation of Christ: "Look, I am coming soon" the prayer of the believer answers: "Come, Lord Jesus!"

> The Spirit and the Bride say: "Come!"
> Let him who hears also say "Come!" Rv 22, 17
> Amen! Come, Lord Jesus! Rv 22, 20

This prayer: "Amen! Come, Lord Jesus!" is the last prayer of the last book of the Bible. It also concludes the prayer of our whole life.

Let us phrase the question honestly: Do we desire the return of Jesus, his flashing presence in our life which, like the light of dawn, with a single stroke rends the heaven of our sadness and our boredom? Or are we really afraid to die?

I would like to submit the following point of interest to you: Whereas we usually make a big deal about death and often to seek to anesthetize our agony with the drugs of life's pleasures, the righteous people of the Bible, who lived according to the heart of God, did not worry much about death, about survival, about resurrection.[7] Actually, the first explicit witness that we have in the Old Testament concerning individual resurrection is found in the Book of Daniel:

> At that time, many of those who sleep in the land of dust will
> awake for eternal life. Dn 12, 2

We can date "at that time" in a precise way. It is the end of the persecution by Antiochus Epiphanus around 164. This is to say that all the faithful whom we consider as the founders of the religion of Israel: Abraham, Isaac, Jacob, Moses, David, Isiah, Jeremiah, Ezekiel, all the other prophets, all the singers of the Psalms, in short, all the saints of the Old

Testament, lived for almost a millennium and a half without the hope of a bodily resurrection such as we have with the Resurrection of Jesus. Their sadness was expressed in the refrain:

> Death cannot praise you.
> Those who fall into the pit
> no longer hope in your faithfulness.   Is 38, 18

But on the other hand, their whole being, with all the fibers of the heart, was straining to this hope:

> You cannot abandon my soul to the abode of the dead,
> nor allow the one who loves you to see the pit.   Ps 16, 10

What counted essentially for them more than life, more than death, was the grace of the Covenant, that is, their being near to the God of their love in life, in death, and beyond death. It is for this reason they were crying: "You cannot abandon the one who loves you! You the God of love cannot do that!"

Paul expresses clearly this certitude and this hope in the New Covenant when he writes:

> Who will separate us from the love of Christ?...
> Yes, I am sure of it: neither life, nor death...
> Nothing can separate us from the love of God manifested
> in Jesus Christ, our Lord.   Rom 8, 35, 38-39

While he was going from Antioch of Syria to Rome to undergo martyrdom there, Ignatius wrote to the Christians of Rome:

> I am writing to all the churches, I send word to all: it is with great heart that I shall die for God... Allow me to become food for the beasts: it is through them that I will get to meet God. I am the wheat of God; I am ground by the teeth of the beasts to overcome the immaculate bread of Christ... It is in full life that I write to you, desiring death. My earthly desire has been crucified. There is no longer in me the fire for earthly wood. There is no longer anything but a living water that murmurs in me and says in my heart: "Come to the Father!"[8]

3. The Priestly Prayer

In the Gospel of John, Jesus concludes the farewell discourse with a long prayer of intercession and oblation. We find in this prayer an echo of the homily and paschal praise that Jesus uttered at the Last Supper. Since the sixteenth century, this prayer has been called the "Priestly Prayer."[9] Here

Jesus is consecrated as an offering to the father and brings with him his disciples who are going to continue his mission in this oblation.

We also note that Jesus sometimes speaks as if he were already risen. Thus he affirms that he is no longer in the world, that he has completed the work of the Father, that he has glorified him on earth.[10] One could then consider the Priestly Prayer as a type of transtemporal preface that Jesus pronounced before his Passion and Resurrection,[11] a preface that the early Church would have taken up in the celebration of the Eucharist, which is memorial of that Passion and that Resurrection.

An Eternity of Love

This prayer is one of strange beauty. It fascinates us intellectually because it leads us to the threshold of the world of eternity. We are so frail before the mystery of God!

Jesus prays for his disciples. He affirms that the Father loves us with a love similar to the one with which he loves Jesus:

> You loved them
> as you have loved me.   Jn 17, 23

The very mission of Jesus was to reveal the Father in order to make his love come upon us:

> I made your name known to them
> and will make it known to them more
> so that the love with which you love me may be in them
> and that I also may be in them.   Jn 17, 26

This affirmation is the last affirmation of the Priestly Prayer. It closes in this way the first part of the Gospel of John, the book of the seven signs. It is placed just before the account of the Passion thus signifying its importance. We are confronted with the mystery of God in us. And this mystery is the following: The unique love which rests upon the unique Son is the same love which also rests upon the children of adoption.

It is surely a wonderful, unprecedented affirmation to say, "God loves us." But now we must add that God loves us with the infinite love with which he loves Jesus. We must add even further that he loves us with the same eternal love with which he loves Jesus. For the love of the Father for the Son is a love of eternity:

> You loved me
> before the creation of the world.   Jn 17, 24

Each person is a person of eternity. Each love of God for us is an eternal tenderness, without beginning or end. Each one of our existences is as young as God himself. Before the creation of the world, before the fifteen or seventeen billions of years of the existence of the universe, when nothing existed yet before the explosion of the initial furnace, before the time when there was not yet time, in the universe where there was not yet our universe, when God reigned alone in the immensity of his immensity, God thought about me, thought about this little thing without consistency whose existence, as Scripture says, is as ephemeral as the grass of the fields and the flower that blooms.[12] He fashioned each fiber of my heart; he shaped each one of the billions of cells that constitute my body; he modeled each one of my thoughts; he invented every one of my words.

These very words that I am writing or pronouncing were presented to him before the billions of billions of years of the universe's existence. In a word, he has loved me eternally.

God exists as the Father who loves his Son in the unity of the Spirit. It is in this love that his existence is built, if one can say it. God exists—as unheard of as it is to think it—only as he includes me at each moment, that is, eternally, through grace, in that love that builds his unity at the same time as the unity of the universe and each one of its marvels.

An Eternity of Glory

Perhaps, you are thinking that we have lapsed into exegetic or mystic delirium. Perhaps we have not read the Gospel well? No. The more we read the Gospel, the more this eternity of love plows our heart and takes root in it. In fact, what Jesus says about eternal love, he affirms also about the glory in which he wants to make us participate:

> I have given them
> the glory that you gave me.   Jn 17, 22

And a little later, he says further:

> I want that where I am,
> they also may be with me
> and that they see the glory
> that you have given me.   Jn 17, 24

Seventh Sunday of Easter

Now that this glory that Jesus gives to us on behalf of his Father is also a glory of eternity. It is, Jesus says:

> The glory that I had with you
> before the world was created. Jn 17, 5

In biblical vocabulary, the "glory of Yahweh" designates God himself in the brightness of his splendor, in the radiance of his majesty, in the infinite weight of his riches. This glory of God is incarnated in Jesus. According to the Letter to the Hebrews, he is "the radiance of the glory of the Father."[13] And the glory of Christ is man saved according to the wonderful formula of Irenaeus:

> The glory of God
> is living men.
> And the life of man
> is to see God.[14]

By allowing us to share in his divine glory, the Father fills us with the splendor of his light, with the plentitude of his life, with the riches of his love. And this glory is the glory that shines on Christ "before the world was created," before these fifteen or seventeen billions of years which represent our feeble way of speaking about eternity and which are not even the breath of an instant in comparison with eternity.

How difficult is it for us to speak about the mystery of God with human words! How hard is it to articulate the love of God with human concepts! How impossible it is to imagine an eternity of love!

What then, can we say? Perhaps only that there is nothing to say. At the threshold of the world of eternity, our only response is our praise, our blessing, our thanks to God. Paul has the same teaching as John. He affirms in the Letter to the Ephesians that we have been blessed and predestined "before the creation of the world" to be holy and blameless in his presence in love, to the praise of his glory.[15]

May we respond to Christ Jesus in this Sunday's Gospel by making each moment of our life a "praise in his glory." Amen.

CONCLUDING PRAYER

Thus prayed Jesus:

> *"Father, you loved me before the creation of the world...*
> *may that love you have for me be in them"*

Before the creation of the world and its young beauty,
before the first day of the billion years of the age of the universe,
when no light yet existed to measure the length of time
and only the peace of your love hovered over the nothingness
in the infinity of your eternity,
Father, you loved me.
You showered me with blessings in your Son Jesus.
You wanted me always before you
in your love, to be a "praise of your glory."
What can I say to you, Father, except:

> *Thank you forever and ever!*

Before the first sun burst forth from the darkness
and after the first dawn was born on the horizon,
before the song of the first night lulled the stars to sleep
and the first nebulas traced for you their rounds of joy,
in the infinity of your eternity,
Father, you wanted my soul.
In your light you revealed its most secret places;
you loved it in your Son Jesus.
You adorned it with beauty in the image of the splendor
of the Firstborn
What can I say to you, Father, except:

> *Thank you forever and ever!*

Before the hills were brought forth
and the depths hollowed out
and the first daisy unfolded astonished petals in the meadow,
before the first nightingale surprised the silence of the deep
with its song,
and the first trout leaped with joy
in the blue foam of the torrent,
in the infinity of your eternity,
Father, you predestined my body,
you even chose the color of my eyes.

331

You loved me in your Son Jesus.
You want my eyes–my eyes!–full of your light
to see you face to face on the last Day.
What can I say to you, Father, except:

Thank you forever and ever!

Before the first heart capable of eternity was fashioned and the
first smile of love was born in the cradle of lips,
before the first kiss of a husband bloomed for his wife
and the first child was born
from the womb of its mother,
in the infinity of your eternity,
Father, you wanted my heart.
You prepared for me the works that I would accomplish,
not because you needed them for your glory
but because my heart needed them for its beauty.
You loved my heart like the heart of your Son Jesus.
When you come on the last day
to gather it from the dust
and when it shines for eternity in your splendor,
what can I say to you, Father, except:

Thank you forever and ever!

Father of Jesus and Source of the Spirit, we pray to you:
Never cease to look at the place
that you have prepared for us from all eternity.
See, we are coming soon!
Our whole life is only a path of return to you.
Let us enter now into your home
with all the angels who are our friends,
and all the saints,
to celebrate the infinity of your eternal love
forever and ever. Amen.

NOTES TO SEVENTH SUNDAY OF EASTER

1. See Acts 6, 3 and 15.
2. See Acts 7,58 and Heb 13, 2.
3. See Acts 6,3,510;7,51.
4. See 2 Pt 1,19 and Rv 2,28.
5. Rv 7,14.
6. See Rom 13,14 and Rv 2,28.
7. One will remember the Sadducees, at the time of Christ, denied the existence of resurrection (cf. Mt 22,23; Acts 23,8) under the pretext that they found no argument in favor of this belief in the written law.
8. *Letter to the Romans*, IV, 1-3; VII-2.
9. It seems that it was the Protestant theologian David Chrytaeus (1531-1600) who first used this formula.
10. See Jn 17.4, 11-12
11. It is clear that in the transcription of the discourse of Jesus, the redactional work of John and his community is particularly important.
12. See Ps 103,15.
13. See Heb 1,3.
14. *Against Heresies*, IV, 20.7.
15. See Eph 1, 4-6.12.

PENTECOST SUNDAY

READING I (VIGIL)   GN 11, 1-9

A reading from the book of Genesis

At that time the whole world spoke the same language, using the same words. While men were migrating in the east, they came upon a valley in the land of Shinar and settled there. They said to one another, "Come, let us mold bricks and harden them with fire." They used bricks for stone, and bitumen for mortar. Then they said, "Come, let us build ourselves a city and a tower with its top in the sky, and so make a name for ourselves; otherwise we shall be scattered all over the earth."

The Lord came down to see the city and the tower that the men had built. Then the Lord said: "If now, while they are one people, all speaking the same language, they have started to do this, nothing later will stop them from doing whatever they presume to do. Let us then go down and there confuse their language, so that one will not understand what another says." Thus the Lord scattered them from there all over the earth, and they stopped building the city. That is why it was called Babel, because there the Lord confused the speech of all the world. It was from that place that he scattered them all over the earth.

The Word of the Lord.

READING I   ACTS 2, 1-11

A reading from the Acts of the Apostles

When the day of Pentecost came it found the brethren gathered in one place. Suddenly from up in the sky there came a noise like a strong, driving wind which was heard all through the house where they were seated. Tongues as of fire appeared which parted and came to rest on each of them. All were filled with the Holy Spirit. They began to express themselves in foreign tongues and make bold proclamation as the Spirit prompted them.

Staying in Jerusalem at the time were devout Jews of every nation under heaven. These heard the sound, and assembled in a large crowd. They were much confused because each one heard these men speaking his own language. The whole occurrence astonished them. They asked in utter amazement, "Are not all of these men who are speaking Galileans? How is it that each of us hears them in his native tongue?

We are Parthians, Medes, and Elamites. We live in Mesopotamia, Judea and Cappadocia, Pontus, the province of Asia, Phrygia and Pamphylia, Egypt, and the regions of Libya around Cyrene. There are even visitors from Rome—all Jews, or those who have come over to Judaism; Cretans and Arabs too. Yet each of us hears them speaking in his own tongue about the marvels God has accomplished."

The Word of the Lord.

RESPONSORIAL PSALM   PS 104, 1. 24. 29-30. 31. 34

R/. (30) Lord, send out your Spirit,
  and renew the face of the earth.

Bless the Lord, O my soul!
  O Lord, my God, you are great indeed!
How manifold are your works, O Lord!
  the earth is full of your creatures.

R/. Lord, send out your Spirit
  and renew the face of the earth.

If you take away their breath, they perish
  and return to their dust.
When you send forth your spirit, they are created,
  and you renew the face of the earth.

R/. Lord, send out your Spirit
  and renew the face of the earth.

May the glory of the Lord endure forever;
  may the Lord be glad in his works!
Pleasing to him be my theme;
  I will be glad in the Lord.

R/. Lord, send out your Spirit
  and renew the face of the earth.

R/. Or: Alleluia.

READING II   I COR 12, 3-7. 12-13

A reading from the first letter of Paul to the Corinthians

No one can say: "Jesus is Lord," except in the Holy Spirit.

There are different gifts but the same Spirit. There are different ministries but the same Lord; there are different works but the same

God who accomplishes all of them in every one. To each person the manifestation of the Spirit is given for the common good.

The body is one and has many members, but all the members, many though they are, are one body; and so it is with Christ. It was in one Spirit that all of us, whether Jew or Greek, slave or free, were baptized into one body. All of us have been given to drink of the one Spirit.

The Word of the Lord.

GOSPEL   JN 20, 19-23

A reading from the holy gospel according to John

On the evening of that first day of the week, even though the disciples had locked the doors of the place where they were for fear of the Jews, Jesus came and stood before them. "Peace be with you," he said. When he had said this, he showed them his hands and his side. At the sight of the Lord the disciples rejoiced. "Peace be with you," he said again.

"As the Father has sent me,
so I send you."

Then he breathed on them and said:

"Receive the Holy Spirit.
If you forgive mens' sins,
they are forgiven them;
if you hold them bound,
they are held bound."

The gospel of the Lord.

INTRODUCTORY PRAYER

Father of our Lord Jesus Christ
and source of the Holy Spirit:
We praise you and we bless you for your Church
that you brought into being on the day of Pentecost.

Today again, send your Spirit upon us:
to loosen our lips for your praise,
to burn in our hearts with the fire of your love,
and through the voice of the risen Jesus, our brother,
may he help us to sing the marvels of your love

in all the tongues of the earth.
To you be glory
forever and ever. Amen.

HOMILY

All the Christian feasts are like flowers blooming on the stems of the feasts of Israel. And all the feasts of Israel sink their roots into the history of the chosen people.

It is in this history that the Christian Pentecost is also rooted. This feast celebrated the gift of the Spirit of Jesus to his Church.

Pentecost calls to mind the old agrarian feast which, in its origins, marked the end of the harvest which was fifty days after the offering of the first sheaf of the fruits of the harvest.[1] Today in the Christian Pentecost, this harvest is formed by the faithful who enter into the Church. The old Pentecost celebrated the gift of the Law at Sinai; today in the Christian Pentecost, this Law is the law of the Spirit of Jesus. The old Pentecost called to mind the conclusion of the Covenant with the people of the Exodus; today in the Christian Pentecost, this Covenant is the New Covenant of the risen Lord.

The first reading which is offered for the Mass of the Vigil is that of the Tower of Babel. How does such an old story introduce us to the celebration of the new Pentecost?

Indeed, the path which leads from Babel to the Christian Pentecost, from Genesis to the book of the Acts, is long. It crosses not only the whole Bible, but even the whole history of the chosen people. Furthermore, it even begins in prehistory, since Babel is situated in the first eleven chapters of the Book of Genesis. Those chapters deal with the destiny of humanity in general. We find ourselves here before God's call to Abraham (in chapter twelve), before the beginning of the chosen people.

But this path from Babel to Pentecost is a marvelous path. It is worth the trouble to get involved in it.

May the Spirit of Jesus be our guide.

1. The Tower of Babel

It used to be that when one mentioned the Tower of Babel, the question which immediately came up was, "Is it true?" And one would put on a sly smile, full of doubts. There was no concern for the religious message of this passage in the Bible.

337

For more than a century, archaeologists have been intent on digging in the sands of the Middle East, in what is called the "fertile crescent," which is the cradle of our civilization.[2] They have discovered not one tower of Babel but a quantity of these towers. They are called ziggurats. It seems that from the fourth milennium, the Mesopotamians had raised sanctuaries on high terraces. The first ziggurat to be excavated–it was in 1845–1851–was that of Nimrud. It was called "House of the seven guides of heaven and earth." It is forty-seven meters high. The ziggurats which are relatively the best preserved are those of Ur, whose construction goes back to the end of the third millenium, that of Urak and that of Aqaqurf, whose height reaches fifty-seven meters today. The ziggurat of Babylon had a particular splendor.

The Ziggurat of Babylon

The ziggurat of Babylon was called Etemenanki, which means literally "House of the foundation of heaven and earth." It was built out of hollow bricks held together by layers of reeds and enclosed in a frame 15 meters thick of baked bricks joined by bitumin. Its base rested on a square of about 91 meters. A set of stairs and circular ramps allowed one to climb the seven levels and reach the summit. There stood the temple covered with blue enameled bricks.

The whole of the ziggurat overhung Esagil, "House of the high summit, temple of the god Marduk, a gigantic temple of approximately rectangular shape. Its sides' greatest dimensions measured 456 and 412 meters.

We know the height exactly thanks to the tables of Esagil preserved in the Louvre: The first level was 33 meters high, the second, 18 meters, the third, fourth, fifth, and sixth, 6 meters each, and the seventh, 15 meters. All this adds up to a total of 90 meters.

We can imagine the extreme fascination that this colossal mass had to exert on the "sons of the desert," the people of Abraham.

It is on this foundation of architectural splendor and idolatrous polytheism that the Yahwist tradition of the Bible presents its account of the Tower of Babel toward the middle of the ninth century. The Bible presents it as a religious teaching. Only scraps remain of historical contacts with the Etemenanki, the Tower of Babel.

The Construction of the Tower

The builders of the tower come from far away and wintry countries "from the edge of the East." I find them rather sympathetic: overflowing with optimism, intoxicated with the spirit of enterprise, starved for a civilizing work, and good workers as well:

> Come! Let us make bricks
> and bake them!
> Come! Let us build a city...   Gn 11, 3-4

The making of bricks seemed like a rather primitive process to the Yahwist author of the account who was of Judean origin. Actually, in Judea, it was enough to bend down and gather rocks for building. And the smallest hill offered a quarry from which the most beautiful, proportioned rocks could be taken, whereas brick was such an ephemeral material for such a gigantic undertaking!

The Hebrew text is very nice. Literally, it says:

> Come, let us brick bricks,
> let us blaze them in the blaze!

Perhaps behind these expressions there is an echo of the Babylonian poem of creation, *Enuma Elish*. The god Marduk speaks in this poem:

> Yes, make Babylon, whose construction you have desired:
> Let its brickwork be built, and raise the sanctuary!
> (They) wield the pickaxe.
> The first year, they molded the bricks;
> when the second year came,
> they raised the top part of...Esagil.
> They built the high tower in stages.[3]

The Pride of the Builders

The Tower of Babel could have become a magnificent prayer, like joined hands extended to heaven. Alas! It went down in pride. At least, that is the way the Yahwist redactor presented it (obviously, he did not carry the "Babylonians" in his heart);

> Come! Let us build ourselves a city and a tower whose summit
> will penetrate the heavens.   Gn 11, 4

The tower, then, really had a religious signification. Far from being a prayer imploring the coming of God, this architectural grandiloquence was pride scaling heaven. One knew in the Bible about those "cities whose fortresses reached to heaven."[4] Of course, we are in the East; exaggeration is customary. But exaggeration is not pride:

> Let us make a name for ourselves,
> and we will not be scattered
> over the whole earth.   Gn 11, 4

In the ancient East, the name of a person is like the duplication of the person. That which does not have a name does not have existence. The poem *Enuma Elish* begins the account of creation in this way:

> When on high, heaven was not yet named,
> when below, the Earth did not have a name…[5]

In return, to affirm one's name, by writing it on a clay tablet, is to affirm one's existence. Uru-ka-gina, the king of Lagash (2351-2341), a city of Lower Mesopotamia, had the following inscriptions written in cuneiform to Bawa, his beloved goddess:

> Bawa carry away the prayers of Uru-ka-gina.
> That is his name.
> The love of Bawa for Uru-ka-gina will have no end.
> That is his name.[6]

The intention of the builders of the Tower is to dominate the whole earth while exhibiting the pride of their name. The psalm said about the proud:

> Their mouths claim heaven;
> their tongues frolic on earth.

In the ancient inscriptions we also see the Sumerians or Assyrians glorify themselves for having built a country with one language. Even today, we know to what point the superiority of a country, whether it be political, intellectual or commercial, entails the diffusion of the language of the "conqueror" to the conquered.

The Intervention of God

God intervenes. To the activities of people who mutually excite themselves through their "Come! Come!" is opposed to the tranquil power of God: "Come! Let us go down!"

There is also a point of delicious irony, as if God were afraid that the tower of clay would penetrate heaven:

If they begin in this way,
from now on nothing will keep them
from doing everything that they desire.   Gn 11, 6

Finally there is this sovereign goodness of God who wants to stop sin.
For the greater the sin, the greater the condemnation will have to be.
God's decision is twofold. He decides to stop the construction by scattering
the builders.

The Lord scattered them
over the face of the earth.
They stopped building the city.   Gn 11, 8

Where God destroys, we cannot rebuild. This was known even in Babylon
as is witnessed in this old Sumerian canticle to the goddess Nisaba,
"creator of god, king, and man," goddess also of writing and science:

Nisaba, where you do not make man stable,
man cannot build a house,
man cannot build a city,
he cannot build a palace,
he cannot establish any king.[7]

Was the psalmist remembering this old Sumerian canticle when he wrote:

If the Lord does not build the house,
the builders labor in vain.
If the Lord does not guard the city,
the guard stays awake in vain.   Ps 127, 1

God's second decision is the confusion of the languages. The Yahwist
redactor links the word Babel to the Hebrew verb *Balal* which mans to stir,
to mix. At the etymological level, such an explanation is false, since
Bab-El means "door of God." At the symbolic level, it is adequate.

Fundamental Questions

The account of the Tower of Babel poses the fundamental questions of
existence. The Bible answers them in the negative.

Is the unity of languages possible? Is it desirable? To be sure. But surely
not at Babel which was perishing in its pride. Babel was seeking not the
unity but the unification of all under its domination:

(Daughter of Babylon), you said:
"I shall be a soverign forever…"
You dwell in security;
you say in your heart;
"I, and I alone!"   Is 47, 7-8

Can we make a name for ourselves? To be sure. Will God not say to Abraham right after the story of the Tower: "I will magnify your name."?[8] Therefore, we can acquire a name. But surely not at Babel, which will become a desert of silence:

Her cities will be changed into a desert,
into parched land and into a steppe.
No man will live there.   Jer 51, 43

Finally, can we meet God? Can we go up to heaven? To be sure. It is the very desire of whoever prays to God. But surely not at Babel. For instead of going up to heaven, Babel was crushed on earth. Addressing the king of Babylon, Isaiah questions him in this way:

How have you fallen from heaven,
Morning star, son of the Dawn?
You said in your heart:
"I will scale the heavens,
above the stars I will set up my throne…
I will ascend to the summit of the black clouds
I will resemble the Most High."
How? You have fallen into the sojurn of the dead,
into the depths of the pit.   Is 14, 12-14

That is how the tower, which could have been a magnificent prayer similar to that of our cathedrals, became a desert, home of "the lynx and the jackals."[9]

2. Bethel

The painful scene concerns Jacob who, through trickery, had taken the paternal blessing which by right belonged to his older brother Esau. Jacob now lived in fear of the terrible vengeance of his brother who had said: "Near is the time of my father's mourning. At the time I shall arise and kill my brother Jacob."[10]

Needless to say, Jacob's conduct had not been irreproachable since he had flirted with a lie. But Esau was not without fault either, since he had such little esteem for his birthright as the eldest son that he traded it for a plate of lentils.[11] Jacob then leaves Beersheba, the tranquil oasis of the south, and flees to the north. He thinks first of all about saving his life, also about getting rich, and finally about becoming engaged. Rightly so, Jacob had declared that the Cannanite girls of the neighborhood were not worth anything, and Rebecca even found them dripping with idolatry. Therefore, Jacob leaves for Haran, the land of his ancestors where he will find, along with the young beauties of his clan, the ancient patriarchal faith.[12] It is on the path to Haran that the marvelous story of Bethel begins.

> He came by chance to a certain place and spent the night there,
> for the sun had already set. He took a stone, placed it under his
> head, and slept in that place. Gn 28, 11

Then, he had a dream. He saw a ladder whose summit reached heaven and whose base was planted on earth. It was not one of those stupid ziggurats made out of clay bricks that the idolaters raised to their false gods, but a light and airy ladder which was cast from heaven to the kingdom of earth.

Here is a marvelous procession. It was not one of those slow processions of pagan priests climbing the circular stairs to the ziggurat, but a joyful procession of angels, a coming and going of messengers from heaven to earth.

Here, moreover, is a radiant vision. It was not the appearance of the god Marduk and his consort, with the pantheon of his grimacing gods, but–and this is the culminating point of the account–it was the appearance of Yahweh himself. He stands before Jacob the wanderer, speaks to him about his father Isaac and his ancestor Abraham, renews to him the promise of possessing the land, and confirms to him the blessing made of old to Abraham:

> All the nations will be blessed through you
> and through your descendants. Gn 28, 14

Therefore, at this hour in the history of humanity, the hope of the earth rests upon Jacob.

Finally, Yahweh gives him the supreme assurance of his presence:

> I am with you.
> I will keep you wherever you go. Gn 28, 15

When Jacob awakens, he cries out explaining at the same time the meaning of Bethel:

> Here is the house of God
> and the gate of heaven. Gn 28, 17

Fundamental Questions

Bethel takes up the fundamental questions that Babel had twisted.

Is there a gate of heaven on earth? Can we meet God? The Bible answers: yes, but not at Babel, but at Bethel.

Can we enter into a dialogue with God? The Bible answers: Yes, but not at Babel, by scaling the ziggurats which are follies of pride, but at Bethel by welcoming the angels who come down from heaven.

Can the nations assemble themselves to receive God's blessing? The Bible answers: Yes, but not at Babel where they are scattered "over the face of the earth," but at Bethel where all the nations of the world inherit the blessing promised to Jacob.

Does God always stay with us? The Bible answers: Yes, but not at Babel, the house of mud, but at Bethel, the house of God where God says to Jacob: "I will be with you!"

Can we build a house to God? The Bible answers: Yes, but not at Babel on a tower of clay, but at Bethel where Jacob met God:

> Rising early in the morning, Jacob took the rock which had
> served him as a pillow and set it up as a pillar and poured oil over
> its top... He said: "This rock that I have set up as a pillar will be
> a house of God."   Gn 28, 18, 22

God abandons to their folly the people who rely upon their strength only, who build for themselves towers to scale heaven, who run through the world with their language. He cherishes those who speak humbly in his presence; he throws them a ladder from heaven; he makes them bearers of his blessing for all people.

Babel is pride; Bethel is humility. Babel is nature; Bethel is grace. Babel is the work of man; Bethel is the grace of God.

3. Nathaniel

Babel, the gate of God; Bethel, the house of God; the gift of God: here are three names which end with *El,* "God" and which are linked in biblical history. This history begins with the call addressed to Abraham; it is continued by Bethel which is opposed to Babel, and it is completed by Nathaniel who fulfills in plentitude the prophecy made at Bethel.

We remember the vocation of Nathaniel. He belongs to the first disciples that Jesus called. It is to him that Jesus speaks about Bethel when he says to him:

> Amen, amen I say to you:
> you will see heaven open
> and the angels of God ascend and descend
> on the Son of man.   Jn 1.51

Thus, the Jacob of messianic times, or even the ladder which decends from heaven– for the images are surpassed when the reality is the Son of God– is Jesus himself. He fulfills the prayer of the Old Testament:

> Oh, that you would rend the heavens
> and come down!   Is 63, 19

He is Emmanuel, God-with-us. He overthrows the audacity of the builders of the Babylonian pantheon. There is no more need to try to scale heaven, since he established his tent in the midst of human prayer.

The Babylonian builders founder in pride by wanting, as it is said, "to make a name for themselves." Jesus humbles himself for the extreme, to death on the cross, and receives from his Father the "Name above every other name."[13]

4. The Christian Pentecost

Jesus is the "Yes" that the Father says to the world in messianic times and in whom he fulfills all his promises.[14]

The Holy Spirit is the gift in which the Father brings to his Church the grace of Jesus.

Is the unity of the languages of the earth, I mean to say, unity in the understanding of love, possible on our earth? The New Testament answers: Yes, not at Babel, but in the Church of Pentecost.

At Babel everyone spoke the same language. They were torn apart, and they no longer understood each other. At Pentecost, they all speak different languages. And they understand each other. Pentecost is Babel in reverse.

Not only does each one understand the Apostles in his mother tongue, but the Apostles begin to speak other languages! Luke insists:

> They were all filled with the Holy Spirit.
> They began to speak in other languages,
> each one expressing himself according to the gift
> of the Spirit.   Acts 2, 4

In short, it was a true deluge of tongues! But one praise:

> We hear them proclaim in our languages
> the marvels of God.   Acts 2, 11

How many people speak the same language but do not understand each other! How many families speak the same language, but the husband no longer understands his wife, and the children no longer understand their parents!

How many people speak different languages but understand each other because they love each other in the love of the Spirit!

The pygmies of the equatorial forest, without knowing a word of French, understand perfectly the smile of the little sister who comes to take care of them. And the nomadic shepherds who pitch their tents at the edge of the Sahara Desert where the first waves of sand are born, understand, without needing a translator, the help that the missionary comes to bring them. And every believer, whose heart is open to love, understands without need of explanation, the joy and the suffering of his brother and sister.

May the Spirit teach all people the language of the Church of Jesus! May this language be one of love!

One People

Babylon wanted to realize the dream of "one people speaking one language": a people celebrating itself, an assembly magnifying its own name, a nation dancing around a tower of clay which claimed to scale heaven.

Is the unity of the human race possible? The Bible answers: Yes, not at Babylon, but at Pentecost. When people revolt against God, they no longer understand each other and are dispersed. When they bless God, they understand each other and are gathered together.

Luke writes that all the nations under heaven proclaim the marvels of God.[15] "All the nations?" Luke gets carried away by his enthusiasm. But it is really true! The faithful of Pentecost represent "all the nations under the sun."

The celebration that Babylon wanted to organize collapses in a silence of death. How poignant is the lamentation over its fall!

> She has fallen, she has fallen,
> Babylon the great!
> She has become a dwelling place of demons…

> The song of harpists and musicians,
> of flutists and trumpeters,
> never more shall be heard in you.

> And the craftsman of every trade,
> never more shall be seen in you.

> And the song of the millstone,
> never more shall be heard in you.

> And the light of the lamp,
> never more shall shine in you.

> And the voices of the bride and groom,
> never more shall be heard in you.   Rv 18, 2, 22-23

How radiant, on the contratry, is the Church-City, the New Jerusalem, beautiful as a fiancée adorned for her Bridegroom! She is not a tower that would rise from earth to heaven, but a city that comes down from heaven from next to the Father to earth! How melodious is the immense voice which cries out:

> Here is the dwelling of God among men…
> He will wipe every tear from their eyes.
> No more death, no more tears,
> no more crying, nor pain.
> For the old world has passed away!   Rv 21, 2-4

Spirit of Jesus, forgive us when we raise our own towers of pride and vanity. Help us day after day to build the temple of your holiness and in this way to welcome on earth that city which is given to us from heaven!

The Dwelling of God on Earth

The seventh level of "Etemenanki," the Tower of Babel, portrays a temple; it is here that the divinity, descending from heaven, was thought to dwell among men. It was "the dwelling of God."

Etemenanki! A prodigious name! "House of the foundation of heaven and earth." What was its history?

Pentecost Sunday

From decay to decay, from restorations to restorations, the tower of Babylon survived until the seventh century. Nabopolassar (625-605) tells us:

Marduk, my Lord, ordered me concerning Etemenanki,
the tower in levels at Babylon, which before my
time had become decayed and had fallen into ruins,
to assure its foundation in the heart of the
inferior world and its summit to make similar
to heaven.[16]

His son, Nebuchadnezzar (605-562) boasts of having completed the works that his father had not been able to bring to a good end.

From all that, today there only remains some sad ruins. As it happens for other masterpieces, the inhabitants of the surrounding area considered Etemenanki as an excellent quarry. They supplied themselves from it with bricks with the stamp of the king of Babylon in order to build their own houses.

And what about Bethel, the cherished sanctuary of the house of Jacob: "I will be with you; I will keep you wherever you go?" From the time of the schism, Jeroboam I (931-910) will make it the principal sanctuary of the North to rival the one of Jerusalem. He will dishonor the holy place by introducing it in the cult of the Golden Calf.[17] Amos curses Bethel, and Hosea will apply to it the nickname of Beth-Aven, "House of iniquity;"[18] there is what became of "the house of God"! The city was destroyed at the time of the Syrian invasion in 724. Nothing remains of it today except the village of Beitin, built on the site of the old Bethel. Bethel, no more than Babel, is not the dwelling of God.

Since Babel, humanity has not ceased to raise towers and build dwellings for God. Some steeples of our villages, some towers of our cathedrals are pure adoration as well as architectural splendors. In their own way they prepare the elevation of hearts and the coming of the Holy Spirit. Other constructions have fallen in the indifference of time and in the forgetfulness of the faithful. Like Etemenanki, they have served as quarries for the neighboring inhabitants. God holds architecture in such little esteem! To the rhetoric of the Gothic or the Roman, he prefers light and airy ladders cast from heaven to the most humble hearts.

And yet, the mystery of Pentecost continues marvelously. Each believer, indwelt by the Spirit, becomes a temple infinitely more precious than Etemenanki and more magnificent than all the cathedrals on earth. And each catechumen receives at his baptism the name "which is above every other name," the name of Jesus.

On this day of Pentecost, make of us, Lord, the temple of your Spirit. Make of us a temple infinitely more solid than the Babylonian ziggurats because it will be built on the Rock which is Christ, a prodigious tower more elevated than our cathedrals because it will be founded on humility. Let resound there the prayer of the partiarchs, the prophets, the kings, the psalmists, the martyrs, all the saints who have built you a dwelling in their heart, also the prayer of the builder of cathedrals who, for your love, have cut the stones, and of "all the nations under heavens." Receive also in our supplication, we pray to you, the prayer of the litle people of Etemenanki who thought to honor you by building their tower. They were living in darkness, but it was nevertheless to you that they were raising their hands; they were mistaken about your name, but they were not mistaken in their love.

With all the disciples of the first Pentecost, with Mary, the mother of your Son, we bless you for the marvels that your Spirit performs in us. Amen.

CONCLUDING PRAYER

Many are the languages of the families of nations.
Diverse are the riches of the peoples of the earth.
But only one Church proclaims your name of Father
in one Spirit.

Come within us, Spirit of the Lord.

Innumerable are the hands lifted to you,
and without end, the murmur of our heart celebrates you.
But only one prayer bows before your majesty
in one Spirit.

Come within us, Spirit of the Lord.

Without end our songs of light resound,
our harmonies sparkle, our rhythms dance.
But only one choir proclaims your immense glory
in one Spirit.

Come within us, Spirit of the Lord.

Pentecost Sunday

Radiant are the splendors of the beauties of our earth;
a flaming light is the joy of our loves.
But only one tenderness gathers us together as a family
in one Spirit.

Come within us, Spirit of the Lord.

Intolerable is the ugliness of our sins,
and hateful, the weight of our faults.
But only one forgiveness radiates from the sun of your mercy
In one Spirit.

Come within us, Spirit of the Lord.

Spirit of the risen Christ,
you distribute your gifts to each of us as you wish.
We give you thanks for the gifts that you place in us.
Keep us in the joy of your service
and in the peace of your love.
forever and ever. Amen.

NOTES TO PENTECOST

1. According to Lv 23.15-16 (Feast of Weeks)
2. See A. Parrot, *Bible et Archéologie*, 1-2, (Paris: Delachaux et Niestlé, 1970). The best commentaries are G. von Rad, *La Bene'se* (Geneva: Labor et Fides, 1968) and C. Westerman, *Genesis*, Coll. "Biblischer Kommentar," (Neukirchener-Verlag, 1974).
3. In *Les Religions du Proche-Orient*, Coll. "Le trésor spirituel de l'humanité," (Paris: Fayard-Denoël, 1970), p. 61.
4. Dt. 9.1.
5. *Les Religions du Proche-Orient*, p. 38.
6. *Inscriptions royales sumériennes et akkadiennes,* Coll. "Littératures anciennes du Proche-Orient," (Paris: Ed. du Cerf, 1971), p 81.
7. Cited by H. J. Kraus, *Psalmen*, Coll. "Biblischer Kommentar, Altes Testament," (Neukirchener-Verlag, 2 Teilband, 1960), p. 861.
8. Gn 12.2.
9. Jer 50.39.
10. Gn 27.41. There is also an opposition between Esau, the hunter who runs in the desert, and Jacob who, through his labor, makes the earth habitable.
    The importance of the traditions concerning the cycle of Jacob is known. These traditions could have been the center around which the more or less independent accounts concerning the partiarchs were grouped. According to a long process of information which lasted nearly a thousand years, these accounts formed the partiarchal story as we know it presently in Genesis.
11. See Gn 2.29-34.
12. See Gn 27.46 to 28.2
13. Phil 2.9.

14. See 2 Cor 1.20.
15. See Acts 2.5 and 11.
16. Cited by A. Parrot, *Op. cit.*, p. 35, note 4.
17. See 1 Kgs 12.26-33.
18. See Am 3.14 and Hos 5.8.

About the Author

Lucien Deiss, C. S. Sp., is a French missionary priest of the Congregation of the Holy Ghost. He was professor of Sacred Scripture at the Seminary of Brazzaville in Africa and taught Sacred Scripture and Dogmatic Theology at the Grand Scholasticate in Chevilly-Larue, Paris.

As an influential member of the Vatican II consilium on the Liturgy, he worked for liturgical reforms. He also assisted in the translation of the International Ecumenical Bible (TOB).

In his desire to create a more biblical church, Father Deiss conducts scriptural and liturgical workshops on every continent. A man of great wit, charm and profound spirituality, he combines his scriptural knowledge and musical talent to help people encounter Christ today.

As an international authority on the exegesis of the New Testament and the Fathers of the Church, Father Deiss has written many books on liturgical, biblical and patristic subjects.

acknowledgments

Alan Hommerding, editor and series director

Laura Adamczyk and Diane Karampas, translators

Sr. Cecilia (nuns of New Skete), cover art

Selections from God's Word Is Our Joy are available on cassette recording. Please contact World Library Publications' Customer Service department, toll-free: 800 566-6150.